THE DAY ONE EXECUTIVE

THE DAY ONE EXECUTIVE

A GUIDEBOOK TO STAND OUT IN YOUR CAREER STARTING NOW

APRIL ARMSTRONG

NEW DEGREE PRESS

THE DAY ONE EXECUTIVE
A Guidebook to Stand Out in Your Career Starting Now

ISBN   979-8-88504-419-6   *Paperback*
         979-8-88504-437-0   *Hardcover*
         979-8-88504-425-7   *Kindle Ebook*
         979-8-88504-426-4   *Ebook*

EARLY PRAISE FOR *THE DAY ONE EXECUTIVE*

"April has, in the most clear, direct, and relatable language, captured the essence of what it takes to be a successful executive. In these disrupted, complex times, exceptional leadership will carry the day—and now, we all have a 'secret decoder ring' to help us on our way."

—THE HONORABLE SUSAN M. GORDON, FORMER PRINCIPAL
DEPUTY DIRECTOR OF NATIONAL INTELLIGENCE

"The Day One Executive is full of practical, easily understandable leadership wisdom that anyone can apply to their own life, starting immediately. Having learned many of these lessons the hard way through the trials and tribulations of life experience, I wish I'd had this book when I was starting out as a young professional. April's advice will help readers to become more self-aware and intentional about their decisions and behavior and to build confidence and agency that will, in turn, lead to a greater sense of control and purpose throughout their lives and careers."

—JONATHAN R. ALGER, PRESIDENT,
JAMES MADISON UNIVERSITY

"For those aspiring to sit in the executive suite—a must read! April has provided a clear playbook for a successful career by providing great examples and tips to build on your strengths, recognize your blind spots, and embrace change."

—MAGGIE WILDEROTTER, CHAIRMAN AND CHIEF
EXECUTIVE OFFICER (CEO), GRAND RESERVE INN;
FORMER FORTUNE 500 COMPANY CEO

"This book is a field guide to success for any aspiring executive. I had the pleasure of working with April on challenging projects for almost a decade, and I recognize her keen insights throughout. With nearly 300 research citations, The Day One Executive is jam-packed with insight yet is accessible and easily readable. An aspiring executive will gain awareness, get pragmatic ideas for thorny problems, and add some new tools to their toolbox for leading change from even a single chapter."

—PAUL SPEER, PHD, CHIEF OPERATING OFFICER,

MARINE BIOLOGICAL LABORATORY,

UNIVERSITY OF CHICAGO

"April writes from extensive research, direct observation, and lived experience. The Day One Executive translates a lifetime of experience into accessible, actionable, and authentic advice that can help individuals and organizations achieve real change and effective outcomes—beginning on Day One."

—MICHAEL C. SMITH, PHD,

FORMER EXECUTIVE DIRECTOR,

UNIVERSITY OF VIRGINIA

ACCELERATED MASTER'S PROGRAM IN SYSTEMS ENGINEERING

"If you work, whether you just started or are a seasoned leader, this is a wonderful resource. Comprehensive, well researched, and exquisitely written indispensable advice makes The Day One Executive your best guide to success!"

—JERRY ABRAMS, ENVISIONEER,

CENTER FOR CREATIVE LEADERSHIP

OTHER POSITIVE FEEDBACK FROM EARLY READERS:

"...critical for any executive."

— C D

"Powerful—I believe in reading this book. I will come away having learned something that could change my career trajectory."

— J L

"A great book!"

— S C

"The Day One Executive demystifies the path to success in the professional world. It's the definitive paint-by-numbers guide for becoming an executive."

— A B A

"An incredible guidebook for every leader."

— B E

"...beautifully written..."

— M Y

"A classic. Like Strunk and White's The Elements of Style for aspiring and new executives."

— A S

"Reads well and is full of good advice."

— P B

"Inspiring and relevant to women of all ages! I would like to purchase a copy for my fourteen-year-old daughter."

—T R

"The wording, the flow, the examples, the personal stories—awesome!"

—P Z

I dedicate this book to Henry, Arthur, and Leo;
Cansen;
my parents;
and you.

"Life is either a grand adventure or nothing."

—HELEN KELLER

Table of Contents

—

INTRODUCTION

———

Leaders may be born, but executives most definitely are made.

WHY DID I WRITE THE DAY ONE EXECUTIVE?

I discovered early in my career there is a huge gap between what many of us learn in school and what it takes to be a successful executive. According to *Training Industry* magazine, nearly half of new executives do not succeed in the role despite corporate investments in leadership development that exceed $360 billion per year.

Even those who make it to the top struggle. Two-thirds of new executives report feeling unprepared for the challenges they would face in the executive ranks by formal development processes of their organization, according to Development Dimensions International, Inc.'s 2021 Leadership Transitions Report, which is the largest study of its kind, spanning fifty countries and twenty-four major industry sectors.

This book aims to close that gap.

My desire wasn't to write one more leadership book, but rather to fill an empty corner of the vast virtual bookshelf with a blueprint for what it means to *be* an executive. *The Day One Executive* aims to empower you to become the executive of your own life and stand out as a future executive starting on "Day One." It is the guidebook I wish I had when I started my career.

WHY SHOULD YOU CHOOSE TO BE A DAY ONE EXECUTIVE?

When you choose to be a Day One Executive, you are in the driver's seat of your career. You expand your sphere of influence and become someone who can make things happen. You become a change-maker.

As a Day One Executive, you won't stay stuck in a bad job or working for a bad boss, because you know you have the power to create, and recreate, your career at all times. Your work has greater impact, which is its own reward, and you also increase your earning power. You will take more risks and reap greater rewards.

Best of all, you get to live your legacy—and you can start right now, wherever you are.

IS THIS BOOK FOR YOU?

I want you to have every advantage. If you've ever wondered if there's some executive code, the answer is—yes. If you were lucky, you learned this through family, country clubs, college, and connections. The rest of us learn it the hard way, and some never put all the pieces together.

Until now.

This book is for you if you are just beginning your career and:

- want to call the shots in your life and career.
- would like to "recession-proof" or "custom-create" your career.
- have found yourself on the outside looking in as others go into the closed-door meeting you weren't invited to.

This book is for you if you are mid-career and:

- feel stuck as others seem to move up in their careers.
- wonder what went wrong when someone else got the promotion you deserved.
- thought you were managing your career well, but somewhere along the line you started wondering, "Am I missing something?"

What if you're a new executive (or even a seasoned executive) looking to take your organization to the next level? This book is for you too.

HOW CAN YOU BECOME A DAY ONE EXECUTIVE?

In order to be the most potent creator of your career—and your life—you must first see yourself as an executive. There is no "wrong" place to start. You don't need a fancy title or anybody's permission to be the executive you were born to be—and already are if you choose it. It's a choice that you have the power to make every day (the good news is, if you're reading this book, you're probably already a Day One Executive at heart).

It's never too early or too late to show up as an executive, though as with financial investments, it pays to start early. Like financial investing, the sooner you invest in your executive capacity the better because the benefits will accrue and compound. Unlike financial investing, there's no downside risk. It's all upside when you invest in you.

Choosing to develop your inner executive is not effortless. For many of us, throughout our lives, someone rewarded us for pleasing others, not for challenging accepted paradigms or going against the grain. You learned to communicate based on largely inherited and unquestioned patterns in your family. You were taught to have the answers, not ask questions. You may or may not have learned how to influence in a way that creates a greater good for all. Yet, that is exactly what success and the future require.

Let the grand adventure of living begin.

Stand out. Start now.

PART I

GENERATE RESULTS

CHAPTER 1

Know the Driving Force of the Business

———

I was working a full-time job and running a demanding business on the side. I thought I had hired a house cleaner. Instead, I found myself with an indoor F3 tornado.

What was the driving force behind the desire to hire a cleaning team? The answer might seem obvious—to have a clean house. But as this situation quickly made clear, it ran deeper: It was to make my life easier. In their frenzied rush to move to the next paying customer, my cleaners cleared anything in their path like Tom Brady throwing a touchdown pass. The house was clean, and it was also in total disorder.

Their work created *inverse* value as I spent hours each week looking for my own stuff like a kid on a treasure hunt. I once found holiday presents stuffed behind a bookshelf seven months after the holidays. Talk about Christmas in July.

Was the house "clean"? Yes. Did the net value of their effort outweigh the cost? No. Did I keep them? No.

THE DRIVING FORCE OF A BUSINESS IS OFTEN MORE THAN MEETS THE EYE

Understanding the driving force of the business—and of its customers—is often beyond what first meets the eye.

"You have to go beyond the job description," John Hinshaw, chief operating officer of HSBC, the world's largest bank outside of the United States, said to me. "Get curious," he advises. The fastest way to gain insight into the driving force of any business is to ask. And then listen. Carefully.

FOCUS ON THE CUSTOMER

John was a standout talent in his first job with a consulting firm that had a regional telecommunications company as a major client. He demonstrated an unrivaled and rare understanding of the driving force behind the consulting firm, one of their biggest clients, and even the client's customers—and the client's CEO noticed.

On his own initiative, John asked every person he met, and even people he already knew, whether they were current customers of the telecommunications company client. If they said yes, he handed them his business card and invited them to call him if they ever had any problems, offering to be their personal customer service liaison. If they answered no, he also handed them his card and invited them to call him when they became unhappy with their current cellular provider and interested in potentially switching service.

These were the early days of the coming telecom boom, and then, as now, customers wanted to reach a real human being who cared when they encountered technical difficulties. John was that caring human. He took it upon himself to personally eliminate one of their biggest pain points. He connected them with someone who could solve their problem.

By way of reminder, John wasn't an employee of that company. He was an external consultant, and a junior consultant at that. But the level of care he showed the client's customers might make anybody think he was a top executive there.

He was a Day One Executive.

It wasn't long before John was reeling in new customers faster than the company's seasoned salespeople. John was also reeling in something else: first-person insight into what mobile customers cared deeply about—so deeply that they would switch carriers because of it, in an industry where customers are notoriously resistant to switching (Lunn and Lyons, 2018).

In 2005, Accenture published a study showing that two-thirds of customers changed telecommunications providers due to three factors: poor call quality, price, and poor customer service. With one friendly conversation at a time, a decade before that study would come out, John was inoculating his client's customers against at least two of these factors in their industry. The regional telecom client began accumulating a ten-year advantage on its competitors, in part because they had a Day One Executive in John.

KNOW THE DRIVING FORCE AND TITLE DOESN'T MATTER

A few years later, the mobile communications revolution now underway, the telecom company asked the consulting firm to develop a digital strategy. John was the obvious choice to serve as the junior consultant on the project. The telecom company CEO invited John and the senior consultant to present the strategy in the company's boardroom.

This was a formal presentation—an unveiling of sorts, of big findings from months of research. Everybody showed up in their best business attire. John's boss graciously invited him to present the strategy since he built the brief, which was aimed at the CEO.

During the presentation things seemed to go well, and then the CEO did something unexpected. He left the room and returned wearing jeans and a casual sweater.

As he settled comfortably back into his seat, others began to shift uncomfortably wondering what was about to happen. He turned to the consulting team and said, "You just presented to me as the CEO. Now tell me how our customers would experience this." The senior consultant was stunned and momentarily unsure how to respond. John wasn't.

Though the least experienced, John was suddenly the most qualified person in the room because he had acquired deep first-person insight into the driving force of the business.

He was aware the future of mobile lay in making customers' lives even easier. The CEO was face-to-face with a Day One Executive, and John represented the consulting company quite well that day.

Verizon Wireless acquired the regional telecom client company a year later. Who do you think they named vice president and chief information officer (CIO)?

John Hinshaw.

THREE DRIVING FORCES
The driving force of a business usually boils down to one or more of the following, regardless of the specific business or mission:

1. Make money;
2. Make someone's life easier (e.g., save them time, make something easier); and
3. Change the world.

For some businesses, it's all three. Let's take a deeper look at these driving forces:

- **Make Money**
  Bluntly stated, money makes the world go round. It fuels economies. It threads through everything.

  It seems obvious with business, but be aware: Even government, nonprofit, and academic organizations don't have much impact (for long, anyway) without money

(Handy, 2002). Universities, nonprofits, non-governmental organizations, and their boards of directors are looking for leaders who can raise and attract funding. Government organizations elevate stewards who can win budget battles and make good use of taxpayer dollars.

Contrary to the cynic's view, money is at the root of a lot of goodness. It gives people and communities more and greater choices. London Business School professor of strategy and entrepreneurship Freek Vermeulen points out in a *Harvard Business Review* article, entitled "Companies Don't Always Need a Purpose Beyond Profit," that increased wages and wealth have significant positive impacts on societal problems including crime, malnutrition, infant mortality, mental health, and well-being.

- **Make Someone's Life Easier**
  Time is one of the truly non-renewable resources. As an executive recently said to me, making someone's life easier, giving someone their time back, is one of the most important things they feel their organization can do. Making someone's life easier also pays.

  The 2020 pandemic accelerated what has been called the "convenience economy," with the sudden and forced shift to restaurant takeout and delivery, grocery delivery, and drive-through retail options that are likely here to stay. Consider these statistics:

  – A McKinsey Global Institute study showed nearly three out of four people experimented with online shopping, such as grocery services, for the first time during the pandemic.

- Even as the world has opened back up, 70 percent of Americans plan to still buy groceries online (Lund et al., 2021).
- A Deloitte report proclaimed that "convenience continues to reign supreme," as more than half of consumers reported their willingness to spend more to get what they need with more ease.

- **Change the World**

Philanthropic organizations, such as the Robert Woods Johnson Foundation, clearly have primary driving forces of changing the world, and it's true for many for-profit companies as well. Pioneers such as Richard Branson and Steve Jobs openly declared the driving force of their businesses was to the change the world. Organizations are becoming more conscious than ever before about being stewards of the earth and the future through sustainable solutions.

A McKinsey study showed that sustainability investments create real profits and business opportunities. Yet, while 84 percent of global CEOs acknowledge this, only a third said businesses were doing enough (Bonini and Swartz, 2014). Opportunities to excel are always at the ready for the Day One Executive.

The idea of businesses' potential as a force for good isn't new. Charles Handy, author of *The Second Curve: Thoughts on Reinventing Society,* writes about the concept of a contribution ethic in business that has long been present thanks to civic-minded leaders. In the *Harvard Business Review* article, "What's a Business For?" Handy writes that "by creating new products, spreading technology and raising productivity, enhancing quality and improving service, business has always been the active agent of progress."

LOOK BEYOND THE OBVIOUS

As my house-cyclones discovered, the driving force of an organization is not always obvious—a subtle distinction can make all the difference. Take Kodak, for instance.

Maybe you've heard the term "Kodak moments." Once the industry leader in photography, and an early mover in the shift to digital photography, it ceded market position irrecoverably by missing a subtle energy present in the driving force of the dawn of digital.

Long before there was Facebook or Instagram, Kodak accurately foresaw the coming changes and made a bold move to invest in online photo sharing. They recognized printing and physically storing photos in a scrapbook would soon be obsolete and created cameras and editing software that allowed basic photo sharing called "Kodak EasyShare" (Tarek, 2005).

But there was a flaw. Kodak executives mistakenly thought consumers merely wanted to store and share photos—to make their lives easier. The actual driving force was more nuanced, and it would change the world. It was more emotional and less transactional than they realized. Customers wanted something more. They wanted to reach across time and space to share not merely photos, but to connect; to laugh, cry, celebrate, and remark on good, funny, and even hard times *together*—through photos.

This hunger for greater, unbroken emotional connection ushered in the rise of social media, enabling people to connect like never before. Customers flocked to burgeoning social platforms that allowed online photo storage and sharing— leaving Kodak for the history books and business school case studies (Anthony, 2016).

CONSIDER THE DRIVING FORCES IN PEOPLE, NOT JUST THE ORGANIZATION

Like organizations, people also have a driving force. Andrew Neitlich, founder of the Center for Executive Coaching, told me if you want to be successful in a company, help your manager—and their manager—succeed. Be curious about *their* driving force, and make it your mission to help satisfy it. Andrew says his early bosses wanted him to make their lives easier (e.g., fewer hassles and more time). My first boss, Robert Beyster, wanted to change the world and did when he founded a company (SAIC) on the radical idea of employee-ownership at every level.

Center for Creative Leadership research on factors affecting the promotion of managers affirms the value of contributing to your boss's success by knowing what matters to them (Ruderman et al., 1994). The most successful managers are aligned to the driving force of the organization.

In their publication *The Realities of Management Promotion*, written by Marian N. Ruderman, they demonstrate a high proportion of managers who received promotions "significantly improved an existing situation by creating something new, such as a product or function, by fixing an existing business problem, or by fine-tuning an already smooth-running operation." They didn't just improve any old problem—their solutions benefitted *the driving force of the business*. Companies awarded 61 percent of promotions to people who had a track record of success with things that mattered most to the organization. (See also the chapter "Master the Golden Pyramid.")

SEEK ALIGNMENT OF YOUR DRIVING FORCE EVERY-WHERE POSSIBLE

Legendary Apple pioneer and engineer Steve Wozniak (affectionately called "Woz") told me an insightful story. While very different as people, both he and Steve Jobs shared a driving force to change the world. Together they revolutionized personal computing, making a lot of money and lives easier for billions of people across generations along the way.

Woz was working for Hewlett-Packard (HP) when he met Steve Jobs. HP's driving force was making people's lives easier and making money, but not changing the world. They couldn't appreciate the genius they had with Woz and passed up repeated invitations and requests by him to help bring his personal computer creation to market. They just couldn't see the future he knew was available and to which he held the key.

Steve Jobs did, and the rest is history.

WHEN DRIVING FORCES ARE NOT ALIGNED

What happens when your driving force does not align with that of your boss or employer? You may feel like Belgian martial artist Jean-Claude Van Damme in the famous Volvo commercial where he straddles two diverging trucks. As they slowly move further apart, he impossibly does the "epic split" in what Volvo public relations manager Anders Vilhelmsson described to the *Wall Street Journal* as "the ultimate test" (Memmott, 2013).

You have choices. In this situation, you could leave. You may also find ways to harmonize your driving force and that of an employer, even where it is not aligned, as Ray Khuo did early in his career.

Ray, an aspiring human resources executive, worked for a company that cut employee benefits because their driving force was making money. It fell to Ray to break the news. This was really hard for him because his driving force was to make people's lives easier, and this was anything but that.

He was aware the company could not afford to keep the employees on staff in light of a worsening financial condition. Ray didn't have the power to alter the business decision but did see he could choose how to implement it. He successfully advocated for more lead time with notice and transition support, and he used his power to communicate the difficult news in a manner that was sensitive to and honoring of the people whose lives would be affected.

Unlike the Better.com CEO who famously fired 900 people over Zoom, Ray traveled to each of the company's field sites to deliver the news personally—something no other manager had ever done in this company (Pisani, 2021). He shared the company's rationale in an open and transparent manner. The job was hard and thankless, and Ray handled it in a way that even the most negatively impacted employees understood and respected. He made their lives easier than they otherwise would have been had he not been the Day One Executive he is.

Ray is now a top HR executive, widely respected both inside and outside his company. Support the driving forces of those around you as best you can as Ray did, even if it differs from yours (unless it is illegal or unethical), and like Van Damme, you will pass the ultimate test.

HOW TO USE A MISALIGNED DRIVING FORCE TO YOUR ADVANTAGE

A friend of mine, whom we'll call Maria, is a Harvard alumna whose natural modus operandi is to excel. "I can't help it," she sheepishly shared with me in a conversation while we munched on banh mi sandwiches from a local Vietnamese eatery. "It's who I am."

This is not false modesty. Wired to be an achiever, Maria is any employer's dream hire.

Yet, she shared with me in a recent annual performance review, her manager gave her a mere "meets expectations" rating. To my friend, who had a career-long track record of only top ratings, this was an affront. She bravely asked to speak with her manager. What she learned stunned her. Her manager bluntly acknowledged that while Maria's efforts helped the company at large, they did nothing to advance the driving force of the specific internal organization to which she belonged.

Maria's passions were people and partnerships, but her division's focus was concerned with systems and technology solutions. Feeling unappreciated, Maria easily could have left the company. Instead, she used this hard but valuable insight to deftly maneuver a change she knew was long overdue to better align her driving force with the organization's by making an internal move.

With her boss's support, Maria found a new position in the company and is now extremely happy doing what she loves—building partnerships. Her efforts are now appreciated and rewarded because they align with the driving force of the specific organization to which she belongs inside of the larger company. By contributing to the future your organization desires to create, you also simultaneously contribute to yours.

THREE QUESTIONS TO ASSESS THE DRIVING FORCE(S) IN PLAY

- What is *your* driving force? What pursuits, activities, or areas do you naturally pour energy into? I recommend a simple but powerful exercise I call "Do-Great-Love." (See chapter 18, "Take the Highest Care of You," for a description).
- What is the driving force of the organization or leader or client you support? If you aren't sure, who could shed light on this for you? Identify these people and talk to them.

- Periodically check in with yourself: Tune in to the level of alignment. Pay attention to your feelings. Even unhappiness or anger can be important clues to your true driving force. What if, rather than being some permanent condition, they are simply pointers? If you sense misalignment, what choices are available to remedy this?

* * *

Like John Hinshaw, empower yourself to be in the driver's seat of your career and life by learning to discern the real driving force behind everything and everyone. Demonstrate your ability to discern this and you will stand out. Like Ray and Maria, even when your driving force does not perfectly align with that of an employer, you can still be true to yourself and open pathways to new possibilities. Here's what not to do: bring F3 tornado energy to the wrong driving force— like those house cleaners—unless you want to blow your career totally off course.

Chapter Checklist:
- The driving force of the business is often more than meets the eye.
- Know and honor the driving force of people and organizations, and you will create possibilities far beyond a job title.
- Honor your own driving force, and seek alignment of your driving force and everything and everyone.

CHAPTER 2

Master the Golden Pyramid

———

The Egyptians built their pyramids to last thousands of years—nearly five thousand years ago.

Friends of mine who have visited them tell me they were mesmerized gazing upon the golden pyramids through the haze of a heat shimmer, marveling at the engineering and sheer execution success they represent. The Great Pyramid of Giza, the largest most intact, is the only remaining of the seven wonders of the ancient world. In an interview with *BBC Science Focus Magazine*, engineer Steve Burrows said what he finds most inspiring about the pyramids is their longevity. "If you asked us to build something today, and you wanted it to last for five thousand years, we'd think you'd gone crazy. I mean, how could you possibly do that?" he remarked incredulously.

Talk about built to last.

Andrew Neitlich, the founder and director of the Center for Executive Coaching, which trains thousands of coaches every year to work with executives, shared at least part of the answer in a conversation about what it takes for executives to succeed. A friend once told him good consultants "get, sell, and execute great ideas." Andrew told me it struck him immediately that this was also what leaders do. Successful executives are not just idea people. They execute well.

In other words, it took more than a great idea to build the Great Pyramid.

WHAT DOES IT MEAN TO EXECUTE WELL?

Executing well means achieving the desired end state, on schedule and within the budget. Project managers refer to these three dimensions of success as a golden triangle because these variables do not exist in isolation. They are in perpetual and inexorable tension with one another and are sometimes called the triple constraints of project management, as Michael Scheiner writes in his article, "The Project Management Triangle (Iron Triangle) and Its Elements Explained," published on the CRM.org website. Each variable, or constraint, exerts a pull on the others.

Let's take a closer look at each:

- **Cost**
  Cost is the total expense to plan, design, execute, and deliver a product, service, or experience. In the case of a service or experience, some costs will take the form of billable labor hours; thus, the amount of *time* it takes to

do the work will drive cost. This variable also includes invisible but very real "opportunity costs," which are basically all the things you could have done with that time or money through other choices but didn't.

- **Schedule**

  This variable seems straightforward enough: it's a deadline, the date by which you must deliver the product or service. Because there are a lot of moving parts with most major initiatives, there are *a lot* of intricate, interrelated deadlines. It's important to understand these relationships and the ramifications a schedule change on one aspect of a project may have on others. Such a shift will likely trigger the need to renegotiate cost or performance or quality expectations.

- **Performance/Quality**

  Performance or quality expectations can be tricky for a couple of reasons. First, they are moving targets. They are dynamic and continuously in flux. People change their minds and may not always think to telegraph this to you. Second, they are not always explicit. People harbor unspoken expectations. Also, there may be a number of people who collectively shape and influence the expected standard—e.g., shareholders, stakeholders, venture capital investors, or influencers.

These variables of the golden triangle exist within a permeable boundary of a fourth constraint—scope.

BEAR IN MIND THE INVISIBLE FOURTH CONSTRAINT—SCOPE

There's a fourth dimension of success, and it's often invisible: project scope. If you imagine the golden triangle described above now as a golden *pyramid*, project scope is the base, the central variable that influences all other variables.

If you haven't yet, you might hear the term "scope creep" one day. This refers to the reality that people's expectations naturally grow and evolve, sometimes beneath their awareness. The *Nutcracker* Sugar Plum Fairy starts dancing. Before they, or you, know it, their expanding vision has outgrown your budget and timeline, and they're unhappy because you can't make their fantasy come true.

As the Program Management One Stop Shop: PM Zone website bluntly puts it, "A lot—Fast—Cheap—Good" is a set of expectations that can never be achieved simultaneously." What happens when project sponsors or stakeholders become enamored of something you don't have budget for? Can you reconcile this? The answer is sometimes—but it gets a lot harder if they run too far afield of what the schedule and budget may allow. Keep your friends close, enemies closer, and your array of stakeholders even closer throughout project duration.

THINK OF EVERYTHING AS A PROJECT

Mastering the golden pyramid is not something you can learn in a book. If this is new to you, think of everything in your world as a project. Start with something small to practice putting the golden pyramid to use. Waiting until you lead a high-visibility project is not the time to start.

UNDERSTANDING THE DOMINANT CONSTRAINT

While all three dimensions apart from scope are always dynamically in play, one dimension is always the key driver, acting as the current constraint on the project. It's critical to get a sense of this—and to be aware that even this can change at any time.

Let's play with a few example scenarios:

SCENARIO #1:

A client asks you to develop a strategic plan. The client's top priority is to "get it right" and have top executives embrace it.

What is the dominant constraint?

Quality may be the dominant constraint in this example. The budget and schedule are likely negotiable to attain the desired outcome of the top executive's satisfaction.

SCENARIO #2:

A company developing a nifty new product for kids wants to have its product ready on store shelves in time for the lucrative holiday season. To guarantee that time frame, the manufacturer will need to charge a premium to accelerate production on the assembly line.

What is the dominant constraint in this example? *Schedule.*

If you miss the holiday shopping season, you have missed the year in sales. That loss of revenue vastly outweighs the extra surge costs. If needed, you are likely willing to exceed the budget, and you may be willing to shave off some quality expectations, but you cannot risk the schedule.

SCENARIO #3:
A company offers blankets labeled for pro sports teams. The company lost its overseas manufacturer, and while domestic options have faster turnaround times, they are much more expensive. The company must decide whether to provide a similar product at a significantly steeper price point or downgrade to a lower quality product to keep the product affordable to consumers and maintain even its minimal profit margin.

What is the dominant constraint in this example? *Budget.*

This product is a commodity, and consumers will only pay so much. If it's too expensive, customers will simply choose a near-identical competitor product, and it will be extremely costly to win them back. The company will probably need to shift to a lower quality product to stay within the price parameters, but it's likely worth it.

Do you see how these variables interact with and influence each other?

WHEN THE CONSTRAINTS CHANGE PLACE

It can get even trickier. The dominant constraint is not a fixed variable. It can change on you mid-stream.

Imagine another, more complex scenario: a group of companies are partnering to construct a multi-billion-dollar data center. Construction is set to start underway soon with an incredibly complex project plan with hundreds of complex interdependencies, including environmental permitting, electrical equipment, public engagement to ensure political support from the local community for the project, and contingent funding that may depend on successful completion of earlier project steps. If the consortium fails to deliver the project for any reason, they will incur hundreds of millions of dollars in penalties and late fees.

The team worked together to plan the project and estimate costs, meticulously factoring for foreseeable risks, and arriving at agreements on a risk-managed budget. At the start of the project, budget was the driving constraint exerting the dominant influence on project execution. Just before construction was set to begin, however, the COVID-19 pandemic sparked global supply chain disruptions, delaying delivery of key equipment. This was followed by inflation also sweeping the globe. Construction would now be unavoidably delayed. The only question would be by how much.

Is the budget still the dominant constraint now?

No. The schedule is now likely the dominant constraint. Why?

Between penalty fees and rising costs from inflation (projected to worsen), if the team misses the scheduled delivery, resulting costs will swamp the relatively small cost impact of surge requirements. If the team is to complete the project in the most cost-effective manner, the original budget must yield to the new driving constraint of schedule.

HIT THE "GOLDILOCKS ZONE"

The challenge is guiding execution of any project into what I call the "Goldilocks zone." This ideal spot is where everything's just right: the product/service/experience meets or exceeds a client's quality expectations, deliverables are on schedule, and everything is within budget.

Here are three pragmatic pro-tips that can help you master the Golden Pyramid and hit the Goldilocks zone.

PRO-TIP #1: ENGAGE STAKEHOLDERS TO SURFACE EXPECTATIONS EARLY

Successful executives enroll others in shaping the expected quality standard. They invite them to take up an oar and row in the water with them toward the desired end-state. Unlike tangibles of budget and schedule variables, expectations are inherently subjective and intangible. They can be elusive because they live in the imaginations of not just one person but often several influential stakeholders who will ultimately judge success and may not see it the same way.

Some questions you can ask to uncover these deeper expectations include:

- What would success *look like*? (This makes the expectation explicit and observable.)
- If this was successful, what would change? What would become possible? (This digs deeper into what may be a hidden expectation.)
- How would we know if this was slipping off track? Who would care? (This shines light on the guardrails, the early indicators of a problem that can help you stay out of a ditch.)

PRO-TIP #2: KNOW WHAT'S "DONE"

Fresh out of school in my early twenties, I moved into a new apartment. My father came to help me move some belongings. He couldn't hide his surprise when he walked into my living room.

"You aren't even close to being fully packed," he said.

"What?" I defiantly exclaimed, pointing to all the full boxes stacked around my home, as if the number of full boxes was the metric.

The following morning, the movers agreed with my father, charging me a premium for the added time and extra boxes it took them to complete the job.

It's easy to underestimate the last mile of a major project. Get clear early and be explicit about completion criteria. Know what constitutes "done"—and, if you aren't sure, what this looks like. In my moving example, it would have been everything is in a box, nothing is on the floor or on a table that is not in a box.

PRO-TIP #3: ACTIVELY MANAGE EXPECTATIONS

Despite the arrival of systems such as Lean Six Sigma and even the Project Management Institute in 1969, most projects still fail (Hardy-Vallee, 2012). One way even a golden triangle can become a Bermuda Triangle and cause an otherwise promising executive's career to vanish into thin air isn't a project running over schedule or even blowing a budget. It's not even the project that fails to deliver to expectations. It's the element of surprise.

"Nobody likes surprises," my earliest mentors drilled into me. The key? Alert in time to avert.

Delivering bad news is not fun, but bad news isn't fine wine and doesn't get better with age. It takes guts to sound the alarm early when a project may be in grave danger, and such courage is the mark of the best executives. The courage to speak even a problematic truth and show a plan to recover will set you apart from other leaders.

Consistently using a simple forecasting system based on the elements of the Golden Pyramid greatly reduce the chances you will ever have to deliver that bad news. Research affirms regular, risk-targeted status reviews can predict risk up to 100 percent. Investment in even basic forecasting can predict risk with nearly 90 percent accuracy and allow executives to focus their time only on at-risk projects. This is a lot more efficient than having to review every project in a portfolio (Hopmere, Crawford, and Harré, 2020).

A WORD ON STAKEHOLDERS

USE A STRATEGIC APPROACH TO STAKEHOLDER ENGAGEMENT
It's tempting to assume you know what success looks like based on your perspective from a handful of conversations with some key people. That's a mistake. Be strategic in how you approach stakeholder engagement.

One of the most common and least appreciated pitfalls that sinks projects is failing to account for all of stakeholders whose support is required for the project's long-term success. A Purdue University researcher called stakeholder engagement and consensus-building around success indicators a "decisive factor" in project success, based on a review of nearly seventy research studies. They noted this as a significant gap in the Project Management Body of Knowledge, the bible for project managers (Scheiner, 2022). Factor for even this one thing alone, and you will stand out (Shah, 2016). Reconciling conflicting stakeholder views can be messy, but don't delude yourself into thinking you can sidestep this. A landmark research study affirmed a critical pitfall for multi-stakeholder projects (which is every complex initiative) is disparity in how different stakeholders view and measure success (Davis, 2018).

I once worked with an aspiring executive who was a rising star in his organization. The top executive sponsor provided him with a catapult moment on a silver platter. The challenge was to develop a joint strategy to guide billions of dollars of shared technology investments in the coming years. The only catch was all the stakeholder organizations would need to sign off on the strategy.

He made his first tactical error when he thought he could shortcut this. Figuring good messaging on the back end would seal the deal, he resisted inviting stakeholders to weigh in throughout the process. In deciding to not risk the mess of dissension, he risked it all.

He went through the motions of collaborative meetings for appearance's sake. Rather than do the messy but central work of negotiating mutually acceptable consensus agreements (which he feared he couldn't control), he gambled the stakeholders wouldn't feel that strongly in the end and would acquiesce with whatever became the pillars of strategy. They didn't.

He also made an unforced error in deciding that pleasing his boss was his primary fundamental metric. He miscalculated how sensitive his boss (who was a seasoned executive) would be to these constituents' interests. Nine months in and two weeks out from the expected delivery date of the strategy, one of the most influential organizations pulled out.

Top executives declined to sign off, unwilling to go to the mat with these powerful interests. The organization, and he, lost standing. All the efforts were for nothing.

MAP THE TERRAIN

It never ceases to astonish me how many executives wing it with their highest stakes initiatives. Stakeholder mapping is a technique where you take a structured look at power dynamics, awareness, and attitudes regarding your project or initiative. You can use the analysis to inform engagement and influence campaigns. Below are some questions you can ask your team and your stakeholders to give you a running start and help you avoid this pitfall:

- Whose support do we need for this initiative to succeed? (Cast a wider net than you think is required.) Who has the power to stand in the way or block it? (Yes, you are wise to involve, not avoid, them.)
- What would success look like from *their* perspective? (Be open to all ideas.)
- What will it take for them to embrace this product or initiative? (Look for everywhere you can say yes.)

KEEP YOUR FRIENDS CLOSE AND YOUR STAKEHOLDERS CLOSER

Asking what success looks like just once is not enough. You must continually put your finger in the wind and check in with stakeholders to ensure previously negotiated agreements remain valid. Like you, your stakeholders are encountering new information daily. People who may have different or even conflicting ideas from your own are influencing them outside of your sight. Just because you talked about it last week, or even yesterday, doesn't mean whatever you agreed upon hasn't changed. It probably has—don't be the last to know.

Some questions to consider to keep everybody on the same sheet include:

- What are some checkpoints to ensure an initiative is tracking with key sponsors or stakeholders' expectations and, importantly, if anything has changed in their expectations?
- Who needs to be a part of these checkpoints?
- How can we document and communicate the modified expectations to keep everybody on the same page?

* * *

In that BBC interview, structural engineer Steve Burrows also noted modern software has allowed researchers to learn something else remarkable about the pyramids: The Egyptians learned from experience. Each successive pyramid improved upon the last, incorporating lessons-learned.

Master the Golden Pyramid, and while your project may not last thousands of years like the Great Pyramid, you and your achievements will stand the test of time.

Chapter Checklist:

- Think of everything as a project.
- Understand the relationship of scope, quality expectations, schedule, and budget.
- Watch for the dynamic inherent tension between the elements of the Golden Pyramid; pay attention to the dominant constraint, which may change.
- Keep your stakeholders close to you and the project: Quality expectations may be in the eyes of many a beholder.
- Understand how you will track progress to include whether the work is progressing to the expected quality standard, on time, and within budget.

CHAPTER 3

Know Your Value

——

Maggie Wilderotter is a seasoned executive. She has led multiple Fortune 500 companies and start-ups, including serving as CEO of Frontier Communications and interim CEO of DocuSign, and served on over fifty corporate boards of directors for public and private companies. She started her career as a secretary.

In a conversation with me about how she got her start, she revealed an attitude that has permeated her entire career: "This job will be different because I'm going to add value." That is the voice of a Day One Executive and someone who knows their value.

WHY IS IT IMPORTANT TO KNOW YOUR VALUE?

Let me be clear: When I say, "Know your value," this isn't about the value of "you." You, as a being, are invaluable. When you know you can *add* value, you are aware of your value. Some part of you has the sense of what you can uniquely contribute, and that value is measurable, quantifiable, and qualifiable both now and in the future.

Business is all about creating and adding value. When you do, like Maggie, you change the course of a future. You also empower you.

Mika Brzezinski is the co-host of the television news program *Morning Joe* and author of *Knowing Your Value: Women, Money, and Getting What You're Worth,* which is a great read, especially for women executives. In her book, she speaks about the importance of knowing your value.

I have a friend, we'll call her Sara, who says this advice helped her immensely when her employer passed over her for a deserved promotion. Sara created an innovative program management organization for a global Fortune 200 company based on her subject matter expertise and team-building skills that enabled the company to manage risks with billion-dollar projects in new, more efficient ways. She was adding value and knew it, and so she was shocked when the company's executives passed her over for a promotion to lead the very group she created and was already leading without a title.

A bigger shock came when she learned the real reason they overlooked her—politics, not performance. The employer told her she was seen by some in the top echelon as not sufficiently ambitious.

The words "not ambitious" struck her like a two-by-four. Sara was stunned—and then angry. Humble, she was not one to toot her own horn, and at that time she was trying to start a family with her husband.

Rather than letting this stick with her, Brzezinski's advice was to know her value and to appreciate and stand in that value, rather than wait for external acknowledgment. That awareness emboldened her to plan her next career move where she became the successful CEO of her own company. Sara is now happier and making more money than she would have even had she received that promotion. Best of all, she is living life fully on her own terms.

A PASSPORT TO ANYWHERE

You don't have to start a company, though, to stand in your value. Knowing your value is a passport to anywhere. Often, reward structures link more to navigating politics than generating value (Kaplan and Norton, 2005). If that is the case, unless that's your game—get out. Stand in your value and move to higher ground.

When you know your value, you know you can make a move at any time you choose, on your terms. You might have a bad day, but you won't tolerate a bad boss. Your awareness of the value you generate will keep you from feeling trapped or at the mercy of a bad boss, unstable employer, or down market.

Let's look at some different ways adding value can show up.

VALUE-GENERATING ENERGIES

In her book, *Joy of Business: What If Business Is the Adventure of Living*, Simone Milasas describes three kinds of energies required in business that each generate value: creators, connectors, and movers. Some people can do all three (often referred to as foundational). All three energies must be present for an organization of any type to thrive.

Let's unpack these to see how they can help you know, and show, your value.

CREATORS

Creators are idea people. Apple computer legend Steve Wozniak (or "Woz," as he is affectionately called) is an example of a creator. Woz created the world's first commercially successful personal computer, which launched a legendary company, Apple, by putting powerful compute power (previously requiring a huge space and even huger budget) into the hands of everyday people (Encyclopedia Britannica Online Ed., 2022).

I met Woz in the course of researching and writing this book.

"I did a lot of projects on the side for love," Woz said in an interview with me. "I read about young engineers who owned a company with their father… how they would work for two weeks without hardly coming out and design things that would save the world."

That's creator energy talking.

"Oh my gosh, I wanted to be one of these people," he shared with childlike glee.

Woz invented the product that made Apple, but if he and Steve Jobs hadn't met each other, he's the first to say his brilliant creation might never have left his garage. Even the most brilliant creators, like Woz, need connectors and movers. Steve Jobs brought those energies.

CONNECTORS

Connectors are natural networkers.

"They are the ones who will talk to everybody," Simone Milasas says in a SoundCloud audio clip entitled, "Create, Connect, Move."

They thrive on the energy that makes me need to take a three-day nap. Take Jeff (name changed), who works with a fast-growing start-up company. He is not the smartest guy on the team, nor is he the hardest working. In a company that works fourteen-hour days, Jeff slides by with eight-hour days.

Jeff is a connector, and because of that, he is extremely valuable to this company. Jeff's brilliance is in activating a network. Under Jeff's spell, money doesn't just grow on trees, it comes from private jets, lavish vacations, and highbrow parties in the Hamptons. When Jeff starts talking about the company's potential, people with deep pocket write checks the size of some countries' gross national product.

Jeff is a proverbial Pied Piper who meets people everywhere he goes. You can't afford to not have Jeff on your team. Like Steve Jobs, Jeff knows his value. He knows that, without him, even the most brilliant ideas in the world will land you donuts, not dollars.

MOVERS

Now consider my friend Jennifer, who is an executive with a major technology consulting company. Jennifer is a mover. Like many hard-working movers, she doesn't particularly care for what she perceives as Jeff's schmoozing. Movers get things done.

Jennifer can perceive what needs to happen *today* to create the future. Like any mover, nothing escapes her notice. You can rely on a mover to know what questions to ask and to know exactly what needs to be done by when.

MAKE IT VISIBLE

Your choices and the value you generate are not dependent on whether others see the value, but it is still important to make your value visible. This isn't about tooting your own horn or blaring over others. It *is* about allowing your contributions to be seen.

As Sara attests, we pay a price when value isn't seen. Betsy Mcloughlin is a global empowerment coach based in the Washington, DC, metropolitan area. She runs workshops to help people acknowledge themselves and points out there is also an emotional toll to this. "What does *not* acknowledging you cost you?" she provocatively asked me in a conversation.

Value is most visible with creators and connectors. Nobody disputes the value of Steve Wozniak's creation. Jeff can point to deals brought in because of specific key relationships he brought to the table. Making value visible can be harder for movers.

My friend Maria, like Jennifer, is a mover. She works at a technology start-up and was instrumental in the success of a $2 million pilot project that generated $13 million in new revenue within its first year. Maria was certainly not the sole contributor—but her mover energy pulled a high-risk project to a triumphant finish, because customers invested in the technology before it was fully built out, a risky but not uncommon practice in the technology sector.

"There are too many disconnected moving parts," she warned the executives. "The project needs a full-time integrator to help ensure project design meets customer needs," she counselled.

The executive sponsors acted on her advice, and the project became a huge success.

It would be easy for Maria to write off her role in the success of that project. After all, many people and many factors, beyond bringing in a full-time integrator, contributed to its success. Yet this project would not have succeeded on its own without her timely, specific, and accurate warning and recommended intervention.

Too often, humble leaders sit back hoping others will see and appreciate the value they contributed to something. Maria knew she had to make this value visible. To do that, she had to make it tangible.

MAKE YOUR VALUE TANGIBLE

Get in the habit of qualifying and quantifying the value you create in tangible form, even inherently intangible value. Attune to specific examples of where you have generated value for your organization, such as new revenues, higher profits, or measurable advancement of its mission (Glassdoor, 2022). Start by looking at the hard costs of you and aim to have a return on investment (ROI) of *at least* a factor of ten on you.

The business case with Maria's technology project was clear: The company more than quintupled its ROI in the first year of the project and scaled and expanded from there. Maria's "cost" (her pro-rated salary and benefits for that portion of time) was a tiny fraction of the budget, an even smaller fraction of the windfall ROI. With her help, executive sponsors could clearly see the tenfold-plus ROI on Maria's contributions and (wisely) fully support her career trajectory.

There's a mutually rewarding investment in play. She's on their radar because she's on her own radar. She knows her value.

WHAT VALUE LOOKS LIKE AT DIFFERENT LEVELS

Value looks different at numerous phases of your career and grows. Early in your career, your value comes from reliability. A team relaxes when they know they can count on you. They expend fewer resources following up on your work, because they know you will deliver. Generating value at the level Maria did is a more advanced proposition, and it's where the money is.

This may come as hard news for some still operating under an "A" for effort paradigm, but value does not come from trying. As Yoda famously says in *The Empire Strikes Back*, "Try not. Do. Or do not. There is no try." (Kershner, 1980). The act of trying is an input cost, it is not value.

One of my clients oversees billions of dollars of information technology investments in various stages of implementation by a federation of organizations. The organizations that receive these funds provide regular status updates to my client to track accountable progress and address risks early. On one occasion, several organizations didn't submit their status updates, and the input from the few who did was slim.

My client's team sent out a routine reminder email and stopped at that, figuring they had done their job. But had they? What else could they have done to carry the ball to the finish line and deliver value?

Here are a few other actions the team could have taken:

- Proactively reach out by phone.
- Escalate the request as needed to ensure it received the needed attention.
- Investigate poor quality input with follow-up questions.

In settling for this, the team ran two risks: Either nothing was at stake and the team was not needed; or everything was at stake and, with no real insight into the risks, big stuff could blow up tomorrow. If the latter was true, the team deprived themselves of a silver platter opportunity to increase their value quotient (VQ).

A FRAMEWORK FOR CALCULATING YOUR VALUE QUOTIENT (VQ)

Your VQ is the value you deliver divided by your cost to deliver it. Calculating VQ is similar to doing a benefit-to-cost (BC) assessment, except I recommend thinking of it in terms of value-to-cost (VC). The fastest way to assess your VQ is to quantify and qualify the value specific projects, initiatives, or roles you support in an organization generate—and then divide the estimated value of that by your relative cost.

Calculating your VQ (which is a product of your VC ratio) may take a little time to dig through, but you are worth it. It will empower you when negotiating your salary and other forms of compensation. Below is a three-step framework to help you characterize and quantify your VQ. Stay with me!

STEP 1: CALCULATE THE VALUE YOU CONTRIBUTE

I outline three elements of value below—tangible, intangible, and future or potential. Itemize your contributions. Add them up, and then weigh them as I describe below.

ELEMENT 1. TANGIBLE VALUE

This is the extent to which you directly contribute to creating or actualizing anything that brings tangible value, such as increasing revenues or profits, saving money or lives, or avoiding loss.

Measurable value may not always appear to be financial, especially with public sector or non-profit organizations, but are still tangible. Often, there are several possibilities for translating even non-financial forms of tangible value into financial metrics. Ask questions, get creative, and look for possibilities.

- **Itemize projects and initiatives**
Make an itemized list of each project or initiative you supported, and the tangible "so what" result to which your efforts contributed or made possible.

- **Estimate what each is worth**
This is usually pretty straightforward. Perhaps it's winning a new deal or proposal, bringing in new clients, raising money, or other forms of revenue or successful cost-saving initiatives.

- **Weigh them relative to your contribution**
Assign a percentage to each activity or result to represent the relative weight of your contribution. Multiply the total value the project generated to the relative weight of your contribution for a relative contribution value. For example, you are not solely responsible for that success. The other people likely also deserve some credit. Be fair and reasonable as others will need to agree how you characterize this is reasonable.

Example: For the sake of illustration, let's imagine you assisted with a number of activities around a new product that yielded immediate new market value of $1 million. Let's imagine there were ten people on the team, and three of you carried the lion's share of the work. Evenly distributed, you might assess a weighting of ten percent to each person on the team. But since the roles and relative value contributed were not equally distributed, you and your two colleagues would have a slightly heavier weighting in the calculation.

Playing the example out a bit further, since three of you played a disproportionate role, you might estimate the three of you delivered 50 percent of the value, and the other players collectively represented 50 percent of the value. Your relative contribution, therefore, might reasonably be 15 percent. Your role might reasonably represent roughly $150,000 of the $1 million in acquired market value. Even if your role was only 1 percent, that is still $10,000 of value you contributed to generating. Keep it reasonable, as you need to be prepared to articulate your rationale for the weighting or range you assess.

- **Add it up**
  Do this for each project or activity that contributed to some major win for your organization. Then add it all up. This is the estimated tangible value that you helped create.

ELEMENT 2. INTANGIBLE VALUE.

Next, estimate the intangible value you helped to create in terms of things the organization values—e.g., lives saved; enhancing the organization's stature, position, or brand. Intangibles are secondary and best when paired with tangible value.

Not all value is immediately tangible. Intangibles are also generative (and some do represent tangible value). Examples of intangible value include access to influential decision-makers, a new competitive edge, and raising an organization's profile, brand, or stature.

Let's have a look:

- **Itemize**
  Make an itemized list of these intangibles such as those listed above.

- **Assign a rough order magnitude estimate**
  Where you can, assign a rough order-of-magnitude dollar estimate around the potential value it represents. Be creative, yet realistic and reasonable. Look to market research sources to get ideas on reasonable benchmarks.

  Qualify the value where it can't be quantified. Be able to describe the bottom-line impact, the "so what," in terms of the driving force of the business. This doesn't factor into the calculation, but it can help round out a compelling fact-based value narrative.

- **Weight them relative to your contribution**
  As in the first example, weigh it appropriately to reflect your relative contribution accurately.

- **Add it up**
  Do this for each project or activity that contributed to some major win for your organization, and then add the sums up.

ELEMENT 3. FUTURE VALUE.

Itemize and assign an estimated value to any innovations you introduced that have significant potential to deliver value in the future. Future value is the least compelling value element, because it is prospective. It will become more impactful when it takes the form of tangible value, but that doesn't mean you can't claim some of the value creation now.

- **Itemize**

  List any specific projects or initiatives that are poised to generate future value. This is the place to itemize any valuable new skills or credentials you acquired that enables your organization to generate value in areas previously inaccessible to them.

- **Estimate the potential value they represent in the future**

- **Weight them with two factors**
  - Factor 1: Likelihood

    Assign a rough estimate based on the likelihood the projected future value will materialize. Multiply the weighing by the absolute number to get a lower number. For example, if you contributed to the development of a prototype product, while it may have real promise, there is no guarantee the product will come to market and be profitable.

  - Factor 2: Your contribution

    Take the Factor 1/Likelihood results and now assign a secondary weighting to each based on the relative impact or importance of your contribution. Multiply Factors 1 and 2 for each project or initiative.

- **Add it up**

  Add up the sum of the above double-weighted numbers.

You have now quantified and qualified the value your contributions helped generate. We need to look next at what it cost for you to generate that value.

STEP 2: QUANTIFY AND DIVIDE BY YOUR TOTAL "COST"

Get insight into *your* cost to the organization.

If you're employed, this includes your salary *and* the financial equivalent of whatever benefits your organization offers you, along with costs to give you office space, a computer, and keep the lights on. Your company likely provides a compensation statement, and you can use that to help you get your arms around this. Your total cost is usually a multiplier on your salary and may be as little as one and a half times your salary in low-margin businesses with minimum benefits to up to, or even more than, two times your salary in high margin industries.

Note that we are not interested here in everything it costs to generate the value. Because we have isolated out your value by weighing the above calculations, we are focused in this step primarily on the cost of you. Here is how to do this:

- **Estimate current costs**

  If you're doing an annual assessment, you could just use your annualized lump sum cost. But if you are doing a spot review and running these calculations around a particular major contribution, you might use a percentage of your costs over that window of time to scale it accordingly.

- **Prorate for the future if needed**
  If you have any future value entries in Element 3 above (for example, if you are a key player on a multi-year deal), consider breaking your costs out over a period of years that track with your future value estimates. Recognize that your future costs are likely higher because of inflation. You don't have to get it perfect, but it will help to show you are factoring for this. The key is to show realism and apples-to-apples comparisons as best you can.

- **Add it up**
  Calculate this.

You now have an estimate of what it cost the company to have you generate all that value. Next, we are going to calculate your VC ratio to get your VQ.

STEP 3: CALCULATE YOUR VQ

Add up the sum totals of the first three value-creating elements above. Divide that total number by the number you came up with in Step 2, what it costs for you to generate that value. This number is your VQ. Ideally, you can show a VQ of at least ten.

Your aim is to demonstrate unequivocally, credibly, and reasonably the value you deliver is significantly beyond your cost, ideally by a factor of ten. Layer the intangible contributions that cannot be quantified financially on top of this to help round your narrative. This is where assets such as being a team player, reliable, and tenure with an organization come into play.

This exercise takes time and may feel clunky at first. The awareness you gain when you break it down will empower you to stand in your strength, because the root of power is value. You might even surprise yourself at the value you are creating.

INCREASE YOUR VALUE QUOTIENT (VQ)

The value you are capable of delivering progressively builds on itself like layers with every experience, but you must consciously choose to develop and grow it. But where do you start? Like Maggie Wilderotter in her first job, start right where you are.

The three biggest ways to increase your value quotient include:

- Choose higher stakes projects;
- Play a larger, more impactful role; and
- Take on more projects.

Additional ways to increase your VQ include:

- **Go the extra mile, or millimeter.** Offer to do something no one has asked you to do. Stay late to help a colleague who has a lot riding on a big presentation to help them ensure a product is truly client ready. If you overhear a manager or client mention an interest in exploring a potential business area, take the initiative to advance the conversation. Where are the problems (often possibilities in disguise)? Sometimes the easiest places to add value are hiding in the things nobody else wants to do, and it doesn't always require going an extra mile. Sometimes even an extra millimeter is all that is required and makes all the difference.

- **Swim outside your lane**. I don't mean swim *over* someone else, but if you see something that needs to be done, even if it's not technically "your" job, if it can add value and you can do it, offer to do it. I was recently in a meeting with government top officials, and the meeting facilitator needed help taking notes. The group was hitting on some really good ideas, and he couldn't run the meeting and type up all of the ideas bubbling up at the same time.

  I was not technically part of his team, but I know how to synthesize ideas quickly and have mad typing skills. I took a risk and jumped in to help him out with notetaking. With his facilitation and my live-scribing assistance, the group nailed the wording of some key agreements in real time that might have otherwise taken weeks of follow-up meetings. The facilitator and the group invited me to support them in their next project phase.

- **Become more efficient**. "A dollar saved is a dollar earned," as the saying goes. As you become more efficient in your own workflow, you add value just by virtue of generating results with less effort. You create space to add value because you have time to think strategically.

  The *Merriam-Webster* dictionary defines effective as "producing a decided, decisive, or desired effect." Efficient, on the other hand, is being "capable of producing desired results with little or no waste (as of time or materials)." Some see efficiency and effectiveness as redundant or even being inexorably in conflict, with effectiveness coming at the expense of efficiency. Producing the desired result is inherent in efficiency, so be efficient.

- **Be curious about context.** In marketing, people say the content is king. But when it comes to adding value, *context* is king. Often, junior staff members do not understand why a more senior leader seems to care so much about something the junior staff member deems unimportant. In reality, the junior staff member is often simply lacking context. A Day One Executive knows this.

The senior leader's request for more persuasive writing is because that leader knows the organization's future depends on whether they receive funding. Their insistence on editorial accuracy is from the awareness that the organization's brand name rests, in part, on its reputation for quality. And demands for deeper backup insight are because top executives have to answer tough questions.

- **Focus on delivering "gold bars," not earning "gold stars."** Angelique Rewers, founder and CEO of Bold-Haus, a company that advises small businesses in strategic development with corporate clients, describes activity-orientation as the pursuit of "gold stars" (credit and acknowledgment for a good effort) versus "gold bars" (money or the result). (Rewers, 2013).

Be aware that some organizations pander to your "gold star" imprinting because it's a lot cheaper to give you praise than to give you a raise. Don't settle for gold stars. Know your value and demand gold bars for the money you are helping someone generate.

* * *

When you are clear and unambiguous about the value you deliver to an organization, you will not hesitate to speak up for yourself when it comes to negotiating compensation. When you work with organizations and clients who appropriately value what you are willing and able to deliver, work becomes fun. I wonder what doors will open to you when, like Maggie Wilderotter, you open the door to your Day One Executive and say, almost prophetically, "This job will be different because I will add value."

Chapter Checklist:

- Consider if you are a creator, connector, or mover—or all three.
- Become conversant in your organization or client's strategy. Familiarize yourself and align your efforts with its mission, vision, goals or targets, and how they structured the organization to achieve them.
- Be thinking from the start what value you can add and how you will demonstrate it. Take the time to collect metrics that can serve as "before" metrics. Examples include measuring levels of awareness and attitudes around an issue to show how these have changed after an outreach campaign. This awareness empowers you to describe the specific outcomes you helped generate tangibly.
- Be cognizant of all the key players so that you are able to describe accurately the role you played in whatever downstream success is achieved without over- or understating those contributions. Claim, own, and acknowledge your value before you expect others to do so.
- Quantify and qualify the value you created last year. Run the calculations. It's tedious but important to have an accurate grasp of your impact on an organization. It takes some time to evaluate, but you are worth it.

CHAPTER 4

Be Strategic

———

"Grandma! You picked Pepsi!"

Four words, uttered by a granddaughter to her grandmother on a sweltering San Antonio, Texas, street corner one regular day in the 1970s proved incredibly strategic. Those words would soon take the country by storm in a brilliant ad campaign. Within a few short years, Pepsi would achieve the seemingly impossible—overtake Coca-Cola to become the nation's best-selling single, soft drink (Associated Press, 1986).

In a Wharton Leadership Lecture at the University of Pennsylvania, John Sculley, CEO of Pepsi-Cola Company during the infamous "cola wars" era (1977 to 1983), regaled the audience with the story of this magic moment. In 1970, Coke was not only king of the cola category, it was the most famous brand in the world. It outsold Pepsi ten-to-one in half of the country.

Yet, Pepsi had something going for it. Unfortunately for them, only a few executives and lab scientists running taste test experiments more closely guarded than our nuclear secrets knew what it was, in the super top secret world of consumer product market research. While consumers overwhelmingly chose Coca-Cola over Pepsi in shopping aisles, blind taste tests conducted privately in Pepsi's labs repeatedly revealed Pepsi's best kept secret—most people preferred the taste of Pepsi over Coke (Little, 2019).

In a bold move, Pepsi executives brought the lab to the living room: They put consumer taste preferences on public display on televisions around the world. Capitalizing on the rise of camcorders, the marketing team invited regular people like the grandmother and granddaughter above on street corners and supermarkets to "take the Pepsi challenge" on camera. They struck marketing gold.

They were being strategic.

WHAT DOES IT MEAN TO "BE STRATEGIC"?

Given the very concept of being strategic originated in a military context, it makes sense we would look there for the essence of what this means. Consider the following joint doctrine note below, describing military strategy, developed by the US Department of Defense. Eliminate the word "military" and you have a comprehensive definition of strategy:

While military strategy is principally a function of creative art, the logic, or science, behind every strategy must be rigorous and founded upon the evidence of history; the arithmetic of available resources; a clear acknowledgment of time horizons and distances; and astute analysis of friendly, neutral, adversary, and enemy interests and will. Developing military strategy requires an understanding of facts and assumptions to inform strategic decision making. Its logic is both inductive and deductive, guiding purposeful action toward its end.

It's comprehensive, if not concise. Traditional SWOT analysis for strategic thinking embodies this. SWOT refers to strengths, weaknesses, opportunities, and threats. Some people prefer to call it SCOR analysis, which refers to strengths, constraints, opportunities, and risks, but they both serve the same fundamental process.

Both SWOT and SCOR approaches invite you to take a systematic look at the internal strengths and weaknesses (or constraints) of your organization and consider the opportunities and threats (or risks) present in the external environment in which you must operate that exert influence on your organization and its strategic pursuits. Ideally, you do this with others. You invite a host of relevant people to weigh in with what they see and perceive and meld the perspectives. You might do this through structured interviews, focus groups, and literature scans.

As discussed in chapter 5, "Build Decision Intelligence," you consult logic and intuitive sources of insight and factor for past, present, and future time horizons all toward informing your thinking on a way forward. While leaders often do this on an annual basis, being strategic is an orientation. It's an ongoing and omnipresent way of thinking and being to ensure you are accurately perceiving the landscape and know where you, and any organization you are stewarding, are going.

The final element is also key: As an executive, one of your prime directives after you set a vision is to orchestrate decisive, purposeful action, and set it in motion.

WHY EXECUTIVES NEED TO BE STRATEGIC

Being strategic is a distinguishing characteristic of an executive and one that will become more, not less, valuable. Michael Useem, Wharton professor and director of the Center for Leadership and Change Management, calls thinking strategically one of three "essential" executive skills (along with communicating persuasively and being decisive, both also covered in this book). In a separate interview in 2012 with Bill Javetski of McKinsey & Company, Useem suggested this isn't changing anytime soon, saying, "Because the world is now more complicated and more uncertain... there will be a premium on thinking strategically."

Just before the COVID-19 pandemic, I was part of a team helping to shape a new executive development program for a federal government agency in the United States. We interviewed chief human capital officers and did an extensive literature scan of hiring and promotion criteria in the executive ranks of public and private sector organizations. The ability to be strategic consistently ranked in the top three traits required to ascend into the executive ranks and to succeed once there.

A *Harvard Business Review* survey of more than ten thousand leaders affirmed this, with 97 percent of respondents citing "being strategic" as the leadership behavior most important to their organization's success (Clark, 2018). Be forewarned:

Being strategic can also mean pretty high stakes. John Sculley, who had such success at Pepsi, went on to become CEO of Apple Computer from 1983 to 1993—and nearly ran Apple into the ground. Steve Jobs personally recruited and hired him, luring him with the promise to change the world. Yet within two years, Sculley was instrumental in the 1985 ousting of Jobs from Apple. Why? Because they clashed on strategy (Terdiman, 2013).

BEING STRATEGIC REQUIRES THE WILLINGNESS TO QUESTION EVERYTHING

In a 2010 interview with Leander Kahney for Cult of Mac, Sculley admitted it was a mistake to take the helm at Apple. At a *Forbes* conference nearly two decades later, Scully publicly, candidly, and humbly reflected on the near-death experience he invoked for Apple. He acknowledged the type of strategic thinking required to shape an industry (as Jobs had done) is different from what's required when you are in an established industry with competitors, which had been Sculley's strength at Pepsi (Terdiman, 2013). Sculley has since called Jobs "the greatest CEO ever" (Kahney, 2010).

In a colossal strategic misstep, Sculley chose IBM and Motorola processors over Intel processors, locking Apple out of commodity processing, a huge trend he failed to see coming. Microsoft, in contrast, capitalized on it and made big bets in that space, giving them massive advantage in the early 1990s with the rise of powerful processors (Kahney, 2010). In a conversation about this story, Peter Beck, a strategic technologist, noted that as CEO Sculley did not have to be a technologist to understand chip architecture. "But it would have been nice," he noted, "if thinking strategically, he would have recognized that the research and development underway at Intel was way ahead of any competitor, and would eventually produce smaller, less power hungry, and much more powerful chips." He pointed out the irony that current Apple CEO Tim Cook *did* think strategically a few years ago and presciently had Apple develop the M1 and M2 chips that are far better than the Intel chips Apple switched to under Jobs.

Apple is nothing if not strategic.

As a leader, being strategic is an inside job first and requires the willingness and ability to be brutally honest about your own strengths and weaknesses and keenly assess yourself in the light of what the future requires. It requires the willingness to challenge thinking and assumptions—including your own—in ways that are threatening to the status quo (or your own need to be right). You can't be strategic if you are not inviting diversity of perspective. As one of my clients likes to say, "Include the 'pizza guy'—someone completely unfamiliar with your effort who may see something you can't see due to your own blind spots" (see chapter 5, "Build Decision Intelligence").

It requires the humility to not assume what worked there will work here. Wharton professor Harbir Singh says creating a strategic mindset is about addressing the most difficult challenges. "If you're not honest with yourself about what those challenges are, your strategy is incomplete," he flatly told Wharton students (The Wharton School, 2022).

Listen to everybody. Start noticing *everything*. Connect dots. Look for trends and patterns. What do you or others see that others don't?

BEING STRATEGIC IS ABOUT MAXIMIZING ADVANTAGE

Being strategic is about anticipating. Someone who is strategic makes the most of every advantage and minimizes, eliminates, or neutralizes disadvantages to gain a decisive competitive edge. Good strategy can enable you to prevail even when the deck seems stacked against you. Ultimately, "competitive strategy is about being different," wrote Michael Porter in his 1996 *Harvard Business Review* article titled, "What Is Strategy?" (Porter, 1996).

As Sculley told the audience that day at Wharton, Pepsi could not compete with Coke in terms of advertising dollars. It couldn't compete head on with Coke's unmatched creative team, powerful brand awareness, and customer loyalty. The "Pepsi Challenge" did what any good strategy does—capitalized on a unique strength (slight customer preferences for taste) and neutralized a debilitating weakness, the inability to compete head-to-head with Coke's advertising prowess. Their street-corner creative ad strategy totally offset that disadvantage.

This applies to your career as well. Have a good look at your own strengths and weaknesses as a professional. What differentiating strengths might you possess that you haven't yet fully capitalized on? Is it time to bring them out more for people to see? As for any weaknesses (we all have them), don't let them get you down or invest too much trying to fix them.

Do like Pepsi and just offset them. In business and in life, get creative before you get discouraged and know so much more is possible when, like Pepsi, you are willing to be strategic.

WHAT "BEING STRATEGIC" IS NOT

I routinely see executives fall prey to some common myths about what it means to be strategic. Let's debunk them now. Being strategic is not:

- **A substitute for action.**
  I once worked with an executive who proudly displayed a sign in his office that said, "I have a strategic plan. It's called doing things." The irony was striking. With that sign, he was broadcasting he didn't understand the fundamentals of strategy and, not surprisingly, he soon hit a career cul-de-sac.

  When you are not strategic, your best efforts could be at risk because, like Sculley missing out on the Intel processor, you didn't see the big one coming. You put your ladder against the wrong wall. Discussing an executive's role in leading change to create and sustain competitive advantage, Michael Porter, of the Institute for Strategy and Competitiveness at Harvard Business School and widely acknowledged as the father of modern strategy, put it bluntly:

  Managers who neglect strategic positioning can wind up like a hamster on a wheel—running hard while standing still.

Running an organization without strategy is like expecting the choir to show up for the Christmas cantata and sing the same song, having never seen the words or the music. Effective executives know the question isn't *either* we do strategy, *or* we get things done. Strategy shapes what the organization is doing, and when, where, why, with whom, and *how* it will do those things.

Sun Tzu's *The Art of War*, written in 400 BC, is widely considered one of the oldest and best tomes on military strategy even today. What Tzu presciently wrote then is still stunningly true today:

"Strategy without tactics is the slowest route to victory."

(Note that while slow, even *without* tactics, strategy is still the route to victory.)

- **A way of thinking reserved only for the top of the organization chart.**
  The ability to be strategic has nothing to do with where you sit in an organization. Retired financial sector executive Cindy Freund's first job was working at McDonald's. She credits her ability to think strategically as early as that first job with accelerating her own career. Being strategic starts with simply paying attention.

"You don't have to be a strategist to be strategic," she told me in our interview. "Wherever you sit, you need to understand *strategically* where the organization is headed and then ensure you're doing everything possible to support that vision." She added that you have a strategic sense of where and with whom you can get things done.

Strategy and tactics go hand-in-hand according to long-time Harvard Business School's *Working Knowledge* blog columnist Steve Robbins. As he wrote, "Success as an executive requires the ability to move freely from strategy to tactics, the ability to understand linkages across organizational boundaries, and the ability to balance short- and long-term concerns." This ability is required no matter where you sit on an organization chart, and the sooner you demonstrate it, the faster you will rise.

- **Fluffy.**
  When I hear someone complain that strategy is fluffy or just "shelfware," it is an immediate tell they have never led real strategy. In Stanford professors Jesper Sørensen and Glenn Carroll's book *Making Great Strategy*, they show that "one factor underlies all sustainably successful strategies: a logically coherent argument that connects resources, capabilities, and environmental conditions to desired outcomes." There's nothing soft about that.

  If you don't have clear and accountable commitment to accomplish clear targets and observable objectives (or whatever you want to call those ultimate outcomes), and a mechanism for mitigating risks and tracking progress, you don't have a strategic implementation plan. You have wishful thinking—and maybe a document.

  Being strategic is about commitment and action: what you will do and what you won't do. Making the tough decision to stop something or close a branch of an organization, or to say no more often in order to guard your time as a leader, is not always easy. Being strategic is not for the gutless or weak-minded, and it's something executives have a disproportionate power to bring to an organization and make happen.

Sometimes being strategic is simply rallying people toward a common vision. To the extent it is the ensuing work that brings it to life, anything that energizes enthusiasm and shared commitment to tackle the hard work ahead is valuable. Don't take my word for it though: Give it a go without that rallying energy and see how it goes.

BE STRATEGIC WITH AND FOR YOU

Being strategic isn't something to reserve just for a job. You can be strategic with and for you.

Before she moved into banking, becoming a senior vice president at one of our country's largest financial institutions, Cindy Freund was a primary influence in my hive of mentors at the nation's largest employee-owned research and development company. She advised me early in my career to supplement my liberal arts education with a technical degree, describing it as foundational for any future career (my sister did as well).

As I peered into my own crystal ball, I saw they were right. Technology would run through everything. I chose to pursue a master's degree in information systems while working full time (which the company paid for).

Information systems wasn't my passion. I wanted a graduate degree in French or to become a mediator or executive coach, but I was being strategic. The advice paid off: Within a decade, the rise of the digital age became real and technology was embedding in everything. I enjoyed wide open spaces where I could now pursue work I loved. A significant focus of my work soon became helping top executives lead the people side of technology-driven transformation change through strategic communication, facilitation, negotiation, mediation, and coaching.

What do you see when you look into the crystal ball? Where is the world going? What strategic choices can you make today to create possibilities for your future?

BEING STRATEGIC IS A CHOICE

As an executive coach, I frequently meet executives who tell me they don't have the time to be strategic. At the proverbial mercy of the tyranny of the urgent, 96 percent of five hundred managers surveyed bemoaned they don't have the time to be strategic. They don't have time because they aren't being strategic (Horwath, n.d.).

There is no such thing as an accidental executive or accidentally successful company. Anybody or any organization who makes it to the top of their game chose to be strategic early on. This happens years, and even decades, in advance. You've got to know where you are going and lay the track before you can run the train over it—months and often years in advance.

In an interview with Michael Useem for *Knowledge at Wharton*, a business journal from the Wharton School of the University of Pennsylvania, Cassandra Frangos, a consultant with executive search firm Spencer Stuart, points out people who aspire to the C-suite "have their eye on the next two or three moves in their career... they are always thinking, 'What's the next experience I need to make sure that I'm preparing myself to be a [fill in the blank]?'" As the Wharton@ Work website puts it, in looking ahead, you're "bringing the future into the present." That is the essence of being strategic.

In business and your own career, you can't change your strategic goals every other day or you would never get anywhere. But you must be prepared to change if something really major changes in the market, the business environment shifts, or technology evolves. "The important thing," Peter Beck wrote me, "is to maintain a strategic mindset. Especially at the beginning of your career, people will try to focus you in a short term tactical day-to-day mindset (which you need to be good at as well); but there is always room for strategic."

* * *

Being strategic is about seeing the whole landscape. Look for and make the most of every advantage you have available. Start where you are. Like with the Pepsi challenge, you don't have to be slick to be strategic. When you are, you might make history.

<u>Chapter Checklist:</u>
Being strategic is a competence you can hone starting now and develop over a lifetime:

- Choose to be strategic. Don't let day-to-day interruptions crowd out the strategic.
- Develop your strategy chops. Read biographies and history books. Former MIT management professor Henry Mintzberg and his colleagues Bruce Ahlstrand and Joseph Lampel compiled a definitive overview highlighting ten major schools of strategy in the classic book *Strategy Safari*.
- Cast a wide net. Invite diverse perspectives. Find strategic partners. Even in your personal life, consult with a career coach, a financial adviser, or legal counsel to ensure you understand your options and prepare for a range of future possibilities. Invite people to help build the future you expect them to buy.
- Invest in strategic relationships. Join industry associations and attend conferences where thought leaders and luminaries gather. Consider how you might add mutual value to each other's lives (see the other chapters in part 2, "Nurture Relationships," for more information.)
- Check your assumptions. Assumptions are like the jet stream with an airplane. If the pilot factors for it, and the winds are in one's favor, the jet stream can reduce friction. However, if the winds change and a pilot does not factor for it, as John Sculley can attest, they can blow you totally off course.

- Be willing to pivot. Being strategic shouldn't lock you in. In fact, the opposite is true. Being strategic is what allows you to know when to pivot.
- Keep choosing. Being strategic isn't a one and done choice. It's a continuous space of choosing from a place of awareness. It's clear, directed action and the willingness to keep choosing.

CHAPTER 5

Build Decision Intelligence

———

Name-calling is rude unless Maria Cypher is doing it.

As cofounder and partner of Catchword Branding, an award-winning naming and branding agency, Maria is a professional namer who has created monikers like VW Atlas, Starbucks Refreshers, and Upwork. Becoming more decisive and adept with what she calls "rapid decision-making" was the single biggest adjustment Maria told me she had to make when she bought out her cofounders and became the majority owner of the agency (see chapter 7, "Operate with Urgency"). To play at this new level, Maria had to build decision intelligence.

DECISION INTELLIGENCE IS A HARBINGER OF SUCCESS

Decision intelligence is effective decision-making, whether yours or your ability to contribute that of others. It is a predictor of future success. A *Harvard Business Review* survey of seventeen thousand C-suite executives found leaders whom colleagues described as decisive were more than twelve times more likely to become a high-performing CEO (Botelho et al., 2017). That same study, which included two thousand CEOs, showed high-performing CEOs decide earlier, faster, and with greater conviction than their lower-performing counterparts.

Building your decision intelligence will increase your value to an organization whether you are making the decision or supporting a decisional process. It's an art and a science, and mastering it is worth the investment. It starts with treating decision-making as a formal process.

TREAT DECISION-MAKING AS A FORMAL BUSINESS PROCESS

On the surface, decision-making is straightforward. Whether you're planning a vacation or formulating strategy, you will follow the same general process—something like the seven-step process below suggested by Concordia University, St. Paul:

1. Identify the decision
2. Gather information
3. Identify alternatives
4. Weigh the evidence
5. Choose
6. Implement
7. Assess the results

Exactly how this process runs will vary by the nature of the decision. While worth it, it can get pretty messy with complex decisions. It's why you need to build decision intelligence.

SIMPLE VERSUS COMPLEX DECISIONS

Simple decisions are low stakes. They usually have a single decision-maker, and the supporting information baseline is readily available. They don't impact a lot of people, and it's not a big deal to adjust course downstream.

Complex decisions are higher stakes and possibly irreversible. They may impact many people. They may have interdependent, nested decisions involving multiple decision-makers who have their own interconnected decision rights. Downstream implementation may depend on voluntary cooperation by others, which can put the results out of your zone of control.

ASSESSING COMPLEXITY

Understanding the difference is key, because you will invest proportionately in the decision process based on complexity. Factors that increase complexity include:

- Compound decisions, meaning they contain nested issues
- Unclear or low confidence levels in the data
- Subjective information baseline
- Political sensitivity
- Permanence or rigidity, meaning the decision cannot easily be undone or changed

- Significant interdependencies, potentially invoking other interconnected decision rights
- Many, or unknown, options
- Stakeholders are wary or unsupportive, or you don't know where they stand; or, you don't have a full grasp of the set of stakeholders
- Little enforcement power

Effective executives don't plow right in with a one-size-fits-all approach to decision-making. They take the time to assess decision complexity on the front end. They set expectations out of the gate for the decision process and lay the groundwork early to allow time for a sound decision-making process, appropriate to the complexity of the decision.

It sounds like a lot of work, and it can be. But the people whom the decision will affect, including you, deserve nothing less.

THE VALUE OF GOOD DECISION-MAKING PROCESS

Decision support pioneer Dr. Ernest Forman has long advocated leaders to treat decision-making like any other formal business process. I was fortunate to have Dr. Forman as a professor while obtaining my Master of Information Systems degree from The George Washington University School of Business.

"We need organizations to view decision-making as a process integral to the success of the organization," Dr. Forman wrote in his blog for Expert Choice, about a ground-breaking decision support system he developed with American management professor Thomas L. Saaty, creator of the analytical hierarchy process method for complex decision-making.

THE PRICE OF INEFFECTIVE DECISION-MAKING

According to a May 2019 McKinsey study, the cost of undisciplined organizational decision-making can be staggering. Consider the following:

- While an executive spends up to 70 percent of their time making decisions, more than half of them acknowledged they do not use this time wisely.
- Sixty-one percent of executives complain as much as half the time spent making decisions wastes their time.
- The study estimated a typical Fortune 500 company squanders an astonishing five hundred thousand hours annually on ineffective decision-making.

That's real money and impact—why would you leave that on the table? What's more, that's real opportunity for a Day One Executive to add value and have an immediate and positive impact.

In an article I authored for the Forbes Coaches Council, I wrote that how you make decisions also bears on your trust as a leader. Both the approach and style you choose can make or break the trust that, as a respected leader, you likely work hard in other ways to preserve and protect. Let's start with a look at style: As you rise through the ranks, and ascend into broader scopes of responsibility, you must evolve your decision-making style into a more participative and inclusive

style in order to be successful and have the impact you are
here to make.

"MUST" EVOLVE YOUR DECISION-MAKING STYLE

The researchers who authored the *Harvard Business Review*
article "The Seasoned Executive's Decision-Making Style"
found that most of us fall into two categories of innate preferences when it comes to decision-making: Some of us need a
lot of information before deciding, and others of us need just
enough to feel we can decide (Brousseau, 2006). The Kolbe
A Index is a validated assessment you can take at home to
give you an immediate sense of where you fall along these
lines (Kolbe Corp., 2021). Katharine Cook Briggs and Isa-
bel Briggs Myers, creators of the most popular personality
assessment on the planet, the Myers-Briggs Type Indicator,
theorized people have innate preferences for facts and logic
or intuition when it comes to decision-making (The Myers
and Briggs Foundation, 2022). There is a place for both as
we'll see deeper in the chapter.

According to the research behind both the Kolbe A and
MBTI assessments, our decision-making preferences are
supposedly innate and unlikely to change much. However,
our decision-making *style* must evolve as we move through
the ranks. It will look very different when you become an
executive compared to a senior manager.

The authors of a comprehensive study of more than one hundred thousand leaders published in the *Harvard Business
Review* went so far as to conclude "failing to evolve in how
you make decisions can be fatal to your career." Lest we be

tempted to dismiss this as hyperbole, their data showed less than one in one billion odds that these patterns were occurring by chance. As the researchers wrote, "This wasn't a fluke" (Brousseau et al., 2006).

First-line supervisors and middle managers ensure things get done, and their decision styles are necessarily more directive or hierarchical. As authors of the *Harvard Business Review* article "The Seasoned Executive's Decision-Making Style" put it, early in your career, "action is a premium." The styles of senior executives, however, "are the complete opposite," the authors wrote.

As leaders move up the ranks, the researchers observed a steady progression toward openness, diversity of opinion, and participative decision-making. The highest performing (and best compensated) CEOs do this more than others. Resistance to integrative, participative, and flexible styles is a tell that an otherwise promising leader may not yet be ready for an executive role.

Many leaders have difficulty shedding approaches that worked well enough for them earlier in their career and got them this far. It can be hard to see those approaches won't work at their new role as an executive. As management professor Thomas Davenport observed in the *Harvard Business Review* article "Was Steve Jobs a Good Decision Maker?" even Steve Jobs changed his famously autocratic decision-making style and acknowledged even better outcomes.

How do you make this shift? It doesn't mean turning to one or two trusted confidants. Speaking of Steve Jobs's earlier decision style, Davenport noted, "Surrounding yourself with brilliant iconoclasts and letting them take turns winning is not the way to build an organizational judgment capability." In an interview with the Stanford Graduate School of Business, Sørensen and Carroll point out, "Too often strategic decisions come down to power—they become about who has the upper hand... It's a terrible way to make strategic decisions" (Kinni, 2021).

Executive-level decision-making requires going beyond yourself and your tight inner circle. You need to do something which is deeply uncomfortable and downright scary for many of us—be willing to not have the answer. Ironically, it's the *not having the answer* that becomes the invitation to others to join forces with you and bring something into being that creates greater for all. People support what they help build.

Avail yourself of the wisdom and perspectives of others. Involving others generates trust and simultaneously enrolls them in the implementation work that follows. Former chief design officer of Apple, Jony Ive, said as Steve Jobs grew as a leader, "Wanting to learn was far more important than wanting to be right."

This doesn't have to mean inviting havoc. You might wonder, Won't including others pull everything off track, drag the process, or degrade quality decision-making? Not if you use a strategic and structured decision approach.

A disciplined approach ensures qualified people are at the table and uses techniques to mediate personalities and calibrate inputs relative to stakes. As the executive sponsor, you still have a voice—possibly even a disproportionate voice. Inviting others in doesn't lock you out. You need to engineer the people side of your success as much as any other aspect.

CHOOSE THE APPROPRIATE DECISION-MAKING APPROACH

Hundreds of corporate and government executives have attended my decision support workshops over my thirty-year career. I have worked with dozens of executives across nearly every Executive Branch department and agency and the private sector in support of high stakes decisions. I've observed them make decisions through one of four approaches: authoritative, consultative, delegative, and consensus.

I developed a simple decision-making framework to help leaders size up the decision and select the most appropriate approach. The "ACDC framework," as I call it (with a nod to the rock band), has its roots in leadership styles researched by Daniel Goleman and other researchers.

- Authoritative: You have the singular authority to make the decision and the power to enforce it. Downstream success does not depend on the voluntary cooperation of others. In crisis decision-making, where there is no time to lose, this is often the most appropriate approach.
- Consultative: Other parties do not have the power to block the decision, but downstream implementation success would benefit from their expertise, insights, or support.
- Delegative: You fully empower another person to make and execute the decision under the mantle of your

authority. You are willing to be accountable (e.g., own the consequences) for their decision-making.

- Consensus: The commitment of impacted parties is essential to downstream implementation success. These parties have equal or even greater power than you and have the power to stop you or not comply.

Leaders lose trust and risk decision quality when they jump into the decision process with major, high-visibility decisions, giving no thought to the most appropriate decision-making approach.

No leader can know with perfect certainty the right decision regarding complex decision-making. Outcomes are never guaranteed and rarely in your control. What if the most important element in your success as a trusted decision-maker was in your control? It is—it's the integrity of the decision process.

WALK THROUGH THE PLAYS

I played soccer growing up, and we did a valuable drill called "slow-motion soccer." In this drill, the players walked the game. Walking the plays seemed frustratingly slow, but it forced both brain and body to slow down enough to see what was happening on the field.

Decision moments that happen lightning fast were observable in real-time. We spotted higher potential plays, and we ran experimental "what if" scenarios to improve decision-making in the future. The result was better real-time decision-making on the field.

The same is true with decision-making at work. The more complex or challenging the decision you need to make, the more you may want to invest in walking through the plays. It may surprise some to learn our nation's top government officials do this regarding high-stakes policy decisions around catastrophic disasters.

I co-led the evaluation of the nation's largest counterterrorism decision support and training program, Exercise Top Officials (TOPOFF), after the 9/11 terror attacks. The program ran on a two-year cycle because the decisions were extremely complex, affecting the entire nation. The outcomes included ground-breaking national policy in catastrophic disaster response as well as improvements to incredibly complex interagency crisis decision-making processes.

Cabinet- and senior-level officials walked through various scenarios over days, including a whole week of full-scale live simulated play, to see what specific results their policy choices and on-the-ground decisions might create. We meticulously reconstructed every major decision to understand when and how leaders began to take action and based on what information and assumptions (flawed and accurate). We looked at how they communicated the decision and what happened as a result. We then ran tabletop discussions to explore the ramifications of potential decisions. All of this was designed to build the decision intelligence of our nation's top officials.

You don't need to go to this extreme to become a better decision-maker, though. What might it change to take the time on the front-end of a major decision to walk through your options and consider what each will create? What value might a periodic retrospective of your own decision-making process add for you? Whether things turn out how you hope or not, the awareness you gain can be very valuable—even when tinged with regret.

LEARN FROM REGRET

In one of my greatest professional regrets, I once received an offer for a lucrative C-suite level position with an exciting start-up company and turned it down. Within five years, a Fortune 100 company bought the start-up for hundreds of millions of dollars, enabling all the executives to cash out stock and comfortably retire.

After meeting the executive team, I immediately sensed this company was a winner. As fortune had it, I had lunch with a former client the same week I received an offer. I causally shared I was considering joining this company, and my client's face went ashen.

He warned me away, sharing that he and the Department of Justice were embroiled in an ongoing lawsuit with this company due to ethical and legal violations. I respected this former client immensely and felt nauseated hearing this. I declined the offer that evening.

It never dawned on me he could have the wrong company (he did).

Had I been willing to ask more questions and ask for more time, I would be writing you from a yacht in Amalfi. I let a huge opportunity slip through my fingers by not feeling

I could risk even a brief delay in giving them an answer. I still feel regret, but rather than beating myself up, I vowed to become a savvier decision-maker in the future.

I have since made some bold and positive life-changing decisions I might have never thought possible, but that experience helped me be more aware of my blind spots. In that case, my positive impressions of my former client (halo effect) and availability bias (my reaction to the information immediately in front of me) blinded me to the possibility he could be wrong.

MOVING BEYOND BLIND SPOTS AND BIAS

We are all subject to unconscious bias that skews our decision-making. The funny thing is how few of us seem to know it, myself included. In what is known as the "blind spot bias," most people think they are less subject to bias than their peers (something that researchers point out is not even mathematically possible).

In research published in the *Journal of Management Science*, scientists found the belief that you are somehow immune to this, and thus a superior decision-maker, has detrimental consequences on decision-making, including decreased receptivity to advice. The best decision-makers acknowledge this reality and take deliberate steps to offset unconscious bias (Scopelliti et al., 2015). They don't go away, but you can mitigate them and make sounder decisions. This can be especially important with group decision-making, where you grapple not only with your own blind spots and bias but everybody's.

SIDESTEPPING GROUPTHINK

The tendency of groups to unconsciously seek harmony at the expense of making the best choices is a phenomenon researchers call "groupthink." If you build your decision intelligence, you don't have to fall prey to it with your decision-making, even in groups. Many techniques can help a group sidestep the dangerous pitfall of agreeing at all costs, but as the leader you must bravely put a stake in the ground and create the conditions for independent thinking, critical reasoning, and evaluation of consequences or alternatives to take place.

Research psychologist Irving L. Janis was the first to conduct research on the term "groupthink" in 1972, defined as "a psychological drive for consensus at any cost that suppresses dissent and appraisal of alternatives." In his book, *The Wisdom of the Crowds*, journalist and former business columnist for *The New Yorker* magazine James Surowiecki demonstrated the opposite is more often true. Large groups of people see a wise course of action and predict the future more than a small group, no matter their intelligence. Blind spots and inherent bias are harder to neutralize in a small group.

Furthermore, according to research presented in the *Academy of Management Review*, when decisions require commitment or acceptance by others, participative leadership is more likely to result in high-quality decision-making than individual directive leadership (Brodbeck et al., 2007). Properly done, group decision support does not automatically degenerate into or settle for lowest-common denominator consensus. Groupthink dynamics are the result of an undisciplined, sloppy, and unstructured decision process which cannot deliver true consensus.

Northwestern University Master of Science in Learning and Organizational Change student Arpita Das Behl offered what I consider one of the best summaries of techniques to sidestep groupthink dynamics: His list includes prescribing guidelines on methodical decision-making processes and techniques such as devil's advocate; the "thinking hats" approach, which encourages divergent thinking from multiple perspectives before narrowing down; and the presence of experts and use of diverse sub-groups as "important factors in moderating and mitigating groupthink."

But what about individual decision-making? How can we challenge or overcome our own blind spots or biases if we can't see them? Science shows you have more innate decision intelligence than you may realize. The question is whether you are maximizing it.

TRUST YOUR AWARENESS
Neuroscience research shows what some have long known—you have phenomenal innate awareness based on accrued experience. In the *Inc.* magazine article "Neuroscience Reveals How Steve Jobs Made Better Decisions, Faster," contributor Jeff Haden wrote of Jobs, "What appears to be instinctive is actually the result of deliberate practice and extensive experience."

Much like machine learning where algorithms get better and better at pattern recognition, Jobs was an astute observer of subtle patterns not noticed by most (Jony Ive described him as the most inquisitive human he'd ever met) (Ive, 2019).

Haden tells the story of a famous chess experiment where grand masters and novices viewed a board pattern, and proctors then asked them to reconstruct it from memory. When the pattern matched something likely to appear in an actual chess match, the grand masters outperformed the novices. When the pattern was random, not correlated with anything in the real world, the grand masters and beginners performed equally.

Why?

The grand masters relied on deeply embedded recognition, accrued over the course of experience with thousands of chess matches. No novice could match this. This often separates masters in any field and allows them to immediately make the right call when the moment requires it (Bilalic et al., 2008).

Like the grand masters of chess, you also have a rich treasure trove of accrued experience upon which to draw from your life. Sometimes it's easier to see it in hindsight with decisions we made that didn't turn out as we would have wished. Have you ever made a decision that turned out disastrously (or wasn't your best choice)? Be honest, did any part of you have an impending sense of doom, however fleeting, but you chose to proceed anyway?

If so, that's actually great news! It shows you have phenomenal internal awareness! You just chose to ignore it. Don't judge yourself—rather, see it as valuable acquisition of awareness and commit to tuning in even more to your body's awareness. You have a built-in internal decision support system with your head, heart, and gut that will never steer you wrong.

HEAD, HEART, AND GUT

In our interview, Maria Cypher spoke of trusting her gut: "I knew the business inside and out, but a lot of [decisions] come from an educated gut feel," she shared. "You have to do your due diligence, but there are many decisions where you must go with your gut." Maria makes use of both of these "brain" centers (and knowing Maria, her heart is in there too).

More than three decades of ground-breaking neuroscience research have shown you can quite literally ask your body for information when it comes to decisions. We have not one, but three brains constituting the complex, functional, and adaptive neural networks, which are the "head" brain, the "heart" brain, and the enteric "gut" brain (Soosalu et al., 2019). They each have a unique awareness. You're *not* playing with a full deck of cards if you rely only on your logical mind.

The field of decision science has advanced more in the last two decades than ever before, primarily informed by large advances in neuroscience shedding new light on the central role emotions play in decision-making. Decision-making is both logical and intuitive. It is also emotional.

THE POWERFUL ROLE OF EMOTION AND INTUITION IN DECISION INTELLIGENCE

The implications of the findings from thirty-five years of scientific literature on the science of emotion are profound for a field like decision-making that has long lauded supposedly superior rational and logical approaches. The bottom line? In the words of these researchers, while cognition has a role, "emotions powerfully, predictably, and pervasively influence decision making" and have "the potential to create a paradigm shift in decision theories" (Lerner et al., 2015).

Carmen Medina is a retired national security Senior Federal Executive and trailblazer who has pioneered a prominent place for intuition in decision-making in some of the most unexpected places. Coauthor of the book *Rebels at Work: A Handbook for Leading Change from Within,* she is also featured in Wharton School professor Adam Grant's bestseller *Originals: How Non-Conformists Move the World* (National Security Institute, 2022).

"The idea that intuition is the much lesser partner of analytic thinking is based on misunderstandings of human thinking processes," she wrote in an article for the Cipher Brief entitled "The Potential of Integrating Intelligence and Intuition." Medina continued, "When a thought or gut feeling enters our mind unbidden, it is likely the product of behind-the-scenes brain work. Many neurologists now think we can best describe the brain as a predicting machine that constantly compares its current perceptions against all its memories. The brain can detect emerging patterns or changes that deserve attention long before the analytic brain comprehends evidence of a new trend."

We ignore this at our peril.

I can hear some of you now thinking, *Hmmm, this all sounds good, but how exactly do I do this? How do I know whether to trust my head, heart, or gut? How do I get unstuck from analysis paralysis?*

A PRAGMATIC WAY TO ASK YOUR BODY

What if I told you there is a groundbreaking technique that can help you access your innate decision intelligence within minutes? The Multiple Brain Integration Technique (mBIT) is a robust, research-based, and simple approach for harnessing all three brain systems. The technique is best done with an mBIT facilitator, but you can also do it by yourself.

Here's how it works:

1. Settle yourself with some slow, deep breathing for a few minutes. Deep breathing activates the parasympathetic nervous system, which is the state we are in when we are calm. It's also where expansive awareness can arise.
2. Then, check in with each brain center. Start with your heart and ask what awareness it has about the situation. Move to your gut and ask what it knows, then check in with your head brain. Receive whatever awareness arises. Don't judge it.
3. Finally, continue to cycle back through each brain center, checking in with each as a new awareness arises and check for congruence.

You will find that you likely begin to feel a sense of peace as new awareness arises. A solution idea, or a next step, may suddenly become completely clear. This isn't to say don't check with experts, but this is a way to have your voice when it comes to your own individual decision-making.

* * *

Building your decision intelligence is one of the most powerful things you can do to advance your career and impact. Decision-makers are force multipliers because decisions generate ripple effects that get larger as you move into greater scopes of responsibility. Be a force for good.

Build your decision intelligence and give yourself significant advantage before you need it most. Just ask Maria.

Chapter Checklist:

- Follow a structured decision-making process for complex decisions. Resist the urge to take a shortcut.
- Embrace a more integrative, flexible decision style. Invite others into decision processes. Consider which of the four "ACDC" approaches is best for the type of decision you are making.
- Consciously offset unconscious bias.
- Use techniques such as the Analytic Hierarchy Process to assess alternatives in a manner that capitalizes on subjective (emotional) and objective (logical) influences on decision-making.
- Gain insight into your own default decision-making preferences.
- Consider how you can further open your decision-making style to become more inclusive, encourage more diversity, and even establish consensus where appropriate—while being decisive.
- Deconstruct some decisions that played out well or not as well to gain awareness.
- Invite your head, heart, and gut to have a voice in your decision-making.

CHAPTER 6

Be a Change Agent

___

"Why was God able to create the world in only seven days?"

JPMorgan Chase Commercial Banking Chief Financial Officer (CFO) Marcus von Kapff teased readers of a white paper with this metaphorical question, which was as playful as it was provocative. The paper's focus was about the challenges of integrating new technologies at the bank successfully. The answer, he wrote in the paper, was because "there was no legacy." There was no old system or way of doing things that anybody would cling to.

Most executives don't have that luxury when it comes to introducing something new. Getting people to let go of the old and embrace change is notoriously tricky. Pulling it off can make your career as an executive.

LEADING CHANGE IS YOUR MOST IMPORTANT ROLE

You may not see "change management" in the job description, but make no mistake, leading change will be your most important role as an executive because it's inherent in everything you do. It will distinguish you because it's hard and so few succeed.

Whereas a manager's job is to *maintain*—to do what we did yesterday, maybe a little better—an executive's prime directive is to *be a change agent*. Some of the changes you may lead may be small, and some may be quite sweeping in nature. In a *Harvard Business Review* survey of two thousand leaders, a whopping 58 percent of respondents reported needing to reinvent their business to survive, up just over 10 percent from two years earlier (Zhexembayeva, 2020).

Nobody else is more powerful than the top executive to bring successful change into being—or to shut it down. According to researchers at Prosci, a global leader in change management, "active and visible executive sponsorship" is the single most significant influence on a successful change initiative. Choose to be an executive, and you choose to be a change agent.

WHAT DOES IT MEAN TO BE A CHANGE AGENT?
Consider the words of the legendary Peter Drucker in his seminal work *The Effective Executive*, where he lists examples of responsibilities of any executive:

- Sensing the future and positioning a company to be competitive in a world that may yet be one to two decades off.
- Identifying and moving into new markets.
- Determining future product or service directions.
- Improving organizational performance.
- Navigating a merger or acquisition.

- Deciding what to start and what to stop—what to shed or "slough off."

What do they have in common? Leading change.

Consider the following:

- According to the US Office of Personnel Management, the ability to lead change is the number one "core executive qualification" required to ascend into the Senior Executive Service in the United States federal government.
- A study by INSEAD graduate business school cites leading change as one of the four most essential competencies top global executives must possess, out of over 160.
- One of the world's leading executive search firms, Spencer Stuart, drawing upon thousands of executive assessments, names the ability to lead successful change as one of the six fundamental traits of the most successful executives.

Is it any wonder the ability to lead change is a chart topper when it comes to most valuable capacities for executives?

REACHING FOR NEW LEVELS OF PERFORMANCE MEANS CHANGE, EVEN FOR YOU

Operational efficiency is necessary for competitive advantage, but it's not sufficient. A National Bureau of Economic Research survey of over one thousand CEOs across six countries showed "leader-CEOs" (defined as those willing and able to lead change) outperformed "manager-CEOs" when it came to corporate performance (Bandiera et al., 2017). The study classified either hands-on "manager" executives (focused on operational efficiencies) or "leader" executives (engaged in the "hard work of changing the company"). It compared before and after financial performance metrics and correlated the results with executives who were later promoted into CEO positions. Manager CEOs did well in organizations that had routine processes, but leader CEOs delivered far higher performance metrics overall.

No matter where you currently are, helping an organization pull off successful change and achieve new levels of performance can be what I call a catapult moment in your career. JPMorgan Chase CFO Marcus von Kapff wrote in the white paper mentioned earlier, "More than any other strategic initiative, the process of digital transformation shows you what you're really made of… The experience can be career defining."

It was for me.

SEIZE THE CATAPULT MOMENTS

A few years into my career, while still a junior employee at the nation's largest employee-owned research and development company with annual revenues in the billions of dollars, I became aware a lucrative and long-held business area in the company was, or was about to be, in jeopardy. The company pioneered a proprietary methodology for managing the integration of hundreds of information systems scattered across the globe. Owned and operated by multiple independent entities, moving them into a modernized, typical operating environment was a complex task. Get it wrong, and billions of dollars, and possibly lives, were at stake.

Each quarter, teams of expensive systems engineers meticulously summarized their findings in manually-updated "fishbone" charts. The charts enabled decision-makers to visualize how and when dozens of various systems would transition to a new operating baseline and old legacy systems would phase out and flagged risks requiring special attention. The engineering was best in class. The process was creaking under its own weight.

It was the early 1990s, and two transformational technological shifts were underway—the rise of the personal computer (thanks to Woz) and the internet. Earning my Master of Science degree in information systems during this time, it was clear the future was digital.

I was looking at dinosaurs. If we didn't want this business area to become extinct, we urgently needed digital transformation. If we were to preserve our competitive advantage, it was unavoidable. It seemed so obvious, but we had what Marcus von Kapff called "legacy," and it ran deep.

My enthusiasm for transformational change in this business made the "graybeards" uncomfortable, as the company affectionately and almost reverently referred to these senior engineers, belying the men's club that it largely was at the time. From their perspective, this was expensive, premature, and unnecessary—and who was I again?

I saw it differently. From my point of view, if we didn't destroy our own business model first and out-create our past successes, a competitor would.

CHANGE AND THRIVE, OR BECOME IRRELEVANT AND PERISH

I wrote what I now call my Jerry Maguire memo, referring to the self-titled film where a sports agent, played by Tom Cruise, has a moral epiphany and pens a memo aimed to improve the company he works for, only to get fired (Crowe, 1996). My memo didn't point to any moral failings, but it pointed to other risks, as I predicted in no uncertain terms we would lose this market if we did not immediately change course.

After submitting my memo through the proper channels, some of the old guard viewed it with amusement. Others ignored it altogether, figuring it, or I, would go away. Some perhaps understandably saw it as a threat to their comfortable status and stature and were unwilling to consider whether there was any merit to the ideas I was offering.

I didn't pretend to have all the answers, but everywhere I looked, all the data and indicators pointed in a single, clear direction of a call for urgent change. The memo went nowhere.

Until...

Weeks later, one of the company's most prominent clients pulled their business. Why? The company wasn't changing fast enough and was holding too tight to the legacy. A few days after that, I received a call. The client who had just cut funding wanted to meet. He had read my memo.

Working collaboratively with this client and a supportive executive sponsor in the company who helped mentor me, we engaged a community and successfully modernized the business area. The benefits became clear immediately: Analysis that used to take weeks took days. Technology freed our engineers to make higher-order use of their time and do what only they can do: foresee risks, issues, and opportunities previously inaccessible while there was time to act.

Looking back, I now refer to this experience as a catapult moment in my career. Fortunately, with the support of the client and mentorship of that executive sponsor, I stuck my landing and established myself as a change agent. Marcus von Kapff was right. Technology transformation was indeed career defining for me. And it can be for you too.

KEEP YOUR CUSTOMER AT THE CENTER OF THE CHANGE

The partnership with the client was the key to the success of the change initiative I described above. Whether you're in business, academia, or government, be clear about who is at the center of your change initiative. Self-serving initiatives rarely go far.

We met Maggie Wilderotter in chapter 3, "Know Your Value." As CEO of Fortune 500 company Frontier Communications from 2004 to 2015, before transitioning into the role of executive chairperson and retiring in 2016, she nearly doubled the average Fortune 500 CEO's tenure of five years. In just over a decade with her at the helm, Frontier grew from a regional telephone company with less than $1 billion in customer revenues to a national communication services provider with over $10 billion in annual revenues.

At a time when nearly 90 percent of Fortune 500 CEOs were (and still are) male, Maggie's a pretty special businessperson. It's no secret why nearly fifty boards of directors sought her out, and more court her to this day: Maggie is a change agent.

In our interview, she shared the key to her phenomenal achievements: keeping the customer at the center of her work.

Early on in her career she shared a secret to her success, "I decided that the most important constituent to serve was the customer. I worked in a technology company that worshipped the technology, not the customers," she said. Like John Hinshaw who also focused on the customer (see chapter 1, "Know the Driving Force"), Maggie said she also "found a niche that could create substantial value," as she put it, by focusing on the customer.

That niche focused on taking on difficult customers nobody wanted. Where other people ignored them, Maggie got closer to them. She listened intently to them, and in doing so, she says she "turned them into zealots" of the company's services.

She didn't stop there.

She started in accounting, when Frontier Communications was a start-up "running out of a garage," she shared. It was growing rapidly and had no marketing. She told the CEO the company needed to change this.

"I was relentless," she shared, pointing out another key trait of Day One Executives: tenacity. "I worked on the CEO for six months," she said.

One day, it paid off. He gave her the green light and put Maggie in charge of marketing. Before long, he had more news for her. The company had decided to set up five new regions, and he wanted Maggie to run them.

"I don't know anything about operations," she warned him.

"You didn't know anything about marketing either," he said with a twinkle in his eye.

Maggie found herself running operations and sales. "Nobody wanted to do this," she recalled, which spelled opportunity for her as a rising executive. She was now doing something few, if any, of her peers at the time were doing—running a profit-and-loss center in her twenties.

Through focusing on the customer, and in becoming a change agent, it wasn't long before Maggie's efforts were helping the company grow market share, which translated into credibility. "I was formidable in my powerbase in the company and didn't even realize it. I had so much more leverage than I thought I did." Reflecting back, she shared the experiences she gained in that role where she led these changes proved to be the most important job that prepared her to be a CEO.

HOW DO YOU BECOME AN EFFECTIVE CHANGE AGENT?

Maggie distinguished herself early and made such a powerful impression in part because she did what so many others don't: She pulled off successful change. Twenty years ago, researchers estimated that 70 percent of all change initiatives fail (Zhexembayeva, 2020). A survey by Boston Consulting

Group estimates the failure rate now to be even higher at 75 percent (Fæste et al., 2019). According to surveys conducted by the Association for Talent Development and Institute for Corporate Productivity, only 17 percent of leaders reported their organizations being highly effective at managing change. This spells opportunity for you as a Day One Executive.

Maggie side-stepped the most common bear traps with change, delivering unquestionable value to the company that continued into its future.

Change isn't cheap when it works. It's even more costly when it doesn't. In the book *Making Change Work,* authors Emma Weber, Patricia Pulliam Phillipas, and Jack J. Phillips document the financial, human capital, and competitive costs of failed change initiatives. Decades of research continue to point to consistent root causes for initiatives that fall flat ranging from weak or absent leadership support at the top, insufficient urgency, and failing to create a powerful enough guiding coalition (Watkins, 2020).

Why be a change agent and risk it all when odds are against you? Because that's when it's fun! And that's when, like Maggie, you can distinguish yourself while having a positive impact.

Here are some tips to help you become a change agent:

- *Deepen your capacity to be strategic.*
  Establishing a credible platform for change requires a strategic understanding of trends, the market influences, and your organization's associated competitive position

and value proposition (see chapter 4, "Be Strategic," for more). Become curious about the future and study it with an eye on what it will take to meet it when it arrives. You don't have to have all the answers. Just be willing to ask questions, listen to your stakeholders, do your homework, and trust your awareness.

The INSEAD study mentioned earlier in this chapter refers to the importance of the ability of executives to recognize new opportunities and trends and "develop a new strategic direction for an enterprise." Your ability to sell people on your ideas hinges on your ability to paint a vision of a compelling future. An article in *Harvard Business Review* describes envisioning as a "must-have" capability (Shoemaker et al., 2013).

- *Develop your communication and influence skills to be ready in the moment.*
  Develop foundational skill in key areas such as communication, stakeholder engagement, and negotiation. Cindy Freund, former senior vice president of one of the four biggest banks in the United States, called both oral and written communication skills "vital" in a conversation with me about leading change.

"You need to articulate, be able to present to a group, and be viewed as confident and knowledgeable," she advised.

In her career as an executive, she worked with hundreds of professionals, some of whom were very good at what they did but couldn't take the next step because they couldn't persuade others above them.

"They didn't bode confidence," she said. "You've got to be able to do that in order to be a change agent." You need to be quick on your feet and ready in the moment.

Cindy told me a story of when she was a second lieutenant in the Air Force and suddenly asked on short notice to brief a group of colonels and a general about a technology the Air Force had invested in. The leaders were wondering about its future funding profile. One officer asked her a pointed question about the plans for deployment. While Cindy didn't know much about the technical specifics, because this was the domain of non-commissioned officer subject matter experts, she knew the technology was important to the mission. This was the one opportunity to gain the officer's support for it. Thus, it was a key moment. Without missing a beat, she shot back without blinking, "We're going to put them in the field."

The officer threw Cindy a curveball, but her confidence persuaded them, and the officers agreed to the proposal. By leveraging her communication and influence skills, she was ready in the moment and was a change agent. "I walked out having sold the idea but also having absolutely no idea what that technology is," she said laughing, referring to the deeper technical details of it.

She didn't need to. She was well-versed in the technology's mission benefit and knew her people depended on it. Like Cindy, you need to know the material so that you can be authoritative when put on the spot for anything in your domain. "Be prepared. Always be prepared," Cindy advises.

This includes being prepared for a curveball. (Just for the record, after the briefing, the non-commissioned officers praised Cindy's handling of his question!)

- *Treat change management as a formal business process.* Too often, executives wing it with change. Whether you bring in the change management consultants or attempt it in-house, you are wise to use a structured, research-based approach when introducing any change. There's no magic to it, but neither are there shortcuts.

The basics of change management are straightforward. I am partial to the Prosci methodology, which moves through a five-stage process and is summarized with the acronym "ADKAR."

- – A—Start by consciously and sensitively yet clearly raising *awareness* of the need for change. This may be avoidance of danger, seizing an opportunity, or both, as is the case in many mergers and acquisitions. It helps to instill some urgency to generate focus.
- – D—The next step is to foster a *desire* for successful change. This will have greater ease when the time comes for the hard work of change, as people now embrace that need for evolution and join forces to help bring it about successfully. They are enrolled and committed.
- – K—With the winds now at your back and filling your sails, the time has come to equip them to help succeed with the changes. Build *knowledge* through training to give people new skill sets and acquaint them with new expectations. Help them bridge

technically and emotionally from what is, and what was, to what will be.

    – A—Ensure people have the *ability* to operate in the new ways. This is essential to building their confidence they can succeed in the new reality that is coming. Where people come up short, have a long runway and compassionate grace period with active support, demonstrating commitment to their success.

    – R—Finally, *reinforce* the change so that people do not begin to slide back into old ways of being or doing. Reinforcement can come by closing off access to old ways of doing things (e.g., shutting down legacy systems) and by celebrating successes big and small to maintain positive momentum through the change arc, which can involve a challenging period where change is resisted sometimes with surprising vigor.

- *Engineer the people-side of change.*
With people being the most powerful influence on the success of your change initiative, it's astonishing to me how many leaders leave this to chance.

I advise my clients to engineer the people side of change as much as any other aspect. I recommend a SCORE formula to help them stay accountable when rolling out a major change:

    – S—Skill sets. Expose your full team to core "people" skills, some of which they may never have acquired, especially in more technical fields. You wouldn't attempt computer programming without specific skill sets in those areas, so why would you attempt to pull off large-scale change without research-proven abilities around leading change?

- C—Commitment. It's not enough to have people's compliance. You need a consensus underpinning, and don't stop there. You must then move the people on whom your success depends into a state of commitment for the end vision.
- O—Ownership. Ideally, all your stakeholders, but especially the initiative's sponsors, must feel a sense of ownership. They must see it not as "your" project, but as theirs. This may require you as the executive to "let go" in order to transfer some of that sense of ownership to them.
- R—Resistance. There will be resisters, some of whom have the power to stop you. Ignore them at your peril.

I recommend stakeholder power mapping as a technique when it really counts. This involves identifying the formal and informal power players and assessing their relative levels of authority relative to the change initiative. Use a scale of negative three (no power) to three (extremely powerful). Then, rate their attitudes—e.g., how supportive they are—on a scale of negative three (totally against the idea and will fall on their sword to stop you) to three (extremely supportive). Do this discreetly and with trusted members of your team. Then, use the results to target strategic influence campaigns and negotiations to win over the resisters. See chapter 9, "Know Others," for more information around principles of influence.

The biggest mistake I see executives make is foregoing this altogether or doing it once. Perform this analysis regularly and routinely at every major bend and with every major change element. It should look like an air traffic control spreadsheet. However you do it, you must identify and neutralize people who could silently sabotage the initiative.

– E—Engage. Too often, leaders fire off an email and hit a town hall message and consider it "done" with change communication. Engagement is an ongoing process, and communications is a two-way relationship. You must actively engage your broad array of stakeholders far longer than you think you need to. I advise executives to let them tell you, "We're good."

- *Say yes to the mess.*
  In its report, "The Science of Organizational Change," Boston Consulting Group warned, "The dynamic nature of business will require organizations to build capabilities for ongoing large-scale change—so they can keep up with evolving technology and competition" (Fæste et al., 2019). Organizations need to build this from the inside out— and it's likely to get messy. Because so few people know how to lead effective change, this is a massive opportunity for you, just as it was for Maggie Wilderotter and me on a smaller scale.

  Gartner, a research and consulting services company, says three-fourths of the organizations they surveyed anticipate multiplying the number of major change initiatives they undertake in the next three years. What's more, leading change is a misnomer, as if there's a singular change. It's never that simple. Any change initiative involves multiple changes. It's messy. Done right for the right reasons, it's worth it. All progress is change.

- *Empathize.*
  It sounds cliché, but it can't be overstated. As a change agent, you're not asking some impersonal organization to change. You're inviting *people* to change, people who are experiencing loss or fears of loss you may not see or perceive.

The "change curve," as it's come to be known, is based on Elisabeth Kubler-Ross's work on grief. It refers to the letting go process and how people respond to loss, uncertainty, and upheaval (Harrison, 2022). William Bridges is one of the leading researchers in change management and perhaps best known for his research on transitions. He distinguishes between the immediacy of "change" and the longer-term and essential work of "transition," which he notes can be rife with a sense of loss.

You must traverse an almost inevitable pit of despair that can show itself as the last vestiges of the old legacy being dismantled but before the promise of the new is yet visible. This is where many give up, but it's crucial to stay the course and get to the other side of it. Be gentle with people, and yourself, through it.

As an early change leader, empathy was a necessary growth area for me. In my zeal to see that business area evolve, and certain of its promise, I couldn't understand the resistance I faced. I had little sympathy for people I saw as standing in the way of the obvious future. I was totally insensitive to the emotional component, seeing it as irrelevant. It's no wonder some of them wanted to stop me.

Bridges writes on his website (and discusses at length in numerous books), "Empathetic leaders recognize that change can put people in crisis. The starting point for dealing with transition is not the outcome but the endings that people have in leaving the old situation behind." Coming face-to-face with this early in my career was one of my biggest growth areas as a leader and opened my eyes to the criticality of the human dimension of change.

As Bridges writes, "Well-managed transitions allow people to establish new roles with an understanding of their purpose, the part they play, and how to contribute and participate most effectively."

* * *

Spoiler alert: When you choose to be a change agent, it may take more than seven days to pull it off. You're not God, and there are likely some sticky legacy ways of doing things in place. Do it right, though, and there will be another legacy that endures when you're done—yours.

Chapter Checklist:

- Leading change is high risk and high reward.
- Being a change agent will help you make a difference and also help you stand out and distinguish yourself. Just make sure you stick the landing if you have a catapult moment.
- Keep customers at the center of any change you propose to lead.
- Say yes to the mess that other people complain about or avoid, as it may be an opportunity in disguise for you as a change agent to create real value.
- Treat change management like any other business process. Factor also for the longer-term work of transition. Leading change requires empathy because it requires people to release something they or their ego may be attached to.
- Buff up your communication skills so you can be ready in the moment.
- Engineer the people-side of success with change.

CHAPTER 7

Operate with Urgency

Seven thousand. That's how many cases the Supreme Court is asked to hear each year. Out of those seven thousand, only 1 percent of those, approximately 100 to 150, will ever come before the Justices (Federal Judiciary, 2022).

The Supreme Court is, of sheer necessity, a model of efficiency. Every case request is screened, reviewed, and determined. (And you thought *your* email inbox was full!) While we might imagine dramatic scenes of attorneys presenting their briefs at the Supreme Court, it's nothing like you see on *Law and Order*. By the time they arrive in Court, the Justices have already read the briefs. They expect to play ball. The attorneys had better be prepared to field rapid-fire questions by the Justices looking now to drill deeper insight to inform their deliberations.

Like Supreme Court justices, top executives don't have time for anyone to tell them what they could read on their own. They've done their homework. They operate with an innate sense of urgency and expect you to know that. They expect to play ball and put some points on the board when they walk into a meeting.

Some non-executives perceive executives as impatient. They *are* impatient—with anybody not honoring their time. They cut to the chase and expect you to do the same. Executives operate with a pervasive sense of urgency.

You should too.

RECOGNIZE INHERENT URGENCY

Describing the drivers of the inherent urgency of business, Maggie Wilderotter, who as you know from previous chapters led multiple Fortune 500 companies and start-ups alike, including as CEO, told me, "It has to be done yesterday. It has to be done fast. The customer doesn't wait, and neither does the competition."

Maggie would know—she took Frontier Communications from revenues of less than $1 billion when she joined as president and CEO to $10 billion in ten years.

Executives are aware inherent urgency is always present. Urgency now can give you advantage even in a distal future. What was fast enough yesterday, or even a minute ago, may not be fast enough tomorrow—or even *right now*. Market forces are dynamic, and the market sets the pace.

Operating with urgency recognizes that everything is in a dynamic relationship with everything else. I have a beach house. News of impending storms can introduce urgency today that was not there yesterday. Regularly ask what the situation requires (weekly, daily, and even hourly in some cases); learn what has become more or less urgent since yesterday; and re-assess priorities regularly. It can be as simple as trusting the wisp of awareness to make a phone call or take an action, and to do it *now*.

URGENCY IS NOT RUSH

Moving with a sense of urgency is not the same as being rushed. Rush is often an energy of sloppiness and desperation. Urgency is clean. If you deconstruct it, you will often find that rush is a result of insufficient urgency earlier—e.g., what you didn't do yesterday. Urgency is an acute awareness today of what tomorrow—or next year—requires that needs to be initiated now.

Executives have incredible demands on their time from multiple sources, which also generates laser-like focus on how they allocate their time. On average, executives work nearly ten hours per day, 18 percent more than employees clocking forty-hour workweeks. Nearly 80 percent of executives work on weekends, and 70 percent report working during vacations (Porter and Nohria, 2018).

Poor time management is not to blame. It comes with the job. As this research points out, these hours are largely unavoidable. Executives generate results through relationships, and every one of their constituencies wants direct contact with them. Time management is an ongoing challenge for executives (see chapter 16, "Prize Your Time").

In the most effective organizations, decisions are made at the lowest possible level. Before you ask for a top executive's time for a decision, be sure you have exhausted all other possibilities within your own power. By the time a decision arrives on an executive's desk for intervention or action, they will expect you have moved it as far down the field as you possibly can within your power.

Acting with a sense of urgency is a distinguishing trait of top executives. Peter Drucker famously wrote in *The Effective Executive* being an effective executive is less about doing things right and more about "getting the right things done." Having a sense of urgency is about sensing what is important *right now* and doing that. They aren't spending much time on and have no interest in matters that are not important right now—and they expect those around them to know the difference.

EMPOWER YOURSELF AND OTHERS TO SENSE URGENCY

McKinsey research shows fewer than half of their survey respondents said decisions are timely. There are many reasons for this, including inexperience. Only 8 percent of middle managers, and as little as 30 percent of senior managers, have exposure to the "big bet" decisions top executives are paid to make that steer the direction of an organization. Many executives have had extremely limited experience with such high-stakes decisions, which are often made by top executives shrouded in the C-suite (Aminov et al., 2019). They may not recognize the factors driving the urgency from the perspective of their boss's. Decision-making workshops can help expose leaders to the array of complex decisions top leaders face.

In my work, the lack of shared urgency is a common flash point with executives who may express frustration at their subordinates as being the cause for slow decision-making and execution. But managers not acting with urgency is only half the problem. Too often, the executives are not sufficiently sharing marching orders clearly, broadly, or early enough so that managers *can* act with urgency.

One executive shared with me that executives may hold contextual information around decision-making too close to the vest, without which managers are in the dark and have no way to ascertain inherent, and possibly even invisible, urgency. In a study of over one thousand private and public sector organizations, a majority of employees (25 percent of whom were executives) said "no" when asked whether "important strategic and operational decisions are quickly translated into action" (Neilson et al., 2008).

The solution?

Empower people to recognize urgency. Create avenues where important "big bet" decisions can be shared throughout the organization, and allow people to understand the key drivers of any urgency.

The *Harvard Business Review* research team also found in working with 250 organizations that clarifying decision rights and designing information flows had a far greater impact in accelerating execution than other levers, including changing the organization structure (Neilson et al., 2008). "Execution is the result of thousands of decisions made every day by employees acting according to the information they have and their own self-interest," they say. Ensuring everybody has the same picture can spur on productive and innovative urgent energy throughout the organization so that decisions and associated actions are moving forward in a timely manner. If you're not sure about the urgency of something, ask.

ESTABLISH URGENCY

As we've covered in an earlier chapter, the most important and valuable role of any executive is leading change. Moving organizations forward is an exercise in continuous change. Assuming what worked yesterday will work tomorrow is not enough. The most common and costly pitfall in leading change is failure to establish a sufficient sense of urgency (Kotter, 1995).

A sense of urgency is a proactive, preventative operating posture, not a reactive one. In fact, while 89 percent of executives surveyed spend some time on crises under normal operating conditions, generally speaking they spend less than 1 percent of their time on crises in any given quarter. A key reason for this is the ability to recognize and act on urgent matters before they escalate into a crisis (Porter and Nohria, 2018). Savvy executives know they have the power to create and impose urgency, which is sometimes necessary to spur others to action.

STEALTH URGENCY CREATES ADVANTAGE

Successful athletes operate with stealth urgency. The competition may be months or years off, but they don't waste a minute. They know what they are doing in their first week of training is as important—and as urgent—as what they are doing in their last week of training before the big competition. They take nothing for granted because what it will take to actually win the day is always an open question. It's what makes spectating so thrilling.

I once had the chance to spend a week watching tennis phenom Bethanie Mattek-Sands practice. As a nine-time Grand Slam doubles champion and an Olympic gold medalist, Bethanie has urgency running in her veins (International Olympic Committee, 2020). Approaching the tennis courts on the day I arrived, I thought I felt an F-18 fly over the far back court. It was just Bethanie returning a serve. I watched in an almost fearful awe, certain the tennis court would pock like the hood of a car after a hailstorm with each hit.

Fun and kind, the "Lady Gaga of tennis," as she calls herself because of her non-conforming fashion, Bethanie operates with the ferocious stealth urgency of any great competitor (Lester, 2011). As a child, she would stick around after practice ended and hit one hundred more balls. Even then, she operated with a sense of urgency, knowing there was no time to waste—and there wasn't. She began pulling toward her future Grand Slam victories and Olympic gold medal then. She left no advantage on the table—and neither should you.

ADVANCE THE AGENDA

Executives highly attune to their agendas—what they are here to accomplish (Porter and Nohria, 2018). They don't have time for excuses and aren't interested in yours. Conversely, they have all the time in the world for advancing their agenda and will make time for you if you can materially contribute to this end.

Top of mind for any aspiring executive should always be the agenda or agendas top executives are pursuing. The adage, "What your boss finds interesting, you should find fascinating," applies. Demonstrate you understand and share their urgency around their agenda and position every encounter with them in the context of advancing their goals, and you will stand out.

I advise clients to ensure any meeting with a top executive reaches what I call "red-velvet rope" entrance criteria, inspired from Michael Port's book, *Book Yourself Solid*. Do not take a top executive's time until and unless you are able to satisfy this. Examples of what I mean by "red-velvet rope" meeting criteria include:

- Make sure the desired outcome is clear and relevant.
- Anticipate the questions they will ask, and ensure you've run the trap lines to have high-quality answers.
- Do your homework before you take their time. Invest in the pre-work required to not merely discuss but materially advance their agenda. This may mean doing stakeholder alignment and consensus-building work on the front end, because executives will expect this if the decision could impact other parties.

What would be on your list? What would your top executives have on theirs? Not sure? Ask.

RESPECT URGENCY

As a Day One Executive, you know urgency is always present. It's omnipresent. Because of this, you make exceptional use of other people's time and your own. A Day One Executive, like an attorney before the Supreme Court justices, *never* subjects an executive to a verbal briefing. Rather, they:

- Communicate the meeting purpose and outcomes in the meeting request and list read-ahead materials they will receive in advance to help frame and contextualize the decisions to be made.
- Furnish the promised read-ahead materials, which contain necessary support for any decisions or "asks," including a summary of the alternatives considered, in sufficient time for them to be absorbed by the executive.
- Arrive ready to frame the decision to be made efficiently and field second-, third-, and fourth-order questions required to bring final clarity needed for the decision.

Get to the point. Executives are interested in the bottom line, and they want you to get to it quickly. Like an attorney before the Supreme Court Justices, arrive ready to play ball.

LEARN TO "STOP, DROP, AND ROLL"

Executives aggressively shun anything not on the critical path. They value their time and are in a continuous question about what needs to be done right now. I can't count the number of executives I've heard bemoan an ability to accomplish the important due to the "tyranny of the urgent."

To avoid this, I recommend what I call the "stop, drop, and roll" method, a technique taught to kids to keep them safe in the event of a fire, which for our purposes means what can I delete, defer, or delegate.

Here's how it works:

- Delete (Stop): It doesn't take long for a task list to feel like your basement closet, stuffed with things you no longer need and never will need again. When in doubt, get it out—make a deliberate decision and *stop* it. Permanently take it off the list.
- Defer (Drop): Anything that doesn't absolutely have to be done right now you can likely defer—so make the conscious choice to drop it, at least for now. You can always pick it back up later when and if it becomes more urgent.
- Delegate (Roll): That leaves all the other things that do need attention to bring them to completion or move them toward decisions. Roll anything that someone else can do to someone else.

DIVING INTO DELEGATING

The stopping and dropping elements above are self-explanatory, but delegating can be messy. Many dread it will create more problems than it's worth and that it's faster to just do it yourself. In the short term, it probably is. But delegating is a strategic choice and investment, not a reaction. Properly done, delegating is empowering to others and is essential to organizational effectiveness.

Beyond this, Harvard researchers have quantified what top executives know to be true: effective delegation literally pays. One study at a law firm showed median partners who delegated earned 20 percent more than those who didn't (Hubbard, 2016). Importantly, they found delegating paid handsomely even when it wasn't cheap. The lawyers who delegated moved from lower-value, routine tasks to higher-value, complex tasks. Clients were willing to pay more to have higher-value work done.

Every good investment requires upfront costs and pays dividends downstream. At its best, delegation creates more for everybody. It's empowering to both delegator and delegatee. See chapter 12, "Be Accountable," for more on how to delegate effectively.

* * *

Most of us are unlikely ever to have a support team and processes as optimized as those of the Supreme Court Justices, but the good news is you don't have to be a model of efficiency to start operating with urgency. Executives don't let people waste their time, and you don't have to either. Hold yourself—and others—to a higher standard before letting them have access to you and your time.

You deserve nothing less.

Chapter Checklist:

- Each day ask, "What requires my attention today?" It may include taking steps toward targets months or even years in the future.
- Deconstruct your "rush." Be willing to see where recent rushes could have been avoided with greater urgency on the front end. Where can you show more urgency today to offset the rush tomorrow?
- Periodically do a "stop, drop, and roll" exercise to see what you can delete, defer, or delegate. Practice delegating and see what changes.
- Ensure every meeting you request with a top executive meets *their* "red-velvet rope" criteria. You can visit www.AhaInsight.net for an example list, and feel free to ask the executives directly. Create your "red-velvet rope" meeting criteria list and share it with your team, or better, invite them to create it with you.
- What questions can you ask to uncover the invisible urgency inherent in anything you are supporting? Where can you invite others into urgency? Rather than just give a deadline, let your team in on what's driving urgency so that they can join you in bringing the necessary action, creativity, and innovation forward.

PART II

NURTURE RELATIONSHIPS

CHAPTER 8

Know Thyself

———

"A passionate zealot," he said with a gleam in his eye. "That's what my favorite professor at West Point would have called you," he added, reaching for a particular military history tome on a voluminous bookshelf and turning almost too easily to the exact page with the quote.

It wasn't exactly an insult, but neither was it exactly a compliment. I wasn't exactly sure what it was.

Here's what I did know: A retired military officer, he was one of the company's top executives. He was inviting me to know myself at a new level.

AN ENTIRELY DIFFERENT EDUCATION

At twenty-eight years old, I was a newly-promoted executive in one of the most successful science, engineering, and technology companies in the world. I had a burgeoning reputation as a positive team player with vision, able to rally people to build collaborative strategies that solved recognized problems. I was unafraid to speak truth to power.

That last part made some people uncomfortable.

In pointing out I wasn't just a zealot, I was a *passionate* zealot, this executive was communicating as gently as possible that I could come on a little strong when I really believed in something. Maybe a little too strong.

That interaction marked the beginning of self-awareness for me as a professional and maturation as an executive. My unwavering enthusiasm, coupled with insistent vision, had helped the company modernize a decades-old business area at risk of extinction in the mid-1990s as the first glimmer of the information age peeked over a sleepy horizon. That new age would soon begin to shred outdated business models. I was earning my Master of Science degree in information systems while working full time. Through that program, I was mingling with some of the top technology innovators who, within the year, would become some of the richest people in the world. I could sense what was coming like elephants who can feel a coming tsunami.

Along the way, I also ruffled some feathers. How could people not see this?

This was the beginning of an entirely different education about leading people: How to influence and engage people in a way that makes them want to come along with you. It starts with you: knowing thyself (and I clearly had a lot to learn myself, or I would have joined those first mover innovators).

WHY CARE TO BE SELF-AWARE?

You are powerful, beyond what you likely have yet acknowledged. And with all power comes responsibility. Conscious care about where and how we wield our own power is a mark of mastery. In my case, it was sobering to discover that seeing the proverbial prophet did not thrill everybody.

Like any trait, this passionate zealot characteristic can be a double-edged sword. It helped inspire and succeed with change that otherwise may not have happened. On at least one occasion, blinded by my own misguided enthusiasm, this same trait may have incinerated a valued relationship. I've had to learn when and how to set the dimmer switch—not turn "me" down but give more care not only to the message but to modulating the energy I bring in the delivery of messages.

Being willing to see yourself, through your own eyes and those of others, can empower you to have more options in how you relate with others. You can create more space of choice when you are able to more consciously contribute to what others value while not divorcing yourself in the process. This skill is indispensable in the professional world.

THE UNIQUENESS OF THE PROFESSIONAL WORLD

Let's face it. The professional world can be messy.

It's a unique space for human interaction, unlike almost any other. In almost every place else, you choose your comrades. But in the professional world, you're stuck with people you didn't choose and you're expected to make it work. If you're lucky, you're bound by a common purpose and mission, and maybe your organization offers some leadership development resources to help you work more effectively with others who may be very different from you.

Your friends have your back. In the professional world, you may have to swim with sharks.

The business world is also remarkably small. As we discuss in chapter 1, "Build a High Value Network," you will cross paths with people in your career several times. Your reputation will always precede you.

It's in your best interest to make relationships work for the long term, even when it's challenging and even when you don't like or trust the person. Your ability to cultivate constructive relationships begins with the relationship you have with yourself and your willingness to know yourself.

THE INESCAPABLE IRONY OF SELF-AWARENESS

Self-awareness begins with a humbling irony. We are not aware when we are not self-aware. In an interview with Angela Duckworth on Guy Kawasaki's tender, intimate, and informative podcast, *Remarkable People*, Angela called self-awareness "the foundation of all personal growth." She went on to say, "Without it you can't unlock any growth. With it, you have the possibility of changing almost anything."

We all have proverbial blind spots, but it's surprising how few people are willing to do the uncomfortable work to truly know thyself. Ten studies involving nearly five thousand people showed that only 10 to 15 percent of people possess measurable self-awareness, according to Harvard researcher Tasha Eurich. Those who do choose to embark on this humbling journey to turn those sometimes-harsh lights on and be willing to know themselves will have huge advantages.

It's an inside job.

INSIDE OUT

Eurich differentiates between two forms of self-awareness: internal and external.

- Internal self-awareness: How clearly we see our own values, passions, aspirations, fit with our environment, reactions (including thoughts, feelings, behaviors, strengths, and weaknesses), and impact on others.
- External self-awareness: Sensitivity to how others view and experience us.

Focusing only on internal self-awareness can be success-limiting because you may be less interested in seeking feedback from others and thus less willing to challenge your own views. Focusing solely on what others think, however, can leave you feeling pretty empty sooner or later in your career. The greatest leaders, she argues, actively work on both "seeing themselves clearly *and* getting feedback to understand how others see them."

Let me be clear here: This doesn't mean you have to receive other people's feedback as inviolate truth and then morph yourself to please them. They also have blind spots and biases.

They are also subjective. It's not that they are right and you are wrong.

Rather, it's about gaining awareness of how others perceive and receive you through their own filters, however accurate or skewed, how you influence an environment, and vice versa.

FEEDBACK FACILITATES GROWTH

Even in nature, healthy feedback facilitates growth. In plant biology, this dynamic is known as the "responding relationship to the environment" (Zhou and Shao, 2008). Awareness of your own interests, desires, and motivations empowers you with greater choice, both in navigating relationships and in pursuit of a personally rewarding career. Becoming aware of your own filters and learning to calibrate your interactions can facilitate greater ease and cooperation with others.

By growing in self-awareness, you empower yourself to have a space of choice rather than solely being subject to triggered, automatic reactions and even risking derailment (see chapter 14, "Don't Derail"). In learning where your buttons are, you will recognize when someone is pushing one. Self-awareness can also insulate even the most caring among us from one of the most prevalent and lethal threats to an otherwise promising executive's career: momentary insensitivity to others (Van Velsor et al., 1995).

THE PAYOFF OF INVESTING IN EMOTIONAL INTELLIGENCE

Our ability to consciously influence others is commonly called emotional intelligence. Daniel Goleman popularized extensive research on the subject of emotional intelligence. He demonstrated that emotional intelligence is at least as important as cognitive intelligence in success (Goleman and Boyatzis, 2017). Research using the Genos Emotional Intelligence Inventory with over one hundred professionals in New Zealand found people with high levels of emotional intelligence performed significantly better in the workplace (Cummings, 2005).

Success increasingly requires the ability to lead change in a global and multicultural context, and while admirable, this is unfamiliar territory for many leaders (Gregersen et al., 1998). Emotional intelligence helps you get results with others in a manner that builds, rather than destroys, relationships. It helps you live not merely the golden rule, but the platinum rule: treating others as *they* wish to be treated (Truninger et al., 2018). Emotional intelligence is a skill set you can develop, and self-awareness is at the core.

HOW TO DEVELOP SELF-AWARENESS

Developing self-awareness is not an automatic by-product of age or experience. While it can accrue, you must commit every day to being a self-aware leader. Here are five steps you can start taking now to gain more self-awareness:

1. JOURNAL

Before I started journaling, l struggled mightily to detect the signal of my inner voice from the noise of other priorities and people clamoring for attention in my life until I discovered a technique called "Morning Pages." Julia Cameron created it, and I read about in her New York Times best-selling book called *The Artist's Way*.

I had the great pleasure of meeting Julia over a Zoom interview, where she described the technique as follows:

"You get up in the morning, and you write, 'This is what I like, this is what I don't like. This is what I want more. This is what I want less.' It's like you're sending a little telegram to the universe with your coordinates... You write about anything and everything."

She advises to write using long hand without stopping until you fill three pages of any journal. Don't judge whether the writing is good or bad, or whether you even have anything to say. In case you're wondering whether it works, Elizabeth Gilbert credits this book and technique with the journey that led to her book *Eat, Pray, Love*.

"Just keep your hand moving across the page," Julia said in our interview. She recommends doing the pages longhand because it works a different part of your brain than typing.

Some people understandably resist journaling because they see it as a lot of work, but what if it could be a way for you to hear your own voice in a cacophony of confusion? Journaling can help you understand your own emotions and triggers, tap your deeper dreams (what I call dreamscaping), and even just provide a helpful record of your choices.

Anthony Tjan, coauthor of *Heart, Smarts, Guts, and Luck*, notes that Warren Buffett, one of the greatest living investors of all time, takes the time to write the rationale for every investment he makes. Over time, his journalistic record-keeping has helped him hone his own powers of insight for what most would agree have been some spectacular investments.

A journal can provide a space where it is safe to dare to dream, catalyzing generative energies within those dreams. They may be outlandish, maybe even wildly unrealistic, but there's an energy in those dreams, and they hold clues to you. I'll never be a professional gymnast, but I am energized by the pursuit of excellence. I'll never be a rockstar, but I'm energized when engaging with an audience. What is it for you?

2. GET CURIOUS ABOUT YOUR VALUES

I once overheard a junior colleague on a team I was leading call me a bitch. She was speaking to someone just outside my office door, thinking I was out of the office. Heat seared through my body like an oil rig fire.

I froze. Do I hide in my office until they leave and pretend I didn't hear it? Do I compassionately confront her?

I chose to confront her out of a genuine desire to understand what would cause her to say this. The ensuing conversation was uncomfortable for both of us, to say the least, and marked another turning point in my life as a leader.

It drove me even more powerfully into the work I do today because it showed me that even when we think we are self-aware, we can still have plenty to learn. I also saw how our own closely-held values can be in conflict with one another.

In my case, I value harmony. I also value results. Sometimes you can have both, but not always. Under pressure, they come into tension, and when pressed, I value results over harmony. I'm willing to sacrifice harmony in the short term, figuring mutual trust will carry the day in the long term.

In the situation with this colleague, however, we had only recently begun working together. She didn't really know me. There was a power imbalance, as I was more senior than she. We had not yet built up the "trust deposits," as Stephen Covey calls them in his book *The Speed of Trust*, in our emotional bank account together. My full court dedicated press for results, which I just assumed she valued with equal zeal, came across as uncaring and insensitive.

While one of the most uncomfortable conversations I've ever had, that awkward conversation opened a door to what became a more authentic, high-trust relationship that likely would contribute to greater relationship resilience going forward.

In the early 1980s, researchers Robert E. Quinn and John Rohrbaugh developed the Competing Values Framework. The business resource blog *FourWeekMBA* has a good summary. It depicts the inherent tension between organizational drivers toward both stability and change, and internal (e.g., mentoring, etc.) and external (e.g., results) priorities. These dimensions are always in a dynamic interplay, but knowing they exist, and that you are also subject to them, can be liberating.

One way to gain some clarity around your own values and where they may compete or be in tension with one another at times is to do this simple exercise periodically:

- Select a handful of values from a long list (you can find such a list in an internet search).
- Next, consider how or under what circumstances any of these values may come into tension.
- Now, if you had to choose only one, which would you choose? If you find yourself hedging, get curious. Under what circumstance does this value take the wheel? When might another win out? How would you know when you are experiencing a value clash with someone else? How could you address that?

This isn't to say you always have to be predictable or are responsible for how other people feel. It is about empowering yourself with greater sensitivity to how you operate so that you can stay in the driver's seat of you.

4. FEEDBACK

There is a lot of controversy these days about the f-word—feedback. And rightly so. It's a loaded word because it's entirely subjective. Feedback can damage if you give it too much power. It can also be a powerful aid in the often rocky path of an executive.

Be selective in whose feedback you invite—everybody should not get an equal voice in your life. As Brené Brown writes in her book *Dare to Lead*, "Get clear on whose opinions of you matter." Look for people who will tell the truth in a spirit of up-building. Be brave and bold in your invitations. Be on alert, for people will sneak in a window or kick in your door with their uninvited ego, projecting what they don't like about themselves onto you, masquerading as a "truth" you need to hear. Don't let them in.

With a sincere invitation and no risk of reprisal, trusted coworkers and friends will offer perspectives that are honest, supportive, and have your best interests at heart. You will know the difference. Opening yourself to feedback is not about becoming who or what everybody else says you should become. It's simply about awareness.

There are many forms of feedback, starting with the gentlest forms first. I'll cover four here: (1) leadership strength assessments; (2) interpersonal direct; (3) performance reviews; and (4) market signals.

Feedback form #1: Leadership strength assessments

We didn't come into the world with operating manuals. Fortunately, there is a wide range of leadership strength assessments on the market. There are two main categories of assessments, both of which have a place in the life of a leader: developmental and appreciative.

- Developmental assessments: These highlight strengths and areas for potential development based on a combination of inputs from you and a diverse array of other people who work with us, including direct reports, peers, partners, and your clients or bosses. Checkpoint 360, Genos Emotional Intelligence Inventory, and the Trust Quotient 360 are examples of these that my company uses.

Done right, with complete anonymity, candor, and a supportive, non-punitive context, 360 assessments shine light on how others experience us. This can often be extremely sensitive and hard to hear, especially for caring leaders. Over time, as we work to hone certain capacities, 360s ideally reveal shifts in how others experience us.

- Appreciative assessments: These shine light on innate aspects of our personalities that are unlikely to change but that you can appreciate in yourself and others. The Myers-Briggs Type Indicator (MBTI), Clifton Strengths-finder, and Kolbe A Index are examples of these types of assessments. These assessments gift you a greater appreciation of yourself and your team, with an emphasis on valuing differences. They give you a new language and tools to help you and others flex in new ways to bridge differences that can naturally escalate into conflict under pressure. Never ascribe to malice that which can be explained by simple personality difference.

My friend Pete Smith, author of *Dare to Matter: Choosing an Unstuck and Unapologetic Life of Significance*, cautions that people can misuse assessments as a way to excuse bad behavior. His concern is that assessments could give people permission to not mature or grow and instead simply shrug and say, "Well, that's just who I am." He's right. Some people surely do this, but not Day One Executives.

My perspective is different. I view assessments as some of the gentlest feedback sources we can receive as leaders. As you move through the business world, you will receive feedback from others one way or the other, whether you like it or not—and whether you know it or not. People want to work with you again, or they don't. They desire to contribute to your work in the world, or they won't. They will refer and recommend you, or they won't. I'd rather know earlier rather than later where those limitations are.

Feedback form #2: Interpersonal direct

In its simplest form, you can always ask people to give you feedback on your working style. However, be aware of the following cautions.

1. Be coachable. "You can't handle the truth" is one of the most famous movie lines ever uttered—spoken by Colonel Nathan Jessup (played by Jack Nicholson) to Lieutenant Daniel Kaffee (played by Tom Cruise) in the 1992 blockbuster film *A Few Good Men* (Reiner, 1992). Demonstrating you are willing and able to hear the feedback is on you. Likewise, ensure anybody to whom you are offering feedback is able to receive it before you offer it.

   In his book *Elegant Leadership*, Andrew Neitlich, founder of the Center for Executive Coaching, defines being coachable as being "receptive to advice, trying out new ideas, and listening to tough feedback." Someone who is not coachable "thinks they already know or can figure it out." He notes this type of person has to be in "*lots* of pain before they ask for, or take, anybody else's counsel."

2. Be alert to disproportionate power dynamics. The more senior you are, the less likely people are to feel safe giving you feedback and the more threatening your feedback may be to them, however well-intentioned it may be. A study by Joseph Grenny, author of the *New York Times* bestselling book *Crucial Conversations,* reveals eight out of ten people feel their boss has an "undiscussable weakness" (Grenny and Maxfield, 2019). Assessments, such as 360s described above, can be helpful, particularly one where the input is truly anonymous. Likewise, be sensitive to this when offering others feedback.

3. Acknowledge cognitive bias and lack of skill. Korn Ferry Institute research shows that most managers are unskilled at offering constructive feedback to "grow talent," with this competency ranking last out of sixty-seven (Rock et al., 2014). Ouch.

Feedback form #3: Performance reviews
Performance reviews are among the most common—and universally dreaded—forms of feedback in a work environment. They may be on the way out, at least in their traditional form, and not soon enough, in my view. They're subjective and rife with unconscious bias.

Performance reviews have a dark and sordid history that dates back to forced labor. Many still largely reflect a punitive, judgmental energy rooted in the view that people don't want to work (Dishman, 2018). Former MIT management professor Douglas McGregor was the first to introduce the radical idea that a manager's attitude impacts employee motivation in his seminal 1960 book, *The Human Side of Enterprise*. His ground-breaking research is still dismantling systems rooted in distrust and subjugation in favor of systems that aim to empower, unleash, and inspire human potential (Dishman, 2018).

In a 2015 Deloitte survey, 58 percent of managers stated traditional performance reviews did not serve their purpose. Corporate Executive Board studies put the number closer to 95 percent (Rock et al., 2014). In a *Harvard Business Review* article titled, "The Feedback Fallacy," Marcus Buckingham and Ashley Goodall argue that worse than useless, performance feedback can be destructive because, at its premise, it assumes the feedback is a) desired by the recipient, and b) the giver is qualified to give it.

Deloitte, Microsoft, Adobe, Accenture, and many other companies have ditched annual performance review systems, experimenting with other forms of feedback. At Deloitte, managers now answer a simple yes or no question about their team members: "Given what I know of this person's performance, I would always want him or her on my team."

To the extent you work in an organization that still does performance reviews, I recommend you write your own review starting now. Pay attention to the results you generate and help others generate. Get clear with clients and sponsors on what's expected from the role you are playing, and what success would look like. Get clear early on the metrics that matter (See chapter 3, "Know Your Value").

Begin tracking them yourself so that you have the foundation for a before-and-after story down the road. Be critically thoughtful of your own contributions. Don't abdicate your own power and leave your story solely to others to judge. Give yourself a voice—a strong voice, backed by data.

Feedback form #4: Market signals

A cherished mentor empowered me early in my career with this simple advice: You'll know you're succeeding when people (customers) come to you with work. If you're busy, you're probably succeeding. If you're not, ask yourself why.

This wisdom empowered me to custom-create a career by attuning to where I could generate value. Rather than wait a year for a performance review, I saw quickly where others came back for additional support, or conversely where they didn't. Market signals are always flowing. Sometimes they are invisible, like a radio wave. Tune your radar to pick them up.

WHEN FEEDBACK GETS LOUDER

Feedback in any form that is not heeded will get louder. Consider the following examples:

- When a board of directors or executive team becomes disenchanted with the performance of a key leader, they let them go.

- When an employee demonstrates they are not open to growth, management will phase them out of the job or the organization.
- When an organization feels they've exhausted their options to get a better result from their contractor, they don't renew the contract.

KNOWING THE CURRENCIES YOU VALUE

Finally, get clear about what *you* value. Money is only one form of currency. It's important to know what's important to you. Other forms of currency include autonomy, meaningful work you enjoy, flexibility, working with great colleagues, status, non-monetary perks, and so much more. Knowing this will help empower you in negotiations, especially in roles where monetary compensation options may be limited. You can increase your options when you are clear on what you value. What are the forms of currency that matter to you?

* * *

The final habit in Stephen Covey's best-selling book, *The 7 Habits of Highly Successful People*, is "sharpen the saw." What if you are the saw? It can be painful or unpleasant to have your edge sharpened, but the payoff is worth it.

Thirty years after that bookshelf conversation at the dawn of my own first executive role, I'm still a passionate zealot. It's what fueled this book. If you're reading this, you, like me, have something huge in your corner that many simply don't—humility and the desire to grow.

Chapter Checklist

- Self-awareness is an inside-out job. It requires the willingness to search inside yourself and to allow feedback from the environment.
- Feedback can be flawed, and it's also invaluable. It's the foundation for effective relationships with others.
- You can ask people for feedback and learn to read market signals.
- Write your own performance review. Give yourself this voice and see clearly where you shine.
- Assessments such as 360s and others can help you see yourself and understand how others perceive you.
- Realize your values (and others') can be in tension with one another. Be interested in discovering where you default to one over another.
- Unheeded feedback gets louder.

CHAPTER 9

Know Others

———

Budgets were tightening faster than a Santa suit after the holidays. Other organizations needed money. Like wild animals circling the tents in search of a meal, the operation appeared to be a lavish buffet. For the Executive Director, whom we'll call Jeff, the heat was on.

Performance had been lackluster for at least a year in Jeff's shop. He blamed his managers.

"They just won't hold people accountable," he complained to me in an initial consultation.

But did he?

A brief observation of a single leadership team meeting revealed a key indicator of trouble: a mismatch between Jeff's words and actions. His stated desire was to create a high-performance team, but his actions revealed something different. Jeff was unwilling to confront some difficult dynamics taking root in his organization. In placating or looking the other way, he was complicit in the organization's downward spiral. His leadership team simply took their cue from him.

Just ask Ron.

Jeff hired Ron, the newly promoted chief operating officer, to help "clean house." Ron was eager to hit the ground running. Taking Jeff at his word about wanting to raise the standard, Ron began instituting stricter reviews of materials produced by the operating divisions before products went to Jeff for approval. The leadership team, unaccustomed to this level of oversight, pushed back at this unwelcome newcomer. Who was this guy again?

Jeff was in a sticky spot. Does he back Ron and demonstrate he was serious about improving performance, or does he leave Ron out in the cold to fend for himself?

Suffice it to say, Ron soon needed a parka.

Like a lot of us, Ron had a lot to learn about truly knowing others.

RESULTS REQUIRE EFFECTIVE RELATIONSHIPS
We don't get far alone. Getting results requires the ability to develop and sustain relationships, which requires knowing others beyond what immediately meets the eye.

As Chris Voss, CEO of the Black Swan Group and former lead international kidnapping negotiator for the FBI, writes in *Never Split the Difference: Negotiate as If Your Life Depended on It,* "In every negotiation, the outcome is a result of another person's decision." Negotiation, he argues, is "all about making the right moves in a world where to get what you want, you have to ask for it correctly… Getting what you want out of life is all about getting what you want from and with those around you."

In short, you need to know others.

MORE THAN MEETS THE EYE

It soon became all too clear that despite his public proclamations and private assurances, Jeff had neither the intention nor the inner fortitude to do what was required to affect the deep cultural change to lift organizational performance in a sustained manner. Ron was in an impossible position.

Set up for failure from the start, Ron's pressure tactics were making Jeff look bad to his subordinates. Rather than risk his own social power, Jeff made Ron the fall guy.

Observing this dynamic provoked an "aha insight" for me. You can't be a "Pollyanna" when making your way in an organization. Be willing to know others, to see them for who they truly are, not who you want them to be or how they want you to see them. Rather than take them at their word, watch actions. Be aware of what makes people tick. Contrary to what he said, Jeff sacrificed performance but not social affiliation—he did not want to look bad.

ADOPT A DISCOVERY MENTALITY.

As Chris Voss writes, our "fears, needs, perceptions and desires are mostly hidden." He goes on to note that "your main goal right from the start should be to acquire as much information as possible through extraction and observation."

That may sound a little impersonal or tactical, but he's right: Always look beneath the surface.

NOBODY WANTS TO LOOK BAD

"Rule number one is nobody wants to look bad," Bilge Emrich shared with me in our interview. Now CEO of a capital projects advisory services consultancy (Astar Advisory), she is a former executive at a Fortune 200 company with more than twenty years of experience in the construction and energy sectors who has done business on four continents.

"The universal unwritten rule that applies to every individual from every culture is that you cannot make someone look bad—especially your boss," she said with a compassionate smile, then added, "and be aware that *their* perception of what makes them look bad may differ from yours."

Having spent significant time doing business in Asia and negotiating with Asian companies, Bilge gave the example of the concept of "losing face," making someone look bad in front of others. "In Asian cultures, it is almost fatal in a relationship sense to cause someone to 'lose face.'"

Not making someone look bad starts with understanding what they believe will make them look good.

FIVE CORE NEEDS OF PEOPLE

Almost anything you desire to accomplish as an executive requires the cooperation and support of other people. It's what Guhan Subramanian, the first person in the history of Harvard University to hold tenured appointments at both Harvard Law School and Harvard Business School, calls inter-dependent problem solving.

This isn't easy, though. It's the reason so many leaders struggle and the reason that AHA Insight focuses so intensively on influence, negotiation, and consensus-building in our work with executives who are leading major change (see also chapter 5, "Build Decision Intelligence").

Your work as an executive is an ongoing series of negotiations with the people whom your organization's success depends on and with whom you achieve it. The best negotiators put themselves in others' shoes. They make it their business to know others.

The first step in knowing others is recognizing we all share what Roger Fisher and Daniel Shapiro, authors of *Beyond Reason: Using Emotions as You Negotiate,* call five core needs. The five core needs are:

- **Appreciation**—Nobody likes to feel unappreciated, unheard, or devalued.
- **Autonomy**—This refers to the freedom to make decisions without imposition from someone else. When someone feels their autonomy is being trampled, they will have no further interest in the content.

- **Affiliation**—Humans have an innate need for belonging. When we feel excluded, the anterior cingulate cortex area of our brain lights up, the same region that activates with physical pain. Pathways of possibility will close off, and we will shut down.
- **Status**—Acknowledging your counterpart's status is a way to build trust and rapport. In contrast, when we feel disrespected, we shut down. "A quiet rage builds inside of you" is how one male executive put it with remarkable candor. Attacking someone's status may be tempting in a moment of frustration, but be aware you are potentially severing the relationship.
- **Role**—This is not only a formal position we may occupy but can also refer to informal roles we take on in a negotiation. We have the power to shape roles with other people that are mutually rewarding.

Violate any of them and you have likely shut someone down. Honor them, and the possibilities that can appear might surprise you. Mutually rewarding deals can appear, where everybody receives more than they otherwise would have, when counterparts honor these needs and stay in creative discussion at a negotiating table (Fisher and Shapiro, 2006).

With this awareness, you're ready to move into some of the more complex and intricate aspects of coming to know others. These next elements won't matter if you're not first honoring those core needs.

I propose four lenses (personality, values, politics, and culture) through which you can observe others. You could consider it a framework that moves from the specific individual (personality and values) outward to interactions with other people (politics) and then further outward to the organization (culture). Let's unpack these.

FOUR LENSES

- **Personality**

  Our personality is often the first thing we notice in people. In allowing others to see you, they are more likely to feel comfortable opening up and letting you see more of who they are. There is no one personality that makes a better executive or leader than another, and all of us are more than meets the eye. Be open about your interests and let your natural personality shine through.

  Many organizations do personality assessments, such as the Myers-Briggs Type Indicator (see chapter 8, "Know Thyself," for more on this). If you have the chance in an organization to take this type of assessment, do it. It demonstrates you are unafraid to be known and willing to be vulnerable.

  Ask about and take an interest in your colleague's activities and passions. We devote significant energy to our passions. It can be in these spaces real relationships can take root.

  I once worked with a highly accomplished man who was a professionally trained ballet dancer. Another former colleague had a metallurgy shop in his garage where he fashioned historically accurate and fully working replicas of medieval weapons by hand (you don't want to get on this guy's bad side). Two women I once worked with sat one hundred yards apart from each other for years before discovering they were both trained vocalists. Their voices could make a statue weep. Everybody's a genius at something, you just have to find out what that is. Getting to know the person behind the persona can melt walls (and make work more fun).

- **Values**

  As we explored in chapter 8, "Know Thyself," we all operate according to a set of deeply held values. In his book *The Nature of Human Values*, trailblazing values researcher Milton Rokeach says relatively few "terminal human values" serve as the internal reference points for our choices, beliefs, and behavior. They are complex, subtle, and often interwoven. Sociologist and researcher Robin Williams (not the beloved comedian) describes values as "complex pre-codings," and "core conceptions of the desirable within every individual and society."

  Often, we jump to conclusions about people. Be curious about who people are and honoring of the experiences that have shaped them, known and unknown. Be willing to let others know some of what has shaped you.

  In my case, my parents raised me in a military home, and we moved during the middle of my fourth-grade year of school. All the kids already had their friends, and nobody needed or wanted a new friend. It was painful. Things got better, but I never forgot what it was like to be alone.

This drives me even today to be sure every person in my sphere feels seen, heard, and acknowledged. Having once been the outsider, inclusion for me is a deeply held value. It likely had considerable influence on my choice to move into executive coaching, facilitation, and mediation work.

Rokeach showed values exist within an intricate order of operations. He demonstrated that by measuring the "relative ranking" of these values, it is possible to predict a wide variety of behavior (Rokeach, 1973). While this research demonstrates values' profound reliability and inexorable influence on our behaviors, these relative rankings aren't always obvious to the casual observer.

Using myself as an example, most people who know me say they find me to be friendly and accommodating. It can take people by surprise when they encounter what they may perceive to be uncharacteristic intensity when someone violates a value of mine I hold dear, such as trust. Those who know me realize this is entirely congruent with who I am, but it can take others off guard.

Values can be complex and more than meets the eye, so hold an almost sacred space of curious non-judgment when it comes to knowing others.

- **Politics**
"There's the org chart, and then there's the org chart," Bilge said to me, almost whispering the last part with a knowing wink as she described how things really get done in organizations. She added, "People who understand the

invisible organizational chart can get results more efficiently without ruffling feathers."

Politics is inherently social. Where two or more people gather in any context with power and structure, politics is likely to be there as well. Power is complex and also simple. Ordinary people "know what it is to have power and they can sense who has it," wrote Henry Mintzbert, one of the world's foremost experts on power and politics in his book *Power In and Around Organizations*.

"You have to learn to read people," Bilge advises. "There are a lot of politics, and it's important to understand what people are really saying. There is always layer after layer."

Eager, idealistic, and ambitious, Bilge distinguished herself early on as a Day One Executive through the exceptional quality of her work. The executive vice president of her Fortune 200 employer asked Bilge to help overhaul the company's capital projects program that oversees thousands of projects competing for billions of dollars in funding. Bilge helped develop a prioritization model that objectively evaluated both financial and non-financial benefits to steer funding to the most deserving projects. The model helped measurably improve the overall return on investment for the company. It also gained the support of even skeptical business units, because they saw that prioritization model was fair and did not favor one business unit over another.

The executive VP and the CEO loved it. The CEO asked her to present her analysis and recommendations to the

COO. Bilge was stunned and totally confused when the COO was "totally dismissive." She would later learn that the COO saw the executive VP as a rival. As someone considered to be the executive VP's asset, she was automatically suspect.

"Even if I put something extremely valuable in front of him, which I had, he was not going to like anything from me because he would perceive it was coming from the executive VP," she shared.

Years later, the business units fully implemented the program despite the objection of the COO, but without her or the executive VP receiving any credit. On the one hand it was disappointing, but also illuminating. She said discovering this opened her eyes to sensitive dynamics not visible on a static organization chart.

Ethnology is a branch of anthropology that "studies the world from the standpoint of its social relations," as the Princeton University writes on its website. In their article entitled, "The Org Chart as Political Map-Making," ethnographers Jasmine Chia and Samuel Hagen caution that while organizational charts have some value in describing formal functional relationships and power lines, they have one significant limitation: "They represent linear hierarchies where human relationships are decidedly non-linear." They advise people "to eschew the imperialistic tendencies of the [org chart] cartographer and recognize an organization for its inherent nature—a complex web of culture and dependencies not easily squeezed into boxes and lines."

"There are a lot of agendas going on," Bilge said referring to that complex web, "especially in large organizations. You need to understand who's in with whom, who doesn't like whom. When one executive doesn't like another executive, you need to understand this," she advises. Trust yourself. If you feel confused, it is a signal that actions are not matching words and is an invitation to be aware. There are probably some politics in play, even if you can't yet discern them.

How do you navigate the often-messy dynamics of office politics? In short, be aware of but don't play politics. Here are some tips to help your intrepid explorer understand and navigate the lay of the land.

- Create an allegiance map. Draw out an informal relationship- or allegiance-based organization chart. Imagine the formal lines and structure or the formal organizational chart fading out and a relational network becoming visible. These lines are thicker than the formal organizational chart lines.
- Remain neutral where you can. Create a reputation for yourself independent of your boss. "Take your reputation in your own hands," Bilge advises. "If you are perceived as someone who is independent and willing to help anybody who is trying to do the right thing succeed, you can transcend those political alliances," she says.
- Keep the organization's best interest front and center. Pledging allegiance to the "right" people might appear to elevate you faster in an organization, Bilge said in our interview, but it is precarious. Remaining

independent may be a slower path, but you will have a stronger foundation. Create a solid foundation with competence and awareness, not allegiance.

- **Culture**

  People behave the way they do in organizations because somewhere, they are being rewarded for it by people in power. This exerts a strong influence on organizational culture. Root out the rewards—be they public recognition and bonuses or more discrete social acknowledgments and special exceptions to the stated rules—and behavior is suddenly explained.

  Rewards often align with relationships (e.g., politics). In healthy organizational culture, reward systems align with stated values. Dysfunctional organizations (and leaders) don't. They claim to value one thing but reward another. As Ron discovered the hard way, expecting a leader to acknowledge a double-standard is like expecting to walk into a buzz saw and not have it hurt.

  At its core, organizational culture, like politics, boils down to two words: unwritten rules. The Society of Human Resource Management (SHRM) points out, "Unlike the mission or values appearing prominently on company walls and websites, in most cases culture remains unwritten" (Grossman 2009). Rewards and allegiances provide the greatest clues to dynamics with others that can otherwise be invisible.

  Once you train your eyes to see allegiances and tacit reward systems in place, it's like putting on night vision goggles. You will see things in the pitch-black dark of night that others can't.

One thing to be aware of—culture is sticky. You're unlikely to single-handedly change organizational culture without positional power at the top. If you find yourself in a truly toxic culture, see it for what it is—and consider making a grateful, and graceful, exit.

* * *

Being willing to know others will give you the foundation for building a high-value network. It can make navigating tricky relational terrain easier. Most importantly, wherever you choose to be, you will have you.

Even still, it never hurts to pack a parka.

Chapter Checklist
- Committing to truly know others is a critical skill, and it begins on day one.
- Remember that nobody likes to look bad in front of others. Make people look good everywhere you can without disavowing yourself.
- Honor people's five core needs. Apologize when you inadvertently trample one (don't judge yourself, just acknowledge it and repair it).
- Hold a space of curious non-judgment when it comes to getting to know other people.
- Research people of interest to learn more about them, even before you meet them. Say yes to social activities

that help break the ice. This lets you see different sides of people and foster new relationships outside of your normal patterns. Make the effort to get to know people's personalities and passions.

- Be willing to see people for who they truly are. As Maya Angelou famously tweeted in 2015, "When someone shows you who they are, believe them the first time."
- Be aware. Don't look only at the formal power organizational chart. Create an informal relationship or alliance-based organization chart. Map out the loyalty lines. Use it as a map to sidestep landmines. Look for the rewards.
- Keep the organization's best interests front and center. Be aware of power dynamics but realize you don't have to play politics to be successful.
- Watch for the often-invisible culture cues and rewards. Learn to speak the language of actions. As baseball legend Yogi Berra famously said in his leadership book by the same name, "You can observe a lot by just watching." Where you see conflicts between what people say and do, trust what they do.

CHAPTER 10

Create a High Value Network

———

You've probably heard the old adage, "It's not what you know, it's who you know…" but have you read the fine print? It's also: how well you know them, what you're willing to do for them, and what they are willing to do for you.

Andrew Neitlich is a Harvard Business School alum and founder and director of the International Coaching Federation (ICF) Accredited Center for Executive Coaching. About thirty-five fellow aspiring executive coaches and I were in a capstone workshop with him when he did a quick and memorable networking demonstration.

He asked us to raise our hands if we could name a billionaire. Nearly every hand went up. He then asked us to raise our hands if we personally knew a billionaire. Three hands remained up. He then asked us who knew a billionaire who would take our call. Two hands remained.

You don't need to know a billionaire to have a high value network. But you do need people who will answer the call—and you need to be that person for others.

YOUR NETWORK IS THE ULTIMATE SUSTAINABLE POWER GRID

At its core, your network is a power grid, and you are at its center. Power in this sense is the capacity or ability to do something; and to direct or influence the behavior of others or the course of events. You possess intrinsic power. You do not need anybody's permission to retain this power, and you are not dependent on anybody to "give" you this power.

Your power has nothing to do with your pay, where you sit on an organizational chart, or whether you even have a job right now. *You* are a powerful person—period. Full stop.

As you enter the professional world, your power extends beyond you. It infuses your influence and contributes to your network, which in turn contributes to you. You can use energy to influence other people and events.

You have power that you may not yet even fully appreciate, and I hope this book will be the beginning of claiming, owning, and acknowledging this. You will become more potent as you increasingly come to see, acknowledge, and appropriately and constructively use your power. One caution is to never use control "over" others. Instead, see your power (which is considerable) as a resource you can deploy to generate greater good for all. Handled with care, your network can be the ultimate sustainable power grid, reliably there for you even in the storm.

Center for Creative Leadership research into three Fortune 500 companies showed 81 percent of promotions came through relationships with someone higher in the organization who helped with visibility (Ruderman and Ohlott, 1994). Your network holds more sway over the arc of your career than any manager or supervisor ever can or will. Create a high value network, and your career becomes bullet-proof.

WHAT IS THE SOURCE OF POWER?

In a conversation with me, Jane (not her real name) shared that a Fortune 200 company retained her during a layoff of dozens of other executives and highly qualified personnel because Jane had an extensive network inside the company.

"I knew people everywhere," she said. "The company knew I could get stuff done." Jane didn't just know a lot of people— she had a powerful network who would take action on her behalf if she called. Her network showed up for Jane because of all of the ways she had shown up for them over the years long before she needed anything from them.

The source of power in your high value network is the generosity in your use of power with your network. When the layoffs impacted her colleagues, Jane could have offered sympathetic ear and left it there. Instead, she took action to help her colleagues facing the prospect of unemployment, some of whom were at risk of losing company-sponsored immigration visas. Jane began using her power and her network to help them find new projects or jobs outside the company. Everybody found a new position. Do you think these individuals will take Jane's call in the future? Absolutely.

WHAT ARE DIFFERENT FORMS OF POWER?

Power is present in every relationship. Understanding power can help you claim, own, and acknowledge yours and use it to build a high value network. John French and Bertram Raven, researchers from the University of Michigan, identified the most widely cited classification of social power. They identified six forms of influence:

- Legitimate—I call this "positional" power, and it is associated with a role on an organizational chart. It is a "loaned" form of power and, thus, temporary. You hold it for however long you are in the position and for the length of time the organization imbues the position with formal power. Don't be seduced by this form of power: It vanishes when you leave the job, or the role de-escalates due to a reorganization.
- Reward—This basis of power derives from your ability to offer something of value to someone else in exchange for something you value. This may be tangible (e.g., promise of bonuses, promotions, a corner office, etc.) or intangible (e.g., approval). This influence is transactional in nature—a person using reward power expects something in exchange.
- Expert—This is power rooted in your expertise. The rarer and more in-demand your skill set, the greater the power it conveys. Name your price when you have a skill or ability an organization dearly needs, and be aware you

have the power to lend this to others to build your high value network.

- Referent—Integrity, admiration, and respect are the core inspirational powers available to all of us. You extend this power to others when you generously connect people in your network on behalf of others or extend your reputational capital on behalf of someone else, such as giving them a job referral. Unlike reward power, someone using this power asks for and expects nothing in return.

- Coercive—this form derives from the ability to take something of value away or threaten someone. It requires the means and the will to follow through on the threat. It may be tangible (e.g., a demotion, firing, special privileges) or intangible (e.g., the threat of rejection, alienation, revocation of favor or a mantle of positional power, etc.). This form of control may be effective, but it is also expensive for its holder. Use coercive power with extreme caution. Misuse of coercive power can backfire. Leaders who want to get things done while also building a high value network are wise to consider this a power of last resort.

- Informational—You've likely heard the adage that "knowledge is power." Information power is available to everybody willing to invest in learning and sharing what they know to help others. Mentors utilize informational power to develop mentees. This power is sometimes mistaken for a person's ability to control the information that others need to accomplish something, but withholding such knowledge is a form of coercive power, not informational power.

John Hinshaw (whom we met in chapter 1, "Know the Driving Force") wielded informational power effectively early in his career before he had real positional power, reward power, or even referent power. Now group chief operating officer and managing director for the HSBC bank, John didn't start his career with extensive family connections or an Ivy League education. He was just generous and thoughtful, and as an avid and precocious student of the emerging internet technology, John had informational power to share.

Informational power took John far early in his career, and as he began to accrue other forms of power, even sparking what would become one of the most important friendships in John's life and career, he shared with me in an interview. As an undergraduate student, John used his knowledge of the burgeoning internet to educate James Madison University Provost and his economics professor, Dr. Russell Warren, about how to use this transformational technology. A year later, Dr. Warren inspired his pupil to do an internship working with technology at the US Embassy in London, which helped launch his career.

WHAT FORMS OF POWER CREATE A HIGH VALUE NETWORK?

The four most enduring forms of power (expert, referent, reward, and informational) have a direct bearing on the quality of your network. Jane used informational power to build rapport inside the company by lending her mentorship to people coming behind her. She used referent power when reaching out to her own network to help her colleagues find new employment. Jane's expert power, combined with her referent power, made her extremely valuable to the company that kept her employed when faced with the difficult situation of widespread layoffs. As a manager, Jane had reward power as well as legitimate power.

To the extent you hold and grow any of these forms of power, you become less vulnerable to the negative use of force by others (e.g., coercive) toward you and less at the whims of undesirable circumstances outside your control. As Jane experienced, your employer can eliminate your job, they can go out of business, or the bottom can fall out of your business. You will move forward with relative ease when you systematically establish a power base and wield it with care with and through a high value network.

THINK QUALITY—NOT QUANTITY

Researchers estimate by mid-career, most people have a mean average of 750 people in their network of contacts (McCormick et al., 2010). Most people accumulate contacts the way a trawler gathers fish—scraping the seabed and dragging a big fishnet behind them as they move along in life, collecting LinkedIn contacts along the way. If you've ever seen a trawler dumping its haul, you know you spend a lot of time cleaning out that net.

A high value network is not an automatic byproduct of meeting people and accumulating names in your contact list or social media accounts. I urge you to put quality above quantity and play the long game with your network. Cultivate and carefully curate it, and realize it extends in all directions, not merely vertically on an organizational chart.

As an introvert, I've never liked the term "networking." It felt so impersonal, devoid of heart and utterly transactional as I entered the professional world. I would do almost anything to avoid a "networking" event. I desired relationships, not a network. Years later, I realized a high value network is exactly that: high quality relationships.

YOUR NETWORK IS A GARDEN

Your network is rooted in a soil of reciprocity. You get to design it, watch it blossom, and decide who is in it. Like any garden, you might periodically need to pull out some weeds. The more you invest in it, the more your garden can give back to you.

If you only expect to receive and are not asking how you can give, it will die on the vine. Neglect it and it will wither. A network is the opposite of transactional because there is no cause and effect. Both parties exist in a space of simultaneous giving and receiving; a mutually chosen relationship with value flowing in various forms, now or in a potential future.

Conscious networking is about generosity, curiosity and caring. To paraphrase former U.S. President John F. Kennedy, ask not what your network can do for you, ask what you can do for the people in your network—and then do it. Support the people in your circle in any way you can before you need them to show up for you. You go first.

PROTECTING THE ASSET OF YOUR NETWORK

Alan (not his real name), a former fashion executive based in Manhattan, New York, shared an important insight with me. He noted you enter the business world thinking a new influx of people will keep entering your life.

"Growing up, you regularly meet new people in classrooms and summer camps, giving you a whole new pool of people every year to choose from as friends. The business world is different," he said.

Once you enter the business world, your network continues to grow and change, but as Alan says, "The influx slows." It also changes less dynamically because people often stay in the same sector or industry, hence the saying, "It's a small world." Alan bluntly cautions, "Stop thinking you'll meet new people and can cherry-pick your favorites."

He likens your business network to a family tree because "you're stuck with everybody to some extent—even the ones you don't like." He laughed and observed, "If you have a family reunion, you're going to have to include those strange cousins and say hi to the mean aunt you never liked."

You can change jobs, but it's not as easy to shed people in a business network, even those you may not like or trust. You must learn to operate with them and make the best of it. I overheard one top executive say recently, "Never burn bridges because you are likely to cross paths with people again—and not just once."

HOW TO CULTIVATE YOUR NETWORK

LinkedIn offers a robust central home for your network. Its value is as a persistent network space even as employers and email addresses may change over the years. How well do you know the people in your network? Now is an excellent time to start if you haven't invested in cultivating your LinkedIn presence and network.

Take a moment to consider the following questions:

- Who's on your contact list? Where did you meet them?
- What made you choose to invite them into the privileged space of your network? What is the basis for their presence in your life's network?
- Will they take your call? Whose call would you take?
- When was the last time you reached out to everyone in your network to check in and see what was new in their world?
- How do you contribute to them? How can they contribute to you?

If you do not know the answers to these questions quickly, your network garden may need tending. I recommend a periodic network audit. Start right now. It's never too late.

HOW TO PERFORM A NETWORK AUDIT

INVENTORY YOUR CONTACTS.

Extract your social media and online contact lists into a spreadsheet or print them out. (Warning: It may look like a circa 1980 phone book.)

ASSESS YOUR NETWORK STRENGTH.

Assess the quality and relevance of each relationship. Use a number between one and five to indicate each relationship's strength, much like the bars in your Wi-Fi network. Give a rating of five for your strongest relationships and one for those whom you have no idea who they are. You may also want to color code using highlighters or Post-it notes to how you know the people (e.g., work, school, etc.) Aim for an average network strength of 3.5.

I recommend placing them in a bullseye graphic with four rings. The center ring holds your most active and reliable relationships, so make it large enough to hold them. Below is an example of how you could tier your contacts:

- Center (5)—You would put your reputation on the line to help them. They are willing to do the same for you. They have the strongest signal.
- Next ring out (4)—You are willing to help the person as long as it doesn't come at any risk or cost to you.
- Next ring out (3)—This person is an acquaintance. You likely don't have a direct personal relationship with the person, but you run in similar circles and have overlapping close contacts.
- Next ring out (2)—This person is a distant acquaintance. You know who they are (generally) and are intentional about their inclusion in your network.
- Outside the last ring (1)—You have no idea who this person is or why they are in your network. You don't necessarily need to delete them, but take care to ensure your true network doesn't get lost in this haystack.

PRUNE AND RENEW YOUR NETWORK.

Consider periodically clearing out those outer-tier contacts to create space for your other relationships to grow and breathe. Reactivate key relationships. Engage with and invest in the people in your network.

HOW TO GROW YOUR NETWORK

Randell Iwasaki leads the transportation vertical for Amazon Web Services (AWS) and is former director of the California Department of Transportation (Caltrans), which manages the country's most heavily traveled transportation system (Caltrans, 2021). He shared a simple secret with me when we were both speaking at the Intelligent Transportation Systems World Congress in Bordeaux, France. He said,

When you go to a meeting or conference, sit next to someone new. You never know the door that person could open.

I've never forgotten this and have found it to be beautifully true.

Growing your network isn't just about growing the number of people in it. It's also about deepening the relationships with the people in it. Here are some ways you can help your network thrive:

SUPPORT THE PEOPLE IN YOUR NETWORK.

Pay attention to what your network is doing and support them in their endeavors. Get on the phone and say hello. Look for where you can offer someone what Adam Grant,

Wharton professor and author of *Give and Take: Why Helping Others Drives Our Success*, calls the "five-minute favor." Some examples include:

- Acknowledge posts online or send an email to acknowledge something they have recently accomplished or to remember a birthday or other milestone in their life.
- Celebrate their victories and acknowledge their sorrows.
- Offer to connect people where it may mutually benefit them.

Do it all from a generosity of spirit, without the expectation of reciprocation. Have the person, not the position, at heart. They, like you, can feel the difference.

ELEVATE OTHERS.

Elevate those who have been there for you when you need it—especially those whose efforts otherwise go unseen or unrecognized. Bilge Emrich, CEO of Astar Advisory, told me in an interview about how elevating others and making them look good helped her overcome strong resistance when leading a major change as a young, up-and-coming executive.

The only woman on an all-male team many years her senior, she was selected by a global construction company to lead significant change in an industry which has traditionally been averse to technology and innovation. She overcame the strong resistance and successfully saw this change to fruition by finding a few brave managers who saw her vision and volunteered to pilot this evolution in their organizations. Using her extensive referent power, she was generous in showcasing the ensuing successes of their organizations. They took a risk in volunteering to go first, and the positive visibility as the changes were now being widely embraced helped to elevate their stature and status.

HOW TO GROW YOUR NETWORK

People often ask me what they can give to their network when they aren't in a position to offer someone a job or fund a new venture. You can offer value to your network in many different ways—access to capital is but one. Be mindful of ethics guidelines if you work for the government before offering any form of value other than your presence (which is invaluable). Here are five other forms of value you can offer someone, including:

- *The opportunity to meet or connect with influencers*—You volunteered on the last three presidential campaigns, and they've invited you to a gala. Are you related to Bono or Beyoncé? Who would value the opportunity to meet these people or be a part of this event?
- *Access to unique or once-in-a-lifetime experience*—Do you have an extra ticket to Formula 1? What unique experience might they value? Who would be fun to share the experience with?
- *Highly valued knowledge, expertise, or skill*—Are you an expert botanist? A musical prodigy? As you become increasingly clear about your areas of interest—professionally and in terms of personal interests and hobbies—you increase your ability to contribute materially to someone else through that expertise. Maybe it's your communication skills in a foreign language, your musical

genius, or your expertise with electronics or engines. Whatever it is, who would value it?

- *Referrals*—Maybe you grew up in France and one of your connections is heading to that very region. You may be able to offer restaurant suggestions or other tips not covered in most guidebooks that could create an incredibly memorable experience for them. Maybe you can offer a timely referral to another outstanding professional expert in a time of need (e.g., doctor, lawyer, accountant, etc.).

- *Presence*—Do not underestimate the power of being in a non-judgmental space with someone. People at the highest levels of power can feel very alone because very few people are willing to tell them the truth or to hold space with them without asking or expecting anything in return. Whether you're laughing with them or listening as they share a part of their lives, making full eye contact and being fully present is an increasingly rare gift in today's world. Presence is not about status or seniority, it's about shared humanity. (See chapter 11, "Exude Presence," for more on this.)

* * *

Remember, when it comes to your network, giving isn't better than receiving—it *is* receiving. Recognize this, and everybody in your network will take your call.

Chapter Checklist:

- Build your professional network by giving and receiving value—now or in the future.
- While your network constantly evolves, its rate of change will slow as you move through your career—nurture your network.
- Think quality over quantity—the power of your network matters more than the number of people in it.
- Understand the forms of power you and others possess and how you can use them to your mutual advantage.
- Periodically do a network audit to prune your network.
- Actively cultivate and support the people in your network; look for how you can contribute to others.

CHAPTER 11

Exude Presence

———

I've never known a superstar, but I've seen how a room responds to my father. My education with executive presence began early watching him. Now a happily retired federal judge and army colonel from the Judge Advocate General Corps, my father has long since hung up his robe. And yet, I see it even today when he enters the pool of his and my mother's beautiful Florida residence. People flock—and float, as it may be—to him.

My dad exudes presence. People feel important, seen, and valued in his presence. And they *are*.

CATCHING LIGHTNING IN A BOTTLE: WHAT IS EXECUTIVE PRESENCE?

Ninety-two percent of HR executives surveyed agree executive presence is integral to leadership (Fillipkowski, 2020). According to Coqual, formally the Center for Talent Innovation, executive presence influences up to 26 percent of promotion decisions (Hewlett et al., 2013). But what exactly *is* it? For something so important, executive presence is notoriously difficult to define.

A study by the American Psychological Association disturbingly acknowledges executive presence is "an unclear concept, but one that reportedly has a substantial influence on successful leadership" (Dagley and Cadeyrn, 2014). Eighty-one percent of people surveyed, while admittedly unable to define it, say they "know it when they see it," or, as I observed with my father, when they feel it.

Writing for *CIO Magazine* in 2020, Shannon Florentine called it an "aura of authority." Writing in a blog on her website, executive coach and researcher Suzanne Bates says it's sending "all the right signals." Stanford University Graduate School of Business lecturer Allison Kluger describes presence as "how you control a room, the impressions you make, and how you affect the people around you" (Duan, 2017). It's your brand.

My dad would say it's all this and then some: It's how people feel in *your* presence. While it may seem like catching lightning in a bottle, you naturally possess presence. You only need exude it.

EXECUTIVE PRESENCE—THE FIRST IMPRESSION THAT LASTS

"Everything speaks," said Pamela Eyring, the president of The Protocol School of Washington, in a conversation with me. This prestigious school is one of the first, and only, accredited school of its kind in the United States. It trains staff at the

White House, the Department of State's diplomatic corps, the Department of Defense, and corporate organizations worldwide in intercultural etiquette and protocol.

Researchers have shown we form first impressions of others, and they of us, within 250 milliseconds of meeting, influencing our perceptions of trust, likability, and intelligence (Swaminathan, 2007). First impressions are proxies for the promises you and your organization represent. Executive presence is the first impression that lasts.

Describing her first job out of high school working with the United States Air Force as a protocol assistant, Eyring observed, "By watching other people's behaviors, we learn how to model attributes that reflect our own personal brand. Demonstrating honor and respect for people from other cultures, and those whose backgrounds and life experiences are different from ours, are ways to express emotional intelligence and empathy for others."

THE POWER OF PRESENCE

Janika LeMaitre, founder and CEO of The Better Professional, shared the following story with me in a *Day One Executive* podcast interview about the power of presence. In her first full-time job at age eighteen, she worked on the banquet team in a five-star hotel. One day, she was walking through the hotel's glorious lobby to the front desk when a group of flight attendants entered in a dazzling flutter of color. Ravishing red hats with enchanting white scarves "cascading across the shoulders" instantly caught her entranced eye. Impeccably dressed and flawlessly groomed from head to toe, these ladies moved in elegant and seemingly effortless unison, Janika recalled dreamily.

"It caught me by surprise," she said. "Instantly, I knew I had to work with that airline. I knew they had standards, and I wanted standards like that." That's the power of a first impression—and the power of presence.

Janika made an immediate career pivot, becoming a flight attendant with that airline. Now an etiquette coach to executives all over the globe, she credits the intensive training she received from the airline with her ability to exude a presence that has graced her career. This airline's clients came from every continent and culture, as Janika said. While every airline provides functional transportation, this company staked its legendary brand on luxury interactions at every level, beginning with the first impressions of its staff.

MORE THAN JUST CHARM SCHOOL

Executive presence is far more than just charm school, it is central to the science of influence. When you exude presence, you invite and entice people to come willingly toward whatever it is you may be asking.

As a kid, I remember my dad discovering a dead cat in front of our house. The cat was on our property, and my dad, while brave in many ways, was notoriously squeamish. He was not about to be the one to dispose of the cat. He called a meeting with three neighbors and shared that "we" had a problem. "We have a dead cat that we must remove," he ceremoniously announced to the neighborhood fellows.

One neighbor, Juan, enthusiastically volunteered his car to drive the cat carcass to a nearby dump, reveling in the ebullience of my dad's presence, and knowing he would go down as a hero in this story as my father always generously shared full credit where it was due. Another neighbor, Frank, figuring this is the stuff of suburban legend, and legends never die, cheerfully grabbed a shovel and offered to lift the cat into Juan's trunk. My dad bought the beer and supported them from the safe distance of the sidewalk, delighted beyond measure, and more than a little surprised, to have the problem solved with such ease—and to see his friends laughing and smiling at their grisly adventure and lifetime memory they all created together.

That is executive presence.

After an extensive review of relevant theory and empirical studies in management, communications, psychology, and social action theory, Suzanne Bates says presence boils down to the fusion of three distinct dimensions—style, substance, and character.

- **Style**
  Style is immediately observable, and while you don't have to wear a red hat and flowing white scarf, Janika's story conveys the immediacy of the impact of style—and ensuring it's working *for* you. Nailing style is less about the latest trend than attention to detail—well-fitting clothes appropriate to the occasion and established dress code.

- **Substance**

  Executive presence, like beauty, is more than skin deep. It's substance, not surface. It's knowing your stuff and being able to hold your own, sometimes and even especially when pressed. It's what Maggie Wilderotter, whom we last heard from in chapter 7, "Operate with Urgency," describes as being able to challenge respectfully.

  In the *Harvard Business Review* article, "Deconstructing Executive Presence," John Beeson describes this aspect of presence as "a sense that you can take control of difficult, unpredictable situations; make tough decisions in a timely way and hold your own with other talented and strong-willed members of the executive team." A majority of 268 executives surveyed picked grace under fire as among the most essential qualities of presence in the CTI study cited earlier.

GRACE UNDER FIRE

It's no fun to be under fire, but that's exactly the conditions when your executive presence may shine most. You may remember the story of my *Jerry Maguire* memo from chapter 6, "Be a Change Agent." In that memo, I suggested modernizing a mature business area to position the company to take advantage of emerging cloud technology. The idea of tipping over a cash cow understandably made a lot of people nervous.

An imperious retired navy admiral who oversaw the relevant business unit summoned me into his boardroom one morning as the idea was gaining steam, admittedly with mixed reception. As I entered, the room fell eerily silent. Looking around, I was the only woman in the room. While not unusual at that time in the technology company, I was encircled by a dozen retired military officers who were the world-wide regional heads of the work in this business area, and it felt a little like being surrounded by hungry lions. It was a little unsettling.

The admiral asked me a single question at point-blank range, attempting to publicly belittle me: What exactly qualified me to think I could know anything about this business since I had never been in the military?

Spotting a Victoria's Secret bag stashed behind his briefcase, I pointed to it and asked if it was for him.

"It's for my wife," he responded flatly.

"What qualifies you to buy lingerie?" I asked, noting that he had never been a woman.

Time stopped. His eyes bore into me, while those of others nearly popped out. By standing up to this bully, I earned the respect of the room and the other gentlemen around the table, many of whom I later learned he had also demeaned. Shocked and amused, they were now eager (if maybe a little afraid) to engage with me around the substance of the idea I was raising. It was gutsy grace under fire. (It wasn't long after he was invited to find greener pastures.)

- **Character**

  Your character also animates your presence. We get to choose how we show up and impact people and change what isn't working for us. Executive presence is putting your best foot forward consistently, day in and day out, not just for that big meeting.

  Pamela Eyring described how, in her early days as a protocol assistant, she was a keen observer of top executives. She noticed how they treated others. Some were kind, even under stress; really listened to others, even her ideas; and made the effort to remember new staff members' names.

  "Those leaders had respect, and as a young professional, I wanted to earn the respect they clearly had," she said.

  Character also includes the willingness to be seen and to be appropriately vulnerable. The most potent executives are willing to let people *see* their vulnerability, says shame researcher Brené Brown, my favorite and probably one of the best-known writers and researchers in this area. Vulnerability is not something we have to work to develop—we are it. We have to work to hide it. Allowing our vulnerability to show is the essence of authenticity as a leader.

BEING AUTHENTIC

Maggie Wilderotter shared with me the importance of being authentic as a distinguishing element of presence. "Anybody can be a successful leader," she said, "but knowing your strengths and weaknesses and not having to pretend will set you apart."

Think of the difference between a cheap reproduction and an authentic antique. The reproduction may boast a flawless sheen, but there's no depth, whereas the antique has a magnificent presence. The antique has power. The imperfections, flaws, and history are a source of its value. When someone tries to cover up the supposed defects of an antique, they paradoxically destroy its value. That isn't to suggest we don't lean in to bridge differences with others or be our authentic selves at the expense of others. (See chapter 8, "Know Thyself," for more on authenticity.)

OVERCOMING BIAS

Obviously, people's judgments on what constitutes executive presence are inherently subjective, and as such they are rife with even unconscious bias. As one example in the APA research cited earlier, when thirty-four subjects were asked to cite examples of executive presence, "the majority of the executives described as having presence were men." This bias can harm people who do not fit these ingrained stereotypes.

When leaders need to work on executive presence, Andrew Neitlich, founder of the Center for Executive Coaching, offered a powerful way to overcome bias. He told me to make the standard visible. Ask the person giving the feedback to describe tangible examples of what presence would look like under various scenarios. "Make it observable," otherwise, you are chasing a moving target, he said.

He advises people to make it scenario-specific, such as a lunch with clients, a meeting with subordinates or top executives, a major speaking event, etc. This doesn't mean you have them conform to the description. Making it visible empowers you to determine whether you feel that's reasonable and helpful and, thus, can take that on board; or whether you feel even that is potentially biased or discriminatory and take additional action accordingly.

In the article "Executive Presence and Biases: 8 Biases and How You Can Use Them to Be More Influential" on the Core Executive Presence website, speaker, trainer, and C-suite coach Devika Das goes even further and advises using people's biases to your advantage. Common also in negotiation strategy, you may as well make the mental shortcuts people already create work for you she says. Choosing to make a great first impression is an example of how you can help yourself capitalize on "anchoring" biases, where people narrow in too quickly on an initial piece of information.

HOW DO YOU EXUDE PRESENCE?

At the risk of sounding like Captain Obvious, at its core, presence is about being *present*. In a digital age of smartphones, smartwatches, and plenty of mental distractions, this is harder than it may sound. Ruminating about the past and projecting into the future pulls you out of the present moment. Like clouds blocking the sun, these interfere with and block your innate dazzling presence from shining through.

We simply can't be present with ourselves or others when we are stuck in the past or time-traveling to an imagined future. We can't be there and here at the same time. We can't exude presence from behind a fortress. Drop your barriers and be present with whatever shows up.

The following tips can help you exude presence, something that will simultaneously require some effort and be effortless:

BE PRESENT WITH YOU.

The singular precondition for presence with another is presence with oneself. Being present with yourself requires getting out of judgment of yourself. As you do this, barriers to you drop, and you become more accessible to yourself and others.

DEVELOP YOUR CAPACITY TO BE PRESENT WITH ANOTHER.

As you get out of judgment of you, you also become more compassionate with yourself and others. You can look others deeply in the eye, because there is nothing to hide or hide from.

Research shows eye contact is a vital nonverbal signal of assertiveness and confidence that builds trust in an "inherently positive way" (Hietanen, 2018). I once ran a workshop with executives who did not know each other and invited them to participate in an unusual icebreaker. I had them pick a partner and, for a mere ten seconds (which proved to be an eternity), gaze silently into each other's eyes without speaking.

Almost immediately, the room began to erupt in stifled laughter and the growing din of conversational release. While the exercise successfully broke the ice, it also spotlighted our collective discomfort just being present with another. Overcome this discomfort, and your presence will startle and stun.

MODEL SOMEONE YOU ADMIRE, BUT BE YOU.

When we think of presence, many of us think of electrifying inspirational figures such as Martin Luther King, Jr. delivering his earth-shaking "I Have a Dream" speech, which infused the civil rights movement with an energy that is thankfully still vibrant, as this crucial work is not yet done. We might think of Abraham Lincoln, Maya Angelou, or a rock star.

Janika LeMaitre recommends being on the lookout for people who hold themselves to a very high standard. "I'm quite curious, I'm inspired, and I think, Wow, that's impressive," she said, describing how such people strike her. Study them, but don't become them. You can still be uniquely you! You can ask yourself what the energy you are admiring in them might look like for you and notice what begins to come to your awareness. It might surprise you!

Looking ahead to the launch party for this book, a friend of mine sent me images of people in capes. At first I dismissed it thinking I could never wear anything like that, but I admired the boldness and something about it stuck with me. Months later, while perusing a Ralph Lauren catalogue, a woman in a gorgeous black cape struck me. I suddenly saw myself wearing it during book signings, and yes, if you come to a book signing, you might catch me wearing a cape!

TAKE A CLASS IN ETIQUETTE.

A class in etiquette can help you fast-track your etiquette awareness. It's the cut above. International norms vary widely, and knowing the cultural nuances can set you apart. As Pamela Eyring said to me, etiquette is ultimately about respect, and "when you show respect to other people, you get that twice full back." Beyond the right and wrong of manners, etiquette is an energy of presence because it's about how we make others feel at ease.

BE PREPARED.

Janika LeMaitre advises people to eliminate even the littlest preventable things that can distract from your presence, such as the unexpected spill of tomato sauce on a white shirt, the zipper that breaks on a dress, or a rainstorm that comes out of nowhere. Plan to attend to finishing touches. Keep an umbrella on hand. Carry an emergency kit with a safety pin, comb, and dental floss. Pack a backup shirt or dress, a tie for men, shoes, and possibly a pashmina scarf for ladies to recover immediately from a fashion emergency when the moment really matters.

TAKE A SINCERE INTEREST IN OTHERS.
As I learned from my father, executive presence is less about you than others. Others respond when you exude a genuine interest in and appreciation for them. Let that be true with every person you meet, regardless of where they sit on an organization chart. People will respond to you like plants to sunlight because, by acknowledging them, your very presence is nourishing and enlivening.

* * *

As a Day One Executive, you are not *the* leader. You are *a* leader. You are a leader with, and of, fellow leaders. People respond to presence. I hope you won't have to put your executive presence to the dead cat test, but if you do, pay close attention to whether you're shoveling the cat or buying the beer.

Chapter Checklist:
- Executive presence is an aura of authority. It exerts a significant influence on your career.
- It is a first impression that lasts.
- Develop executive presence with others by first developing presence with yourself.
- Far more than just charm school, executive presence is a combination of style, substance, and character.
- Presence is how we make others feel.
- If you ever receive feedback that you need to develop this, ask the person to tell you what it looks like—to make it observable.

CHAPTER 12

Be Accountable

Jocko Willink is a trained killer, but not just of bad guys. He kills excuses too.

A retired and decorated Navy Seal, Jocko is a national hero who commanded SEAL Team 3 in attacks against Iraqi insurgents at Ramadi (Covered Speakers Bureau, 2022). He has since authored several books, the first of which is titled *Extreme Ownership*. Despite his notable accomplishments, he may be best known for the cheerless images of his watch that make appearances on his social media, sometimes accompanied by the glisten of sweat on a black rubber floor mat under metal weights.

If a picture is worth a thousand words, Jocko's watch is a silent proof of life symbol of his uncompromising dedication to the discipline of a 4:30 a.m. workout and, more broadly, the unyielding standard to which he holds himself. In his book, Jocko makes it starkly clear he is accountable, first and foremost, to himself, and he invites you to know this freedom too.

Being accountable is one of the most valuable choices we all have available. When you increase your self-accountability, you increase your value. You can take that to the bank.

Accountability is ultimately about integrity. It's being trustable to do what you say you'll do; to deliver reliably. Perhaps you have heard the saying, "How you do anything is how you do everything." Like integrity, accountability is what we do to uphold promises to ourselves and others, even when nobody is watching. Accountability with the smallest things broadcasts the extent to which others can trust you with the more essential things.

ACCOUNTABILITY STARTS SMALL

Start small to develop an accountability muscle. Earlier in my life, I routinely ran carelessly late to business meetings and social events. It didn't seem like a big deal. As I began to value and respect my own time more, I was no longer willing to be late, which started with raising my own bar (See chapter 13, "Raise the Bar").

Two decades later, punctuality became critical when I began doing television appearances. When it comes to live television, the show will go on—with or without you—and if it's the latter, you won't be asked back. Once I made the demand to hold myself accountable, I started honoring the valuable time of my friends and colleagues as much as my own.

AN AGREEMENT, NOT AN ORDER

One of the biggest misconceptions about accountability is that we can "hold" anybody accountable. Like Jocko, healthy people hold themselves accountable. They are accustomed to keeping their promises first—with themselves. They don't need others to hold them accountable.

Accountability is something to be earned, not avoided. It's a consensual transfer of ownership, an extension of trust. Accountable is something we choose to be. It is a level of responsibility we choose to take on.

Accountability is an agreement, not an order.

We can't agree to be accountable for something if we don't first have a full and complete (as much as possible) understanding of what we are signing up for, whether we are willing and able to assume that level of responsibility. Even if the answer is yes, both the assigning party and the delegated accountable party will need to be explicitly clear about what is expected and their respective roles supporting positive accountability (which, with delegated accountability, necessarily includes transparent, public, and consistently reinforced delegation of authority within the relevant scope).

POSITIVE ACCOUNTABILITY

In the healthiest organizations, accountability is not punitive. It is a positive, up-building, and trust-building energy. I encourage leaders to invest more energy around an accountability framework on *the front-end* of a project, setting it up for success, rather than the back-end where the leader must now determine the consequences to people who failed to deliver.

We foster positive accountability when we give visibility and recognition to the accountable parties and every major contributing party from the start. While not caring who receives credit is nice, acclaimed CEO Maggie Wilderotter emphasized the importance of giving credit where credit is due, which is both kind and essential to a culture of positive accountability.

"If a front-line technician fixes something, that person should be recognized. That is the person who figured it out," she said.

FRONT-LOAD YOUR ACCOUNTABILITY FRAMEWORK

Below are six questions you can ask to help frontload positive accountability:

1. Who is the accountable person?
   Executives will often assign a group of people, or "an organization," to be accountable for something and assume the unit's leader will take accountability. This approach can work in mature organizations with high-functioning leaders, but it's a best practice to name an accountable individual. While many people may be "responsible" for aspects of the work, only one person should be accountable for ensuring the successful delivery of the final product. You may decide to identify backup people, but again, there should be a clear delineation of succession authority.

2. Was there a clear and mutual agreement about precisely what's expected, by when, and the time commitment involved?

Accountability is a consent-based process, meaning people must be able to give valid, freely given, specific, informed, and active consent. It may not require a lot of conversation, but it does require a clear discussion. If these elements are not present, consent may not be present, and accountability will be weakened or not portrayed.

Don't be afraid to have a clear dialogue to clarify and understand the request before committing to it. Do not commit or accept accountability for things you cannot deliver outside your control. It is okay to ask questions before saying yes to ensure you understand everything that may be involved before you accept accountability.

As an example, it takes time to travel to and make a four-minute TV appearance. But it takes even more time to schedule, arrange, reschedule, prepare for, and travel to the appearance. It takes up to forty hours to create that four-minute appearance. I learned this the hard way a few years ago when I began doing some local television segments about the Day One Executive. I had not asked enough questions about all that was involved. As the appearances started to stack up, I quickly realized I was over-committed and had to renegotiate the accountable agreements I had made.

Likewise, be clear on the desired result—not just the task or activity. The accountable agreement is not "the act of trying" to get the result. The deal is to ultimately deliver the result. When you show up at a restaurant and order a burrito, you don't want to receive tortilla shells, beans, and cheese at your table. You expect a burrito, and you're probably not happy if it's cold. Nail these expectations down to include where it's all going—what is the ultimate desired end-result?

3. When and how will delegated accountability be communicated?
Accountability in an organizational context is often delegated authority, a conferred authority. The executive with the authority needs to communicate the delegated authority clearly and broadly. If you are agreeing to be accountable for something for which someone else holds the authoritative power, you must do so before accepting the delegated accountability. Without that leadership mandate, you are likely to feel undermined or "cut off at the knees" down the road when the going gets rough, which it will if you are leading any change.

4. What is the agreed follow-up approach?
Agreeing to a follow-up plan should be part of the initial conversation and should happen before accepting responsibility. As a means of sound risk management, this is key since goal posts can move without your awareness. As an executive, invite the responsible party to shape the follow-up process in a way that works for all parties and to live up to your end of the agreement.

5. Is the person capable of fulfilling the commitment?
Another common pitfall with positive accountability is assigning someone not qualified for the work. We'll

call my client Nan. As a chief operating officer of a major organization, Nan was seething. A team member was not delivering, and it was beginning to feel like insubordination.

"Doesn't he know he is accountable?" she fumed one day to me. It felt like pushing water uphill. After she shared what she required, I asked her how she knew the individual was qualified to be accountable for the work. She gave me a quizzical look. I invited her to consider the following questions:

- Did he understand what she was asking? How did she know?
- Did he have the skills, competencies, and experience to reliably deliver it?
- Did he have the power (e.g., the relationship capital and other resources) to deliver?
- Is he competent to recognize potential warning signs and whether the initiative is on track?

Nan softened. She had never considered this. She realized she was expecting something totally unreasonable from this individual. The person in question was silently miserable and stressed, afraid to admit he had no idea how to meet her expectations. She thought she had an accountability problem, and she was partially right—except it wasn't his problem, it was hers. But it was also a fit issue—the individual was not a fit for the role, and ultimately Nan was able to help him find a better role where he could thrive.

6. How will we support accountability?

One of the first things I ask when people tell me they have accountability problems is how they are reinforcing and supporting accountability. If you notice, I frame this question as a "we" question, and it uses the word "support" rather than "enforce."

Most leaders with accountability problems on their teams give me a blank stare when I ask this question. Tools and processes don't have to be expensive or fancy, but they have to work. Whether you use automated systems or simple spreadsheets, the key is to make the following visible and trackable by all:

- The observable outcome(s)
- Associated success indicators
- Key milestones and interdependencies
- Roles—e.g., the accountable, responsible, consulted, and informed parties (e.g., the RACI construct)
- Risks and warning signs of risk—basically, how we will collectively know if the project is sliding off the rails
- How you will monitor progress—e.g., will you do a weekly review? A daily review?

It sounds like a lot of trouble, but if you do these things, you'll sidestep accountability issues.

BEING ACCOUNTABLE MEANS MITIGATING RISK

If you've ever been to the Everglades in south Florida, you know that everywhere you look there are gators. Business is like the Everglades—gators everywhere, either mitigators or alligators.

Risk mitigation is about looking ahead and requires focusing on your sphere of influence and factoring realistically for your circle of concern. In the best-selling book *The Speed of Trust*, Stephen Covey writes about the importance of getting crystal clear on what's within one's "sphere of influence" and "circle of concern."

Planning your commute in a manner that accounts for the possibility of traffic is in your sphere of influence. The traffic itself is not, it is in your circle of concern. You can factor for but cannot control your circle of concern. It's important to know the difference.

Leaving nothing to chance is standard operating procedure for a Day One Executive. Risk mitigation isn't about banking on how things go "most" of the time. It's looking to ensure things go well all the time. It's putting the preventative or mitigation measures in place for the 10 percent of the time things don't go smoothly.

Here are some examples of risk mitigation measures I began to employ in television appearances:

- Leaving two days early for TV appearances (factoring for unforeseeable weather or flight delays).
- Asking the producers for any special driving directions I should be aware of (factoring for unanticipated road construction or the possibility of having to park three blocks away).

- Driving to the TV studio the day before the appearance (in case GPS goes haywire the next morning).
- Doubling or tripling the estimated commute time in case tomorrow will be the day something shuts the highway down.
- Bringing two extra phone chargers in case one stops working.

PREPARATION PAYS

Preparation pays, and the payoff grows as the stakes grow. A friend of mine is a CEO of a biomedical company. Fond of the saying, "Chance favors the prepared," she told me a story of where preparation paid off for her company when the unknown struck out of the blue.

At a time when many US medical supply chains "failed," to quote a joint PBS-Associated Press headline from October 2020, their production factories did not have one day of closure in the pandemic, she shared.

"We did not explicitly prepare for COVID, but because we had prepared for so many other scenarios, we discovered we were in fact also prepared for COVID" (Mendoza and Linderman, 2020).

Like what she's told me many times in conversations, as CEO she doesn't just feel accountable to numbers—she feels accountable for protecting people's lives, while also protecting employees' jobs. "No matter what is thrown our way by chance, if we are prepared, we have a favorable outcome," she shared with me.

CREATE A TRACK RECORD FOR ACCOUNTABILITY

New professionals frequently ask me how to stand out when they don't yet have experience or subject matter expertise. My answer: Start wherever you are and create a track record of accountability. Demonstrate you are someone others can trust to deliver, and contribute to a healthy accountability partnership.

Never do a job halfway. A job half done is worse than a job not done, because someone paid for *something*, and they still received nothing. When you are the Day One Executive and your organization is creating a project or service, it's your job to take it all the way to the finish line.

Choosing to be accountable is an empowering choice. It doesn't require perfection, but it is a consent-based choice to *take full responsibility* for carrying something to satisfactory completion. If you can't for any reason, say so.

The most dangerous excuse is the one you make and *believe*. Because you won't see that as an excuse, you'll see that as an explanation, a valid reason. And "reasons" are excuses in disguise—they will keep you from your fullest potential. When you see yourself as 100 percent responsible for everything, you don't stop until you get the desired result.

In your career, this is true as well. Maggie Wilderotter spoke to me in our interview about what she called the importance of taking control of your destiny and vocation.

"Until you decide to take ownership of your career, you will never get where you want to go," she said.

* * *

The invitation to be accountable for something is an honor and should not be taken on lightly. When accountability is absent, there can be many things in play, including a healthy accountability construct never fully put in place. In that case, more often than not, we may have *assumptions*, not accountability.

You don't have to take the extreme ownership Jocko Willink does and get up at 4:30 a.m. to be accountable. But like Jocko in his pre-dawn workout ritual, ensure there is no daylight between your words and deeds.

Chapter Checklist:

- Accountability is an honoring of self and others. It makes no excuses.
- Accountability is ultimately about integrity. It's being trustable to deliver reliably.
- It starts small. How you do anything is how you do everything.
- It's a two-way street. Follow the accountability checklist before you accept or delegate accountability.
- Being accountable for an outcome means mitigating risks. Either way, you have gators: mitigators or alligators.
- Positive accountability methods can get you farther than punitive methods.
- Without a complete accountability construct, you have assumptions, not accountability.
- Create a track record of accountability.

CHAPTER 13

Raise the Bar

———

Nearly two hundred years after his prime, Paul Cézanne wooed me to his hometown of Aix-en-Provence, by way of the National Gallery of Art. It was a quiet weekday—just him, me, and about four dozen of his masterpiece paintings and sketches.

Paul Cézanne is one of many influential painters of his time, yet even still, he is distinguished among his peers. Credited as an artist who "founded new traditions," his unique style pioneered new directions in abstraction that would influence Pablo Picasso and Henri Matisse (MoMA, 2021). Cézanne wasn't just great. He raised the bar.

If you want to distinguish yourself in your profession, raise the bar.

BECOME A BAR RAISER

There was once a time when Amazon sold books. Just books. Last year, a friend of mine furnished her entire home from Amazon.

A company that sold its first book in 1994 is now omnipresent in more than three hundred million customers' lives. Poised to overtake Walmart as the largest US retailer, JP Morgan analysts recently called Amazon the "fastest growing [business] at scale," with gross merchandise volume growing significantly faster than both US adjusted retail sales and US e-commerce overall (Palmer, 2021).

Blazing growth of a company like Amazon brings with it a host of ethical dilemmas and challenges, which the company is working to address through initiatives such as raising wages, upgrading benefits packages such as paying college tuition, and improving factory conditions (Dastin, 2021). Admittedly, they surely aim these measures as much at maintaining competitiveness in a tight labor market at least as much as attaining any altruistic ethical ideal.

One thing is certain: Amazon doesn't take its growth or future success for granted. It is not resting on yesterday's laurels or assuming yesterday's vaunted standards still apply. Amazon *is* the standard for customer convenience. Amazon lives and breathes the adage renowned blue-chip CEO coach and author Marshall Goldsmith coined, "What got you here won't get you there."

Raising the bar is one of Amazon's core operating principles (along with starting every day as though it is day one). It doesn't just proclaim this on a poster hanging in its corporate headquarters, it is infusing this into its very DNA through its hiring process. Being a bar-raiser is a job—in fact, it's *the* job title of thousands of leaders whose sole responsibility is to assess whether candidate new hires are bar-raisers. They're on a quest to ascertain how committed prospective hires are to moving their own goal posts forward.

MOVE YOUR OWN GOAL POST

I frequently hear complaints among consultants about customers always "moving the goal post." But that is precisely what bar-raisers do. They pick up the market's goal post and move it.

When one of my nephews was young, he went through a brief woodworking phase. Whittling a twig one day into an arrow, he periodically checked the pointiness of the tip. He showed his handiwork to me and, touching the point of his arrow, it felt like it actually could puncture. "It could be sharper," he said with a wry grin, and continued perfecting his creation. He is a bar-raiser.

Some people find the idea of continuously raising the bar exhausting, but what if it could be exhilarating? What if it was the key to continual reinvention in your career? What possibilities would that create?

TODAY'S STANDARD IS A LAG INDICATOR

I'm a huge fan of Guy Kawasaki's podcast *Remarkable People* because his mission dovetails with my own: he's out to make you remarkable. In a recent episode, his guest was blogger, writer, and philosopher Mark Manson, who spoke about Chicago Bulls legend Michael Jordan's legacy.

Manson said, "Everybody thinks Michael Jordan was always in a good mood, but he was always pissed. He was never satisfied. Nothing was ever good enough for him." Jordan was always curious about what possibility lay around the corner.

It sounds like a catch-22 in today's culture where perfectionism is the enemy of good. Expecting perfection of yourself and others can be toxic. The joyful, curious pursuit of it, however, can be thrilling and allow you to discover greatness you never knew you possessed. This isn't to say have outrageous expectations and then beat yourself up when you miss the mark. Rather, like Michael Jordan, invite yourself into the thrill of the chase of what's possible.

Here's a key thing to get: Today's accepted standard is a lag indicator, an indicator of what we valued *yesterday*. Tomorrow's standard may not yet be visible, but it is out there. Be aware: Whatever today's standard is, it is fading. It may still be visible, but you can bet it's on its way out like a sunset.

The new standard is ephemeral, and it's arising right now. It is an energy. It exists in people's minds even if it hasn't yet taken tangible form. It's the task of the Day One Executive to perceive this and meet or exceed it. Set it. Do this, and you will be a trendsetter.

RAISE THE BAR, AND YOU NEVER KNOW WHAT YOU MAY CREATE

In the movie *The Founder,* we learn the story of how two brothers founded McDonald's (Hancock, 2016). In one scene, we see the brothers preparing to open their first store. They're pretty sure they've thought through every detail, but they test their assumptions in accordance with the age-old wisdom to measure twice, cut once. They undergo a series of simulations—first, walking through the restaurant's full-scale blueprint design chalked out on pavement, and later, with their full staff going through the motions of full operations.

Like children in a make-believe restaurant, they pretend to take orders; prepare fake fries and hamburgers (according to exact specifications using estimated preparation and transaction times they calculated); and collect money all to discover unforeseen bottlenecks in their process or floor design.

Such inefficiencies would affect customer experience and revenue throughput, so they iron this all out in advance through the simulation. Only then do they finalize architectural designs and build their first namesake restaurant. There were plenty of hamburger joints in 1940s America, but few are still here today. The McDonald brothers raised the bar and, in doing so, created an industry.

McDonald's has since expanded to more than thirty-eight thousand franchised restaurants worldwide and weathered extreme changes in the market, including a significant shift in consumer preferences toward more healthful fare. Raising the bar still permeates the company. McDonald's revamped menus to meet consumer demands for more healthful food on the go, streamlined offerings to simplify operations in the pandemic, and is pioneering mobile technology to continue to deliver convenience customers have come to value since the McDonald brothers' first store (Maze, 2022).

THE LITTLEST EDGE COULD MAKE ALL THE DIFFERENCE

It's both incredibly hard and remarkably easy to stand out. The little things make all the difference. Pamela Eyring, president of The Protocol School of Washington, gave the example to me about the increasing rarity of hand-written thank-you notes in today's digital world. She mentioned research that showed when two people being interviewed have the same qualifications, and one sends a hand-written thank-you note, this candidate has a 5 percent greater chance of getting the job. That may not sound like a lot, but it's all about edge (another way to look at this is that they run a 100 percent chance of making a positive impression with this action).

You don't always have to go the extra mile to stand out. Sometimes, it's enough to go the extra millimeter. The littlest edge can make all the difference.

Handwriting a thank-you note takes time. It's faster and certainly easier to do nothing, or to shoot off an email. In a world where few do this anymore, when you take that extra step of care, you are raising the bar.

BETTER YOUR LIFE AND THE WORLD BY RAISING THE BAR

The choice to raise the bar will likely lead to opportunities you cannot foresee. It will create possibilities in your life that you could not otherwise imagine. Pamela Eyring had no idea when she took her first class in etiquette at age eighteen that she would one day own one of the most revered protocol schools in the world. She notes that as people around you observe you and your standard, they will tap you for roles with more responsibility and visibility because they view you as someone they can trust to carry a legacy forward and represent the brand, as the school's founder did when she passed the mantle to Pamela.

Raising the bar is how we create a better world. In the *Harvard Business Review*, Lily Zheng says, "Now, consumers and employees are raising the bar." From more aggressive commitments to diversity, equity, inclusion, and accessibility to real investments in sustainability, organizations have the power to help change the world by raising the bar. Zheng observes in order to attract customers in the future, companies will need "a new paradigm that imagines a healthier and mutually beneficial relationship between companies and the communities they interact with."

THE THRILL OF THE CHASE

There's a thrill of the chase when you choose to raise the bar. How much fun can you have in the pursuit of possibility?

Don't do it for the adulation when you choose to raise the bar. Most won't notice or care about your hard work. When people imagine a painter like Cézanne, they tend to imagine him sitting tranquil in a field, cranking out masterpiece after masterpiece. They have no awareness of the investment in the craft, the series of sketches and oil prototype paintings that precede the masterpieces they know and love. They have no appreciation for the countless hours spent working alone, poring over meticulous detail, with no guarantee at the time it would become a masterpiece.

But like you, it did become a masterpiece. Your name, like Cézanne's, will be known far and wide when, like him, you choose to raise the bar.

Chapter Checklist
- Choose it. Raising the bar starts with choosing to be a bar-raiser.
- Become an astute observer. Notice what the standard is, and then exceed it and bring others along with you.
- Where have you raised a bar? What difference did it make? Keep a log of your bar-raising contributions. This log may help you in an interview or salary negotiation.
- Choose to be a lifelong student of excellence. Recognize and celebrate it in others.
- Ask yourself and your team, What would it take to make this 10 percent better?

CHAPTER 14

Don't Derail

"You need to get in here—and now."

Jon's boss (not his real name) was impatient. Jon was the human resources manager for a company spiraling in the wake of the sudden departure of several key executives. The timing couldn't be worse, as he was under extraordinary stress with a personal crisis: His sister was in a coma after being hit by a truck while on a military deployment. "It was a terrible situation," Jon recalled in a conversation with me.

One particular day, he watched a new executive fire a long-time loyal vice president for refusing to be the company's hatchet man. After years of being criticized for being "too passive," Jon erupted. "Who are you?" he asked the new executive incredulously. "You got here five minutes ago," referring metaphorically to the executive's recent arrival.

Jon derailed.

They fired him that day.

Fortunately for Jon, this derailment wasn't career-ending. Within a few weeks, he received a second chance at a new company. Not everyone is that lucky.

WHAT DOES IT MEAN TO DERAIL?

The Center for Creative Leadership, which has studied career derailment for decades, defines derailing executives as "those who, after reaching the general manager level, are fired, demoted, or held on a career plateau."

Up to the point of derailment, these leaders have often been marked as having high potential for advancement, carry impressive track records, and have performed solidly in leadership positions. But then something goes wrong, and an otherwise promising career goes off-track.

Perhaps, like Jon, some don't realize they are operating under extreme stress. Others rise only to forget where they came from. A client of mine shared the importance of not growing such a sense of self-importance that you forget about all the people who helped you get there. "Suddenly they are too important for the little people," she said.

The Leading Effectively Staff at the Center for Creative Leadership (CCL) put it bluntly, "Even leaders with impressive track records have weaknesses or knowledge gaps that, if left unaddressed, can truly wreck their careers."

YOU ARE THE ONLY PERSON POWERFUL ENOUGH TO DERAIL YOU

Many people expend a lot of energy worrying about others thwarting their ambitions. The most dangerous career disrupters aren't likely to be other people, though. It's more likely to be you.

CCL outlines the following five primary causes for derailment:

1. Difficulty **adapting to change** (the most frequent cause of derailment)
2. Difficulty **building and leading a team**
3. Failure to **deliver business results**
4. Lacking a **broad, strategic orientation**
5. Problems with **interpersonal relationships**

Knowing the most common derailers can empower you to take action now to avoid them. John Lybarger, PhD, MCC, an organizational development consultant and author of *Coaching Public Sector Leaders*, reassures, "You don't have to be perfect. You can make mistakes and still rise to the top." However, there are some mistakes to avoid at all costs. Robert and Joyce Hogan (and later, Development Dimensions International) identified eleven specific behaviors that can singularly derail an otherwise promising career (Chamorro-Premuzic, 2017).

DERAILMENT BEHAVIORS

Steer clear of these eleven landmines so you don't accidentally step on any.

1. Approval Dependent—*seek and need praise or reassurance from others, particularly from people higher in the organization.*

People with this trait are overly calibrated to care what others think. As a recovering people-pleaser, I have decades of experience working through this. People-pleasing can be an asset when it helps produce superior work, but you turn on yourself when you are dependent on that approval. The antidote? The more you acknowledge yourself, the less you will require it from others.

2. Argumentative—*skeptical, tense, perhaps paranoid or suspicious, focused on protecting their interests, and likely to resist coaching and feedback.*

The daughter of a lawyer and former college debater, I admit I've had to watch this one myself. Rising through the ranks as a young female executive working with the military on primarily male leadership teams, I had more than one encounter with people in power on the way up that caused me to feel defensive and self-protective. I had to learn to find my voice, assert my ideas, and have my own back in a way that did not carelessly careen into conflict. Learning to listen and negotiate from a place of seeking joint gain was instrumental in helping me change this. Letting go of the need to be right was also liberating. While individuals may indeed have ulterior motives, it's helpful overall to assume noble intent while staying aware.

3. Arrogant—*overly self-assured or confident, resulting in poor listening and dismissal of feedback from others.*

Arrogance is a shield for a deep-seated lack of confidence. If you find yourself talking over others, defensive when people offer constructive feedback, and unreceptive to the give-and-take required for effective collaborative relationships, consider seeking out a trusted coach and investing to build up your authentic confidence.

4. *Attention Seeking**—gregarious, charming, and persuasive, perhaps excessively so, which can result in becoming melodramatic and self-promoting.*

This trait is a blinking light, and by design, on public display. As with arrogance, attention-seekers are overcorrecting for their own perceived shortcoming with excessive wit and charm. When you're knocking it out of the park, you won't need to seek attention, the attention will come to you whether you desire it or not.

5. *Avoidant**—while seemingly pleasant and cooperative, tend to be preoccupied with their own agendas and may prefer to address issues covertly (avoiding more direct solutions), thus being perceived as procrastinators, manipulative, or stubborn.*

I worked with a manager once with significant and visible accountability issues on her team, but she was unwilling to address the issues directly. Reluctant to confront, she would be wholly sympathetic to each party without ever being willing to draw a line in the sand. With an avoidant leader, the net effect was a failing organization, tanking morale and dwindling respect for her leadership.

6. Eccentric—*creative and, accordingly, different from others, perhaps to the point of being unorthodox or odd.*

I once worked with a brilliant up-and-coming leader who was one of the smartest people in the organization, but he wore T-shirts to work, regardless of the audience or occasion. That attire is de rigueur in some organizations and roles, such as coding shops, but the organization he chose as his place of employment was very formal. Non-conformity has its place, but if you desire to rise, pay close attention to the personality of the work space.

7. Imperceptive—*not naturally inclined to read others' behavior, intent, and motivations.*

This person is out of touch, unable to read the tea leaves. Picking up on subtle cues is an important capacity for any executive.

8. Impulsive—*impatient, unpredictable, and inclined to act before considering the consequences of actions.*

If you've ever had an indecisive or reactive manager who fires decisions off half-cocked, you've seen this trait. This can derail you as an executive because your decisions carry more weight. People have real feelings, and you can't always walk back the consequences so easily.

9. Perfectionistic—*micro-managers, controlling, and demanding of others.*

Demanding (and doing your part to support) excellence for the betterment of all is one thing. Demanding perfection so that you can look good will derail you.

10. Risk Averse—*indecisive, too deliberate, or reluctant to take unusual or unconventional actions due to overemphasizing the prospect of failure.*

This person routinely misses the decisive windows of opportunity, and no one can rely upon them to strike when the iron is hot. If this is you, see chapter 5, "Build Decision Intelligence."

11. Volatile—*have difficulty controlling their emotions and are perhaps moody and quick to erupt in anger.*

Jon, who you met in our opening story, fell victim to this derailer in his explosive reaction to the firing of the VP. The Hogan "Dive into the Dark Side" website notes, "When the pressure's on, the line between strength and weakness isn't always clear—drive becomes ruthless ambition, attention to detail becomes micromanaging." When you see yourself going off the rails, catch yourself in the act and take a breather as a circuit breaker.

Under the right conditions, every one of us is susceptible to one or more of these dangers. Antidotes include committing to managing stress (see the next section on "Resilience") and doubling down on self-awareness.

DOUBLE DOWN ON SELF-AWARENESS

While anybody is at risk of derailment, high achievers like Jon run a 26 percent higher risk of spinning off the track than their less ambitious counterparts, according to research by Korn Ferry. That same research found people who are not self-aware and overstate their abilities run a sixfold increased chance of derailment. Executive coach John Lybarger puts it bluntly, "All derailments can be traced back to a lack of—or underdeveloped—self-awareness" (Lybarger, 2019).

DERAILERS CAN BE CONTEXT-SPECIFIC

Derailers can be tricky. As leaders move up in organizations and job demands change, things that in one role are strengths can become weaknesses, and some early shortcomings that may not have mattered in lower-stakes roles can suddenly matter. As you progress in scope of responsibility, be aware expectations for how you show up may change. Challenges that can take on greater significance include insensitivity to others, failure to delegate, and overdependence on a single advocate or mentor (Van Velsor and Leslie, 1995).

Transitioning from one sector to another, or even one corporate culture to another, can also present challenges when behavior acceptable in one place is not acceptable in another. In my interview, Andrew Neitlich, founder of the Center for Executive Coaching, shared the story of a client who recently retired from the military and transitioned to the private sector. Richard (not his real name) was a popular leader in the military who deployed and saw combat. In that culture, his bombastic personality and successful track record helped him make a name for himself. People looked past his rougher edges.

The corporate C-suite had a very different culture. Andrew was working with Richard to smooth out his executive presence, and things seemed to be going well—until they weren't. One fateful day, Richard made a remark that a female subordinate experienced as harassment. He was disciplined, and his career progression stalled.

"Be yourself—sort of," Andrew said wryly. It's extremely important to understand and differentiate between one's personal and professional environments. In the workplace, you are a representative of your employer's and client's cultural and ethical standards. Frustrations you might feel comfortable showing to your family or friends may be inappropriate in the workplace, as Jon discovered. As Richard learned, behavior that may be acceptable, understood, or dismissed as a quirky sense of humor in your personal circles or even in a different professional environment may be offensive in another setting.

PREVENT IT IN THE FIRST PLACE

Here are some tools to shore up your internal resources and prevent derailment.

- **Invest in self-awareness**. The best defense is a good offense: Start now to invest in self-awareness, and be willing to take a hard look at yourself. This isn't about changing yourself into something or someone you aren't. It is about acquiring the ability to flex and be sensitive to the people around you and the environment in which you have chosen to work.

Empower yourself with cognizance and conscious choices. Look around and look ahead. Don't wait to invest in your future self. Derailing is a painful and expensive way to gain awareness.

- **Get an executive coach to build emotional intelligence.** It's one thing to take a conflict workshop and learn new emotional intelligence skills in a classroom, but putting those new skills into action in the moment can be scary. Like learning to ride a bike, you can't just read about it to learn it. Eventually you have to get on the bike. Anyone who has learned to ride can attest you will fall several times before cruising confidently down the street. Coaching provides a safe space for you to fall, dust yourself off, and continue toward your chosen path.

- **Regularly discharge stress.** The risk of derailing rises exponentially with stress. Taking a proactive approach to stress release is one way to help stay in the driver's seat of your choices. When you balance your sympathetic and parasympathetic nervous systems, you operate in a space of maximum awareness and conscious choice. (See chapter 18, "Take the Highest Care of You").

* * *

Now a widely respected HR executive known for his authenticity, courage, wisdom, strength, and empathy, Jon recently received recognition as a "Top HR Professional to Watch" from a major publication. However, he confided the pain of being fired earlier in his career still reverberates.

"It went from terrible to terrible," he remarked somberly. "That moment has never left me. That is why I am the leader I am today."

Hopefully, your journey to your fullest potential won't have to be quite as painful as Jon's. After all, you now have an advantage Jon didn't have early in his career as an executive: You know the derailers and can steer clear of them.

Chapter Checklist:
- You are the only person powerful enough to derail you.
- Educate yourself on the derailers to empower yourself to steer clear of them.
- Be aware that behaviors that may be acceptable with your family or friends may not be acceptable in the workplace.
- Derailing can be career-ending, but it doesn't have to be. For a rare few it can be elevating. Whether, and how, you choose to grow as a leader makes all the difference.
- Be proactive in managing stress, as this is a top trigger for derailment of an otherwise promising career (see the next section, "Cultivate Resilience").

PART III

CULTIVATE RESILIENCE

CHAPTER 15

Be the CEO of Your Life

———

It was 4:00 a.m. on a crisp autumn night, and I awoke in a cold sweat.

I was going to marry a man I deeply loved in a matter of months. He made me laugh, and we shared the same faith and family values. He seemed to be my perfect match. Everything was going exactly according to plan—*his* plan.

Had we thoroughly discussed a shared vision for our life, such as where we might want to live or how we would make decisions together? No, but I figured those particulars must just come later. Fairy tales never include these details.

So, when the man of my dreams surprised me one evening at dinner with an engagement ring, I said yes. Isn't that what you're supposed to say when someone you love asks you to marry them? A gnawing anxiety soon set in.

It soon became clear we were not on the same page initially, with small things showing up that were not consistent with what I thought we had agreed upon. What scientists call "cognitive dissonance" soon set in. When he nervously informed me one afternoon that he had accepted a job in another city without consulting me—I was speechless. Every cell in my body said "no."

As the world slumbered away that one night, I felt terror, dizziness, and nausea grip me. I was experiencing a panic attack. My body was screaming: "I can't do this!"

By "this," I didn't mean just not getting married. I realized I also couldn't continue to live on autopilot—where others decided, and I passively went along for the ride. As the morning dawned, a larger awareness emerged: I had been living my life on a moving sidewalk, and it was time to step off.

Looking back, I now see this was the moment I became my life's chief executive officer (CEO).

GET OFF AUTOPILOT AND START CHOOSING

According to Money Inc., one of the best-selling board games of all time in the US is a classic called the Game of Life. In this game, players roll the dice and automatically move along however many spots the dice show. Based on where a player lands, they are instructed to attend college, get married, or start a family (Lee, 2019).

Playing the game decades later with my nephews, I saw it now through my more experienced adult eyes. The game's logic imposes subtle yet powerful "norms" on players as you passively choose whatever the dice put before you. In 2015, Hasbro commissioned a survey of kids to modernize the game's choice options. The new careers included singer, secret agent, professional athlete, scientist, and, the top pick, video game designer, among others.

Even so, the game still ties your financial fortunes to the whims of chance, not through any direct, creative, proactive action by you. A single misstep locks you in. You are powerless to make a different choice later in the game.

It struck me this game illustrates a larger cultural meta-narrative, where the choice set can appear limited, and certain things are supposed to happen in a particular order. You go to school, get a job, have 2.5 kids, and live happily ever after.

Or do you?

A 2019 Pew Research Center survey shows things are changing, as only about half of Americans over the age of eighteen are married, down from 72 percent in 1960 (Geiger and Livingston, 2019). The divorce rate has remained relatively stable over the last decade, at around 41 percent, leaving many people still needing to take the wheel of their lives sometimes unexpectedly (US Census Bureau, 2022). In the United States, approximately thirteen million bereaved spouses must pick up the pieces of their lives, in the midst of profound grief, and find the strength to move forward, rebuild, and create new joys on terms that may be entirely different than anything they ever imagined (Stockton, 2015). Learning to choose for yourself isn't selfish, and it shouldn't be a luxury. It should be part of a core curriculum of adulting.

CHOOSING FOR YOU

In his blog, "Creating the Right Attitude for Success," motivational author Jim Rohn wrote, "If you don't design your own life plan, chances are you'll fall into someone else's plan." He went on to say, somewhat tongue-in-cheek, "And guess what they have planned for you? Not much."

One of the first choices I made when I became CEO of my life and truly began living was to take the reins and become aware of every aspect of my life. Like a new CEO coming into a company, it took some doing to wrap my arms around where I was, where I desired to be, and what it would take to generate that.

I had to be willing to do some things that were not always comfortable:

- See the good, bad, and ugly of what I had been creating in my life and call myself out where I was not living up to my own espoused values.
- Look at the future I was creating with current relationships and behaviors, and cut my losses with people and behaviors that no longer made sense for the future I desired.
- Give myself permission to dream beyond what even I had ever thought possible.

Becoming the CEO of your own life is the best preparation you can have to be a Day One Executive.

START WITH THE ENTERPRISE OF YOU

Nothing is a more precious resource or asset you will ever steward than you. Your life is priceless. *You* are priceless. Your "life" is an expansive creative canvas on which you can create the masterpiece of you, and it deserves the most phenomenal leader and steward—you.

Becoming the CEO of your life may feel overwhelming if, like me, you feel new to this. It means looking choices right in the eye—not judging them but being willing to acknowledge what they created. It means becoming financially aware. It means no longer making excuses. It means taking responsibility for every aspect of the life and living you are creating and recognizing your power to change anything not working for you.

SHOW UP AS ALL OF YOU

In their book, *Extreme Ownership*, former Navy Seals Jocko Willink and Leif Babin speak to the radical idea of taking responsibility for *everything* that happens in your life. Just browsing Jocko Willink's social media scares the excuses out of me. I'm afraid even his picture will hear me, so I don't dare utter an excuse near my phone. He doesn't tolerate excuses because excuses and lies (including the ones we tell ourselves) become veils that dilute our potency in the world (see chapter 13, "Raise the Bar").

Jocko demands you show up as all of you. You should too. Taking responsibility for everything in your life doesn't mean blaming or berating yourself when things go awry. It means no longer sitting idly in the passenger seat, waiting for someone else to get you to your destination, and instead getting into the driver's seat.

Choosing to take responsibility for your life, even the most challenging circumstances, is an attitudinal orientation that opens you to greater choice and to the energizing and healing wellspring of gratitude (Seligman, 2002). It can be confronting, and it is also liberating. Whether things are great or you feel like you'd like to see some big things in your life change, things can get better as you step up even more and become the CEO of your life.

You may be wondering, *What does it mean to be CEO of your life? Where do I start?* You don't have to do this alone. Let's look to some of the best CEOs out there to help guide us as we step more fully into this role for our lives.

FIVE ATTRIBUTES OF THE BEST CEOS
University of Southern California Marshall School of Business Dean Geoffrey Garrett, former dean of the top-ranked Wharton Business School at the University of Pennsylvania, observed the following five attributes of an effective chief executive after listening to the CEOs of major companies, including American Express, Vanguard, Dow Chemical, and the University of Pennsylvania. An effective CEO is:

1. Creative enough to develop a vision.
2. Empathetic enough to implement it.
3. Has clear priorities that account for the important people in your life.
4. Makes and follows through on good decisions.

5. Recharges regularly.

What if these could offer a starting point for becoming the CEO of your life?

Let's break them down.

1. DEVELOP A VISION

Clear vision is a foundational element of business success. It is an essential and ongoing process to take the reins of your life and create a joyful and generative life and living. Here are some questions you can ask yourself annually:

- What are my heart's desires for my life? (Let it rip! Don't limit yourself!) If I didn't have to limit myself (e.g., if money wasn't an issue), what would I choose?
- What would it take to have that energy in my life? What could I choose today to bring more of these energies into my life?
- What is standing in the way? Where do I hold myself back?

Don't worry if you don't feel like you have perfect clarity on this. You don't have to get a literal vision of your future for this to work. It's enough to get a sense of the energy of what you desire.

You can then do what personal empowerment coach Emily Russell calls "energy shopping"—begin to pull in experiences and relationships congruent with that energy. Sometimes, even small changes can help you shed the things in your life that don't bring joy. Another way to look at it is to consider how popular vlogger Casey Neistat defines success: "It's not how much time you spend doing what you love. It's how little time you spend doing what you hate" (Kukolic, 2018).

Stay continually in touch with your sense of vision, as it may change. Take yourself on an annual visioning retreat. After my engagement ended, I began taking a secluded long weekend once a year in an historic log cabin built in the early 1800s. I called it my Little House in the Big Woods (Armstrong, 2018). Taking this time for me creates the space for my own powerful visioning to come through. I call it getting into my "godspace," reconnecting with my purpose, what I'm here for now.

It's fun to see what shows up when you ask. Here are some other questions you can ask yourself:

- Who am I at my core? What are the golden threads that run through my life?
- What are my secret aspirations I dare not tell anybody for fear of looking foolish?
- When I look back on my life, what would I like my obituary to say?

The key is to welcome anything that may arise, however outlandish, and not judge it. Again, this is less about achieving a literal dream and more about tapping the energy of those dreams.

You don't have to get away or go into seclusion to connect with your vision. In my interview with the legendary Julia

Cameron, she emphasized the gift of her Morning Pages technique in inviting your vision to come through from the faraway place of your kitchen table (see chapter 8, "Know Thyself," for a description). I used this technique for a year before making significant changes in my life, and still do it for tune-ups.

Whatever route you choose, the simple act of connecting with yourself will invite in a new, enlivening energy. The person who knows what she desires gets what she wants. As you take the helm of your life, you exude an air of confidence—a person going somewhere interesting, because you are. Wherever you are going will be interesting to you. Step now into the boardroom of your life and never be bored in a room again.

2. IMPLEMENT YOUR VISION WITH EMPATHY

Empathy is the ability to understand someone from *their* perspective. Unlike sympathy, emotions felt for someone, empathy is a shared experience felt *with* someone (Miller, 2022). Choosing to act with empathy isn't just a kind thing to do, it's also pragmatic. In an annual survey conducted in 2017 by Businesssolver.com, as many as 84 percent of business executives agreed empathy drives measurably better business outcomes.

Empathy is harder than it looks, and it is a skill worth developing. Start with the people around you as you offer your support to them, and seek their support with your evolving vision. Realize that whatever your dreams and visions are, you need the support of others to achieve them, and some of that may impact others. That is where empathy comes in.

You are not alone if you aren't sure how empathetic you are. Sixty percent of the executives in that study bravely admitted to struggling with being empathetic. Further, only 14 percent of employees in the study rated their workplaces as sufficiently empathetic, which suggests this is an area many of us can likely grow in.

3. HAVE CLEAR PRIORITIES THAT ACCOUNT FOR THE IMPORTANT PEOPLE IN YOUR LIFE

CEOs have clear priorities. They guard their time and do not invest it in people or activities that do not contribute to those priorities (see chapter 16, "Prize Your Time"). This is why CEOs and other top executives have people known as "gatekeepers," who require you to go through them before you can get access to the executive. Executive assistants are the most common gatekeepers. They know everyone in the executive's life and where each person falls on the relative priority listing.

As you progress in your career and life, there are likely to be more demands on your time, not less. You will become more in-demand. Top CEOs are unapologetic about not giving time to anything and anyone who does not meet the criteria for entry. They don't need you to like them.

For many of us, the only access criteria to our lives is that someone asks. The colleague who is looking for a distraction can sail by and get access to you. Change that, effective immediately.

Increasing research in the field of social networking shows the unconscious influence others exert on us. The Framingham Heart Study is one of the largest, longest-running studies that looked at relationships between networks of friends and family and their influences on lifestyle factors, behavioral choices and health. The study found astonishing correlations within social networks in everything, from weight gain to smoking to medical conditions. This was true even as you moved beyond the primary relationships (e.g., the influence of a friend of a friend).

Be the gatekeeper to *your* life. Don't let just anyone intrude. Institute what I describe in chapter 7, "Operate with Urgency," as red-velvet rope criteria for access to you.

4. MAKE AND FOLLOW THROUGH ON GOOD DECISIONS

CEOs are action-takers. They know it's not enough to make a decision—the fortune is in the follow-through. You have to take action to unlock the value.

Don't get hung up on getting it "right" or perfect. Do what's necessary to make the best decision with the available awareness, and then take action. They are willing to choose, notice what the choice creates, and choose again (see chapter 5, "Build Decision Intelligence").

Fortunately, you are equipped with the world's most efficient decision support system on board—in your body. This intricate system still confounds scientists with its amazing abilities. Learning to tune into your body is as simple as asking wide-open questions. One of my favorite questions to ask is,

"What future will this choice create?" This isn't a question that has an immediate answer. Instead, it's more like unfurling a sail and seeing whether and where the wind catches.

Another tool I like is to ask myself if something I'm considering feels heavy or light. This isn't a cognitive "thinking" exercise. It's a sensory exercise. Notice whether the energy in your body opens up and expands, or contracts and becomes dense when you consider a set of possibilities.

Your body has an innate knowing, and a choice that brings a sense of lightness will bring more of that as you make and actualize that choice. Choices that feel heavy or contracted are not true for you, or at least not now (Douglas, 2014). Had I known this when my boyfriend of the time popped the question, I would have said no and began asking more questions.

Do a retrospective periodically. Keep a journal of your choices, then look back and assess what they created. I keep an annual record now of significant decisions I make each year—from financial investments to personal and career choices. It's fun and enlightening to look back on them. The exercise can strengthen your connection with you and empower you to acknowledge yourself as the CEO of your life.

5. RECHARGE REGULARLY

When I began my career, I did not recharge regularly, and it nearly killed me.

Feeling like I needed to prove myself as a liberal arts major in a science and technology company, and one of only two women in the technical or early executive management ranks, I went into overdrive. I poured myself into what I saw as one thing I had going for me: my work ethic.

I could outwork just about anybody. I pulled multiple all-nighters and occasionally worked three days straight without sleep. Is it any wonder I devoted an entire section of this book to resilience?

A decade into my hard-charging career, I began experiencing a low-grade fever, numbness in my legs, and extreme fatigue. Several doctors told me I was potentially dealing with up to three auto-immune diseases, including chronic fatigue syndrome, lupus, and even multiple sclerosis. If I kept heading in this direction, I was foreclosing on my ability to go the distance.

This news scared me straight into a meditation class with a Chinese man who was at least one hundred years old (I've seen younger redwoods in California) and became a turning point in my life. Through this class, I gained the dim awareness of how disconnected I had become from my body. I slowly began making lifestyle shifts.

In addition to becoming more honoring of sleep and reeling back my work intensity, I began experimenting with a range of techniques to help physically discharge stress from my body, including Himalayan salt caves, sound bowls, and a somatic technique called Access Bars®, which I now teach, where a practitioner touches thirty-two points on the head to physically release stress from the body. It's like de-fragging the hard drive of your brain.

Recharging is now a priority in my life. From workcations to keeping a beach chair in my car (because you never know when you might pass a beautiful park on your way home from the office and need some pop-up sunshine), I am ready to recharge on a moment's notice. What are your favorite ways to recharge and renew?

* * *

A few years after I chose to become the CEO of my life, I was speaking to a large group at a fundraising event. Someone in the audience gave me the greatest compliment I've received yet after the talk. They said watching me speak was like watching a Ferrari. As a Formula 1 fan, that really lit me up. I'll also never forget it because it was reflective feedback to me that I was finally, really, and truly alive.

What's your favorite race car? Whatever it is, you can have that energy too. Whatever it is, like a Ferrari, nobody wants to step into it and then ride on autopilot.

It's so much more fun to drive.

Chapter Checklist:
- Get off of autopilot.
- Kill your excuses.
- Make time for visioning.
- Have and live clear priorities.
- Choose and follow through on decisions.
- Let your body help guide your decisions.
- Keep a journal and do a periodic retrospective of decisions to see what your choices are creating.
- Don't worry about getting it right or wrong. Know you can always choose again!
- Make time to recharge regularly.
- Becoming the CEO of your life is exhilarating. It's empowering to create the enterprise of you. Step now into the boardroom of your life and never be bored again.

CHAPTER 16

Prize Your Time

———

"I'm struggling. There just isn't enough time to get it all done."

My executive coaching clients and friends have this common lament. I see the toll this kind of stress takes with executive coaching clients, and I've experienced it myself. As I mentioned in the last chapter ("Be the CEO of Your Life"), I was once diagnosed with three auto-immune disorders due to pushing myself beyond my limits.

Time is money, as the saying goes, and it is also your most valuable non-renewable asset. While you can use money to create time and you can use time to create money, you can always make more money, but you can never make more time.

As a Day One Executive, it's time to prize your time.

MANAGE YOUR ENERGY

A shaman friend of mine, Dava Money, once mused there is no such thing as time management. Being a little "woo

woo," she does not believe "time" exists. Instead, she speaks in terms of energy management.

"We do not 'manage' time, April. We manage our energy," she would say.

As a former triathlete, I saw her point. Triathlon introduced me to an entirely new relationship with the concept of time. In race environments, I became palpably aware of time ticking and my need to make every moment count. I also had the experience of time flying, or going too fast, and time crawling, where mere seconds can feel eternal.

I started my business a decade ago, and like triathlon training, being an entrepreneur forced me to become judicious about where I expend my precious life energy. Energy wasters fell away quickly, leaving me with more purposeful, conscious, and enriching uses of my life force.

Today, I work a lot—twelve hours a day is not uncommon—but I follow my energy. I wake up early and work for two hours before I see my first client. I have a lot of structure during the business week, but on the weekends, I "chunk" my time into energy blocks. I think of my day as having six energy "slots" as shown below:

- Early morning
- Late morning
- Lunch
- Early afternoon
- Late afternoon
- Late evening

Rather than scheduling everything into a time slot, I bin the items on my "to do" list into energy slots. I also give myself the choice of what to work on based on what requires my attention in that moment. I rate the items around importance and urgency, and renegotiate urgency where possible. Other than when something is truly urgently required, I invite myself to choose which items feel most fun today to tackle.

THREE CATEGORIES OF TIME

When I started AHA Insight, the "math" of my life changed. I quickly noticed the value of my time and divided it into three categories:

- *Category 1: Revenue-Generating*

Any investment of time that generates revenue now or in the future (i.e., client services, business development, etc.). The majority of my time goes to this. (If you have a job, this is likely the majority of the time you spend at the office.)

- *Category 2: Things Only I Can Do*

This category consumes the next largest chunk of time. As much as I would like to, I cannot outsource going to medical or dental appointments. To date, nobody else can hit the gym for me. While I can outsource tax preparation, I require awareness of the lifeblood of my business, so I require I understand the financials and review them with my accountant and bookkeeper.

- *Category 3: Priceless*

Spending time with my family and friends is priceless to me. Contributing to others through community service is dear to my heart. Going for a hike in the woods, a big adventure, or a relaxing vacation; hitting the gym; and curling up with a good book or escaping into a fantastic movie or series is relaxing and reviving. It seems there is never enough time for this category. I guard this category, and I prize the quality of this time as much as any quantity.

Marie Kondo is a Japanese organizing consultant known for helping people clear out closets. She clears clutter by asking if it sparks joy. You need to "Marie Kondo" your life. If it doesn't spark joy, stop doing it if you can.

Create as much space as possible in the last category. I pay ruthless attention to category two activities (things only I can do) and aim to keep it to a minimum. Discipline and delegating is essential to keep this category under control.

If you prize your schedule, consider periodically tracking your time to maintain accurate awareness of how you are investing valuable assets and ensure it is working for you.

TRACK YOUR TIME

Periodically, especially when I feel I just don't have enough time, I do an audit. This exercise helps me to monitor and maintain the ideal time distribution across these categories. You can use the insight to consciously rebalance these investments where required.

This technique involves tracking your activities and coding your time in fifteen-minute increments for three typical days. Use a time-tracking app, a spreadsheet, or a notebook, but commit to rigorously documenting and then coding every increment of your time. Establish whatever categories work for you to gain the visibility and insight you need.

Some people suggest just using a calendar as your basis for your time audit, but there is one limitation. Invisible activities don't show up on a calendar. As I describe in the next section, these are some of the biggest time bandits in your life. Relying on a calendar alone might obscure the biggest culprits that impact your day the most. Our whole purpose here is to excavate every minute since, like pennies, minutes add up.

The benefit of this exercise is to create more awareness of what your choices are generating, not to judge them—or you. Have a neutral look at where your time is going. Then, start with the easy places to claw back your time. In one of the most comprehensive time studies on CEOs, Harvard researchers tracked over sixty thousand hours of the time of twenty-seven CEOs, coded into fifteen-minute increments. They found a surprisingly high amount of time (11 percent) went to routine tasks that CEOs could delegate to direct reports or significantly curtail by raising the standard, e.g., tightening up sloppy meetings (Porter and Nohria, 2018).

Let's play with the three-step methodology my company uses to help government and corporate clients lead change. This same framework can help you change how you invest your time. The three steps are assess, heed, and align.

Here's how you can use it to help you prize your time:

ASSESS, HEED, ALIGN
Step 1: Assess

Ask yourself some of the questions below to understand where you do your best work:

- Where or under what circumstances am I most productive?
- In what type of environment am I most productive?
- What approaches have worked well for me in the past to shut out distractions?

Take an even closer look at your three-day time audit. Look for patterns. Subcategorize the time if it helps.

Rate your satisfaction with those activities and people. On Guy Kawasaki's *Remarkable People* podcast, author guest Cassie Holmes spoke on this. She recommended rating the activities on a ten-point scale according to your overall positivity in the block of time.

I suggest breaking your rating into two categories: your *level of satisfaction* with how you spent the time, and the *fun factor*.

- Level of satisfaction: This dimension will give you a sense of the overall effectiveness with which you are using your time. This can be a powerful pointer to activities where you can possibly free up time that may be coming at too great a cost.
  In an example from my life, as a first-time author, the publisher required me to ensure I formatted the nearly three hundred research citations in this book in accordance

with the Chicago Manual of Style, one of several editorial style guides. Writing a book with any publisher is a mammoth undertaking, and I wrote this book over a period of ten years while running a demanding business and serving on two boards.

I initially set out to do it myself. My thinking was, *Why pay someone to do something I can do?* A few chapters in, I realized I was moving through mud. I'm not a professional editor, so every citation required anywhere from ten to fifteen minutes of my time to research the specific format based on type of citation (e.g., book, article, podcast, etc.) and more time to properly research and format the details of each citation.

All of this came at the expense of the one thing only I could do—implement the structural edits required for each of the twenty-one chapters of this book by the deadline.

Suddenly, I had the "aha" insight I could not afford to keep doing this. If I continued, I would not make the deadline. I outsourced the citations and engaged support.

- Fun factor: Assessing your use of time through this lens will give you a sense of the activities in your life from which you derive the greatest happiness and joy. Fun and joy are among the few inexhaustible fuel sources. They are the ultimate renewable energies. Looking at your time through this lens will help you continually reorient to your north star.

This lens can apply to vocational as well as leisure activities. Legendary founder and CEO of Science Applications International Dr. Robert Beyster retired at age eighty because the time he spent building a pioneering paradigm-shattering employee-ownership culture was both deeply satisfying and fun for him. A "radical idea that proved wildly profitable" motivated him, as *LA Times* journalist Tony Perry put it. This idea was that a company owned by employees rather than investors would create an even bigger pie for everybody. He was right.

A nuclear physicist by training, his vision as reported in the *LA Times* was simple.

To create a good place for people—the company's engineers and scientists—to work… where people would be free to identify and pursue new business opportunities and then be rewarded for their successes.

He started the company with $10,000 of his own money. It was worth $8 billion when he retired (Perry, 2014). Running SAIC was fun for him.

Step 2: Heed

This step is about identifying the changes you will make to help you take back your time. In my case, I realized I was willing to do something I wasn't open to earlier—hire a private editor to help with the citations. In another example, a client shared with me something she realized worked well for her. She noticed when she was out of the office for morning appointments, nobody bothered her, yet when she was in the office, people stopped by or emailed her nonstop. She decided to experiment with working from home for the first two hours of the morning.

Step 3: Align

This step is the action. Here you actually make the change to better align with your desires and values and see what shows up. In my case, I followed through with hiring the private editor and am so glad I did it. It easily returned sixteen to twenty hours back to me that I was able to reinvest in structural edits and other higher value activities only I could do. My client now works from home for the first two hours of the morning every day and is so much more satisfied.

THREE OTHER WAYS TO RECLAIM YOUR TIME

Three other techniques to reclaim your time include building in buffers, instituting access controls, and building your team. Let's take a closer look.

- **Build in buffers**

  One of the most significant issues with time management is invisible time thieves—all the unanticipated things (and people) that arise in the day that rob you of the precious time you allocated for something else. They walk away happy, and you are left feeling empty with a "to-do" list that isn't any shorter.

  The answer? Build in a buffer. Research shows we underestimate what it will take to get something done. Even the best of us are subject to this "planning bias" (Buehler et al., 2012; and Forsyth et al., 2008). I advise people to take your daily "to-do" list and cut it in half. This helps you factor for the significant unanticipated and unavoidable interruptions you must attend to (but that are not planned) and also helps offset and insulate against that planning bias.

Some other examples of buffers you can build into your calendar include:

- Commute time to a meeting, including the time it takes to get to your car, get gas, factor for traffic, and parking.
- Adding time on the front- or back-end of meetings. Often, we don't plan for the time it takes to prepare for a meeting or to consolidate our thoughts or take needed actions following a meeting.
- Breaks—your body needs breaks, but our calendars sure don't show it. You don't have to know exactly when you will take the break, but factoring for that time can help you build more realistic expectations about what can get done.

All of these can cause your cup to overflow, and not in a good way.

- **Institute access controls—on you**
  Try to walk into a Fortune 500 CEO's office. You're not likely get past the front desk and gatekeeper without meeting some pretty high bar criteria. They have access controls in place, and you should too.

You can't just waltz into their office because you want to, the way most colleagues likely waltz in your office to chew the hay. Starting now, invite the office gabbers and gossipers to move along. They no longer have free access to you. You don't have to be a jerk. You can be politely busy. If you're worried about hurting their feelings, get over it. They're not the least bit worried about wasting your precious time.

- **Build your team**

  As an entrepreneur, I can't run my business without a team, but you don't need to have a business to have a team. A good team can help you leverage your time for even higher value uses. The best time to build your team is before you think you need one.

  I recommend having two types of teams: a business team and a personal team.

YOUR BUSINESS TEAM:

Your business team consists of the people who provide services essential to keeping your current and future work life running smoothly. They often contribute to category 3 activities. By taking anything off your plate that others could do as well, do better, or even do more cheaply than you, you create more space for greater investment in categories 1 and 2.

If you are currently an executive in an organization, you may have a support team provided for you as part of your role. If you don't, build one. As *Forbes* contributor Kevin Kruse wrote, "If you don't *have* an admin, you *are* an admin." (And by the way, having been an administrative assistant, even an admin can use an admin!)

Who is on your "business" team? Example team roles could include:

- Administrative assistant—manages calendars and appointments
- Communications professionals—e.g., editor who can proofread and advise on content and tone for important written products, including emails; social media coordinator to help support professional media; a photographer for periodic headshots
- Coach—able to help you tap your own awareness for handling sticky situations or advancing your career

What would it create for you if you added any of the above team members to your life? Who or what else would you add to your team?

YOUR PERSONAL TEAM:

Your personal team also contributes directly to offloading category 3 items. If you are running a business, this may be indispensable because your time can otherwise be generating revenue. In my case, writing a book while working in a demanding business would not be possible without freeing up additional time with the help of a personal team. It was worth it to me to pay for support in these areas, as it contributes to the people and small businesses providing the support and to my business, book, and me.

Examples of personal team roles include:

- Personal assistant—Complete errands such as picking up prescriptions, groceries and gifts, post office, and dry cleaning.
- Grocery delivery service—Unless grocery shopping sparks joy (and it does for several of my friends), consider ditching the grocery lines. This service can be a bargain when you factor in gas and your time.
- Housekeeper—Keep your home in order through the cyclone of life.
- Cobbler—Maintain the shine and quality of your shoes. By investing a small amount to care for my shoes, I have saved thousands of dollars over the years.
- Tailor—Wearing pants or sleeves that don't fit detract from your brand.
- Personal shopper—These are available for no charge through many stores (or enlist your friend, who is a born fashionista and loves to shop).
- Well-being professionals—This list includes but is not limited to a counselor or therapist, a personal trainer, and bodywork practitioners.

Who is on your "personal" team? What would it create for you if you added any of the above team members to your life? Who or what else would you add?

* * *

Maybe you've heard people say, "Keep your eye on the prize."

Prize your time. Your life is the prize, and this is the time of your life.

Chapter Checklist:
- Manage energy, not time.
- Do a time audit to gain awareness of how you are investing your time.
- Build a buffer into your schedule.
- Institute access controls to you.
- Build your team.

CHAPTER 17

Be Unstoppable

———

"You'll be a liability. You're not fit to do the required lab work," they said.

Mohammed Yousuf was in his twelfth grade, dreaming of a future as an engineer, when he heard these words by the school's department head and panel of dream-crushers. Stricken with polio as a young child in India, Mohammed can't walk without assistance. He uses leg braces and forearm crutches, and his school denied him entry into their technical mathematics program solely because of his physical disabilities.

For many, hearing these words would mark the end of our road. Not Mohammed.

He went on to earn not one, but two engineering degrees: a Bachelor's and Master's of Science degree. He has worked with two of our nation's most successful automakers and is now an executive with the United States Department of Transportation where he helps make transportation systems accessible to all people. He has also since founded and serves as president of the EquallyAble Foundation, which empowers people with disabilities globally through access to education, equipment, employment, and inclusion.

"I'm not even sure how my twelfth grade self knew to persist," he said to me in our conversation more than forty years later as tears of quiet awe and gratitude moistened his eyes. I felt a hushed reverence as he acknowledged and thanked the courageous child in him that made the choice to persevere against all odds.

Doing the work he dreamed of in boyhood, he is making transportation systems accessible for all people and empowering people with disabilities globally. Mohammed is unstoppable.

CHOOSE TO MOVE THROUGH FEAR

One of the most potent choices you can make in your life is to be unstoppable, but this isn't always an easy choice. Many things try to stop us in our lives: fear of rejection, failure or success, and the unknown. Fear of the unknown may even be *the* fundamental fear, say authors of a study published in the *Journal of Anxiety Disorders* (Carleton, 2016). One thing is certain though: It can feel daunting to choose through fear.

Fear can be like the shadow cast on the wall by a child's finger puppet. Depending on your perspective, it can look like a giant monster. It's only when you flip on the lights you suddenly see it's merely an illusion.

When you find yourself tempted to withdraw or shrink back from that opportunity you feel called to pursue or that risk you desire to take but fear, step back and be willing to ask, "Am I really in danger here, or is this just fear looking big and scary?" Every successful person has felt fear, but one thing distinguishes them: They turn on the lights to dispel fear and choose to be unstoppable. If Mohammed could persist in the face of some of the most disempowering words that any of us could hear, we surely can too.

THE TREASURE YOU SEEK

What if the reward of choosing to be unstoppable is greater than anything you can possibly imagine? Joseph Campbell is a towering figure in the power of myths, best known for his collaboration with George Lucas on the *Star Wars* saga. To paraphrase one of his most memorable quotes, "The cave you fear to enter holds the treasure you seek" (Osbon, 1991).

The metaphorical reference went literal for me on a visit I made to Sandia Cave while in New Mexico for a television appearance. I read about this cave in the Cibola National Forest located outside of Albuquerque as a kid. Archeologists and paleontologists view the cave as an important prehistoric find, which contained ice age animals from woolly mammoths and mastodons and evidence of some of the first recorded human inhabitants of North America, dating back at least ten thousand years.

As a kid who dreamed of being an archeologist (once digging for hours in a friend's yard looking for dinosaur bones in a Virginia suburb—hey, it could happen!), I long dreamed of one day visiting this cave. When I found myself within an easy drive of it, I was determined to visit. Imagining myself in this cave after all these years was sunshine and unicorns… until I found myself at the end of the path that led to the opening rather than the mouth of the cave. A rickety metal spiral staircase that clung to the rock face of the cliff greeted me. Like Jack's beanstalk, it led up into an endless sky.

I felt sick to my stomach. This was nowhere in my fantasy. I was terrified of heights, and I was sure I would fall to my death.

I knew I had a choice: I could turn back and never see this cave or dig deep and talk myself through what it would take to scale this stairway to hell. I chose the latter and am so glad I did. (You can read how I did this in my blog post on my website and check out my vlog: www.AprilArmstrong.live).

Entering this cave proved far more than the fulfillment of a long-held dream. It was a physical representation of pushing through feelings of fear that in years past would have stopped me cold. It reminded me of Neale Donald Walsch's quote from his *New York Times* bestseller *Conversations with God*, "Life begins at the end of your comfort zone" (Walsh, 1997). Dr. Paula Anderson is an organizational psychologist and president and CEO of PACE Consulting that works with organizations. She is also a licensed clinician and a diversity, equity, and inclusion advocate. She wholeheartedly agrees with Walsch. As she told me, "Nothing grows in a comfort zone. Growth doesn't happen in a comfort zone."

REJECT REJECTION

Most people will do anything to avoid rejection—even if it means sacrificing their dreams or not going for that promotion. In fairness, rejection isn't just unpleasant, it physically hurts. Scans using functional MRI technology show our brains react to rejection in the same way as physical pain (Kross et al., 2011).

The National Social Anxiety Center notes that fear of rejection has primal roots. Being part of a tribe meant survival, and the isolation of rejection could mean death. Our bodies can't differentiate between the chemicals that arise from the truly life-threatening situation today and the rejection that, while painful, is unlikely fatal in modern times (Rodriguez, 2015). The hard-wired neurological system we inherited from our ancestors, ironically designed to protect us, can hold us back—if we let it. What if there is another choice available to us?

In a conversation with me about rejection, Dr. Anderson affirmed it's normal to feel those fears because, as she said, "nobody likes to be rejected." She offered me a reframe a friend once gifted her: You may find that a "no" may be a "no" in the moment, but what if you chose to let it simply stand for "next opportunity"? She advises people to say to themselves, "*This* may not be the opportunity for me, but there is a *next opportunity* out there, and if I stop here I won't find it. I have to keep going."

If fear is hard-wired into us and a primal response, is all hope lost? Not at all. What if you could feel the fear and do it anyway, as the saying goes? What if it didn't have to be significant? (It's not.)

LOOK FOR THE GIFTS WRAPPED IN GARBAGE

I recently spoke with a friend whose husband had just lost his job. She said he felt devastated.

"What if this is a gift wrapped in garbage?" I asked my friend.

"What?" she asked, incredulous.

I shared with her how sometimes we receive gifts in what I call "garbage wrap." It's like holiday wrap, except it's ugly. It can even stink. I know because I've had my own share of gifts wrapped in garbage—but don't let that wrapping fool you.

What if the disappointment is merely a symbolic taking out the trash of your life, clearing the way for something new and even better to enter? In my friend's case, her husband had been deeply unhappy in his job for a long time. He found a higher paying job with far greater growth potential and a collegial group of colleagues he loved.

My friend Betsy McLoughlin is a former corporate executive-turned-global-empowerment coach. She is also a longtime cancer survivor. She received a gift wrapped in garbage.

"Almost twenty years ago, when I was diagnosed with cancer and required six months of brutal and daily chemotherapy treatments, we received a double whammy," she told me.

Her husband's employer laid him off the same week her treatments began, and she wondered how they were going to survive.

Her husband's layoff was a gift wrapped in some stinky garbage she ultimately was very grateful to have.

"It turned out to be such a blessing because Dan could drive me for treatments. The protocol became progressively more aggressive and debilitating—many days, I would not have been able to drive myself—and I am not sure how I would have made it through without him with me during treatments," she shared.

Dan also helped run their shop at the time, keeping that business afloat.

"Things don't always end up how they may at first look on the surface," Betsy mused, reflecting on it all and the unexpected silver linings she also encountered along the way.

WHAT IF REJECTION EVEN CREATES?

Jonathan Alger is president of James Madison University (JMU), a nationally ranked public university nestled in Virginia's glorious Shenandoah Valley. JMU's Board of Visitors unanimously selected Alger to serve (JMU, 2022).

Under Alger's leadership, JMU has done a steady climb to national prominence, including the number one most recommended university according to a poll by *Times Higher Education* and the *Wall Street Journal* (*Times Higher Education*,

2019). They also have the most employable graduates and recently moved from regional to national-level status (Cramer, 2022).

Jonathan Alger and his wife, Mary Ann, a business executive herself, are the most personable leaders the university has ever had. As a member of two advisory boards at the university for the better part of a decade, serving as president of the College of Arts and Letters, I can personally attest they take a sincere and personal interest in the lives of the students, engaging with and encouraging students across campus every chance they get. The Algers mentor thousands of students and go so far as to say if you haven't experienced rejection, you're selling yourself short.

"If you haven't been rejected, you are not pushing hard enough, not trying hard enough," President Alger said in our interview. He added, "You are not opening yourself to taking risks or considering options."

First Lady Alger agrees that rejection isn't something to avoid. "It's just a part of the path," she advised cheerfully. "Sometimes you meet people and develop relationships even through jobs you *don't* get," she noted in our interview. So, not only is rejection not the end of the road, but it's also *part of the yellow brick road to your dreams*? Yep.

"As a businessperson who did a lot of hiring over the years," she added, "I have to say there are people who impressed me even though I didn't hire them—but I'd still love to help them." Rejection creates.

ONLY YOU CAN STOP YOU

We often worry about other people stopping us. Counting ourselves out—rejecting ourself first to spare the pain of being rejected—is one of the many ways we destroy ourselves. You are the only person powerful enough to stop you.

Have you ever hesitated to apply for a job that interested you, or throw your hat in the ring for consideration for an opportunity you might love to have, because you feared you were not qualified or not sufficiently prepared? Chances are you have, according to the research (Mohr, 2014). Counting yourself out—rejecting yourself first to spare yourself the pain of being rejected—is one of the many ways we stop ourselves.

In one survey, researchers asked more than one thousand American professionals why they chose not to apply for a job for which they weren't qualified. The most common response by a factor of two over any others was: "I didn't think they would hire me since I didn't meet the qualifications, and I didn't want to waste my time and energy."

As researcher Tara Sophia Mohr writes in a *Harvard Business Review* article, "What held them back from applying was not a mistaken perception about themselves, but a mistaken perception about the hiring process." She went on to say, "They didn't see the hiring process as one where advocacy, relationships, or a creative approach to framing one's expertise could overcome not having the skills and experiences outlined in the job qualifications." As she says, "[you may] not need to try and find that elusive quality, 'confidence,' [you] just need better information about how hiring processes really work."

What would it create if you never counted yourself out first? What would change for you if you gave yourself permission to go boldly after your dreams?

GO BOLDLY IN THE DIRECTION OF YOUR DREAMS

Growing up in the '70s and '80s, I was a big fan of the 1970s hit sitcom *Three's Company*, which starred the zany and beautiful Suzanne Somers, a beloved American actress, author and entrepreneur. The racy show featured three housemates, one male and two female, who lived together to save money (Nicholl et al., 1976–1984). I had the opportunity to meet Suzanne at Harvard University when we were both there to speak about entrepreneurship.

She shared how she fell in love with acting in high school. When she saw notices of an audition for a television role in a major new Hollywood show, she was instantly interested. Her only acting experience to date, however, was playing the female lead role in *Guys and Dolls* in a small-town high school theater production. She had never been on a professional audition and didn't know audition protocol.

With nothing but a bus ticket and a book of her own poetry she had written as a teenager, she showed up on the production lot. Looking around the crowded audition hallway, she noticed all the other candidates had résumés. She had her book of poetry.

Some people would have turned back at this, certain they didn't stand a chance. Not Suzanne. Unstoppable, she held her head and proceeded with the audition. Her courage paid off, as she received a callback.

She waited to be called back in for the follow-up audition on a bench outside the theater when none other than Johnny Carson strolled by. He greeted her politely as he passed. Recognizing him instantly, she flashed her dazzling smile and introduced herself, dropping that she had just received a callback for the new show. He wished her luck, and she gave him the book of her poetry as he turned the corner. It proved even better than a résumé, because it was a memorable and unexpected gesture.

She got the role. Not only that, but Johnny Carson invited her to be on his show. The rest, as they say, is history. Suzanne simply chose to be unstoppable, and so can you.

THE EASE OF UNSTOPPABLE

Being unstoppable doesn't mean forcing or demanding one's way. It's a commitment you make to yourself to not give up prematurely on your dreams just because you aren't as experienced as others, such as Suzanne in that first audition. It's about staying open, even in the face of what may appear to be seemingly insurmountable obstacles, as Mohammed Yousuf did. As he said in our interview, "You have to believe that even if there is a rejection or stop at some point, it doesn't mean that is the end." He added, "It's like being a stream of water. If you try to put an end to it, it's going to find other ways to move."

It's about having your voice. It's steeling yourself against any fear of rejection and going for what tugs at you. It's not counting yourself out.

REGRET STINGS LONGER THAN REJECTION

Dr. Anderson told me part of what makes rejection so hard is that we take it personally. A healthy mindset would feel the emotions and move forward, but for some of us, this may trigger something from our childhood. We may have experienced rejection from parents or other authority figures, and for some of us, a fresh rejection can seem to confirm our worst fears we've ever had about not being good enough, or something similar; or surface old memories of being picked last for the kickball team, as I was on an early elementary school field day.

It's no fun—but it doesn't have to stop you.

Dr. Anderson told me one powerful antidote to this can be inviting yourself to "forward think" five, ten, and even twenty years into the future. Ask yourself, "What will my life be like in twenty years if I don't do this? What will I feel?"

She pointed out regret is even bigger and more lasting than rejection. "Rejection will pass," she said. "Regret will not pass."

This wisdom has propelled me through multiple personal risks I've taken with my business and even writing this book. When I wanted to throw in the towel and give up, the awareness of the regret I would feel haunted me and propelled me forward. I knew without a doubt I would live to regret it if I didn't take the risks and go for it. "Use regret to embolden yourself," Dr. Anderson advised.

THE STRONGER THE DEFENSE, THE MORE PRECIOUS THE TREASURE

Ironically, whatever you are avoiding the most intensively may be the very thing you most deeply desire to do or be and—teaser alert—probably already are.

It was for me.

Maybe it was the hair. I was in the seventh grade at Luther Jackson Junior High School. I had a Dorothy Hamill haircut gone bad.

It would be at least three months for it to slowly grow out. It required more and heavier hair to pull that look off. (If your hair didn't spin out like the seats on a swinging chair ride at an amusement park when you twirled, you had no business getting the Hamill haircut.)

Terrified of public speaking and lacking in self-confidence on a good hair day, I had an assignment to deliver a speech on a current events topic in six weeks. This timing could not be worse.

I wasn't alone in this fear. The National Institute of Mental Health reports nearly 75 percent of people experience anxiety in public speaking. *Psychology Today* cites numerous studies that say many people fear public speaking more than death (Drevitch, 2012).

My parents helped me tighten the speech structure and writing. My dad, a masterful public speaker, patiently coached me for hours. He attempted to coach me on connecting with an audience, projecting my voice, and modulating my volume.

It wasn't working. I stormed out of the room in a torrent of tears, certain it was hopeless, when he tried to make me rehearse it again and again. I felt the terror I felt after friends coaxed me to go on a famed rollercoaster with an upside-down loop when the safety bars locked. Little did I know, much like that roller coaster, when the fated day finally came to deliver the speech, I loved it and couldn't wait to do it again.

Years later, as an executive coach and facilitator, I still get that same upside-down rollercoaster feeling in my body when I do a public speaking event. While my stomach still does somersaults, I now know I feel so alive connecting with an audience, and I no longer let it stop me.

Little could I ever have imagined behind that well-fortified granite wall of fear lay my heart's deepest desires and the most rewarding element of my career—speaking. Had I never been willing to take those chances, I never would have discovered the vocational joy I now feel so fortunate to enjoy.

The stronger the defense, the more precious the treasure. Become curious about what you are defending. There is likely a treasure there waiting for you to claim. What if it didn't require defending?

Where is fear holding you back? What if you are far more powerful than you know? What if, like Mohammed Yousuf, you chose right now to become unstoppable?

* * *

I asked Dr. Anderson why we should persevere in the face of even likely rejection. She thought for a moment and then answered, "Because there's greatness on the other side. There is something waiting for you on the other side of your comfort zone, and you will never find it if you stop."

Mohammed Yousuf is living proof of this. But don't take his word for it. Try it out for yourself.

Chapter Checklist
- Choose to be unstoppable—you are the only person powerful enough to stop you.
- Move through fear—feel the fear and do it anyway.
- What if rejection didn't have to be significant? What if it was even a gift (albeit wrapped in garbage)?
- Become aware of how hiring processes really work—qualifications and confidence are not always prerequisites, but some other elements are.
- Rather than judge fear, be curious about what it seeks to protect. Whatever it is, what if it didn't require defending?

CHAPTER 18

Take the Highest Care of You

———

Maybe you've heard the story of the goose that laid golden eggs, among the best known of Aesop's fables. The owner grew frustrated his goose only laid one egg per day because he wanted more. One day, he cut the goose open, planning to take all the eggs at once, only to find no eggs inside (Aesop and Winter, 1919).

More than two thousand years after the writing of this fable, this goose and its eggs still have legs. As venerated Berkshire Hathaway founder and investor Warren Buffett said when asked why everybody doesn't follow his investment advice, "No one wants to get rich slow" (PandoDaily, 2013). While the fable cautions against avarice and greed, it's the secondary theme that really grabbed me: Take care of the goose. To go the distance as an executive and enjoy the ride, you have to take the highest care of you. And guess what? In your business and life, *you* are the goose.

FROM WAY OUT TO ALL IN

It wasn't that long ago companies viewed investing in well-being as way out there. Now they're all in. Well-being has gone mainstream. Not only is it increasingly considered good business, the recognition of the costs of its absence are becoming more visible and harder to ignore.

Salesforce research shows 69 percent of employees are currently concerned about their mental health, and 81 percent are worried about their physical health (Salesforce, 2021). Deloitte's Chief Well Being Officer Jen Fisher has her mission to "empower Deloitte's people to be well so they can perform at their best in both their professional and personal lives." According to Fisher, "Many major organizations are rethinking their reward and development programs to include some version of holistic and end-to-end well-being programs. These are now both a responsibility of good corporate citizenship and a key element of an enterprise talent strategy" (Lahiri and Schwartz, 2018).

Microsoft's Japan offices demonstrated the power of a shortened workweek, now catching on in many companies around the world (Chappell, 2019). Major companies, including Google, Goldman Sachs, and Intel, are all investing mightily in well-being (Stewart 2015). In an article for *The Guardian*, Google's head of mindfulness training says, "If you are a company leader who says employees should be encouraged to exercise, nobody looks at you funny. The same thing is happening to meditation and mindfulness, because now that it's become scientific, it has been demystified. It's going to be seen as fitness for the mind" (Confino, 2014).

If the biggest, most influential companies on the planet are starting to value this, I hope you might consider taking the highest care of you. If you're not sure where to start, have a look at the well-being wheel.

WATCH YOUR WELL-BEING WHEEL

Wellness pioneer Peggy Swarbrick's eight pillars of wellness model is among the most robust out there. The Department of Health and Human Services Substance Abuse and Mental Health Administration, corporate wellness programs, yoga studios, and college campuses coast to coast have adopted it (Kobrin, 2021; and Santa Clara University School of Law, 2021). Some have shortened her model, but notably, no one has added a ninth pillar.

Swarbrick defines wellness as "a conscious, deliberate process that requires a person to become aware of and make choices for a more satisfying lifestyle" (Swarbrick, 2012). Let's unpack the eight pillars of Swarbrick's model, along with some steps that you, as a Day One Executive, can take to integrate this into your life in a sustainable way to keep those golden eggs coming, without killing the goose.

1. **Emotional:** Coping effectively with life and creating satisfying relationships

   This pillar is about resilience. Think about growing the ability to thrive despite adversity through the presence of healthy, supportive, and honest relationships, starting with the one you have with yourself.

Some tips for a Day One Executive include:

- *Be your own best friend*—be conscious of your internal thoughts and never say anything to yourself you wouldn't say to your best friend.
- *Engage an executive coach or psychologist*—to help navigate challenging situations that naturally arise during the demands of any workplace.
- *Build a supportive friend group*—to give you companionship and fun experiences outside of work.

2. **Environmental:** Enjoying good health by occupying pleasant, stimulating environments that support well-being

I used to subscribe to the "bloom where you are planted" adage, but I don't anymore. Certainly, this can be helpful temporarily in cases where you may not be able to control your environment, such as military personnel and their spouses and families. The fact is all plants do not "bloom where they're planted." They require supportive soil, sometimes very specialized conditions, and so may you. Give yourself the best by seeking that soil for which you thrive.

Here are some tips to help you bloom where you are planted until you can uproot and move to your best soil:

- *Connect with nature*
  Simply taking a fifteen-minute walk outside can have immense protective benefits on your resilience. Dr. Cheryl Charles of the Children & Nature Network led

a research project with more than sixty reviewers from twenty-two countries and found that nature provides protective and restorative benefits to people. Even short spans of time spent in nature generate feelings of happiness and well-being and improve concentration, even among people with ADHD. Researchers calculated a three-to-one return on investment for every dollar spent creating a green space in urban areas in the form of lower levels of chronic disease, reductions in medications, and faster recovery from illness (Children and Nature Network, 2018).

- *Seek water*
  A few years ago while in Berkeley, California, for training, I had the opportunity to spend a day with marine biologist Dr. Wallace Nichols, author of the book *Blue Mind* and founder of the movement by the same name. In our conversation, he noted scientists have known negative ions found near water lower stress by causing the brain to release mood-enhancing serotonin and reducing blood lactate levels. He described the benefits of being near water of any type, as researchers confirmed through imaging techniques such as CT, PET, and MRI scans, that proximity to water lowers cortisol levels and increases the levels of "feel-good" hormones, such as dopamine and oxytocin, in the brain.

Practically born on a beach and baptized in an ocean, I love the beach—but a lake, river, pond, and even a pool can do the trick. Be deliberate in seeking to spend a little time with water when you can, knowing it is resilience medicine.

- *Nest*

  As someone who is naturally practical, I decided to paint my walls and select furnishings that would really nurture my body. The online magazine *Psychology Tomorrow* outlines several examples where neuroscience confirms what your interior decorator friends have long known—sprucing up your space contributes to your daily cheer and productivity (Taylor, 2016). Science demonstrates how different colors, daylight, and even clutter affect our moods. Whether in your home, office, or home office, choose even small things to create a cheerful, nurturing, and supportive environment reflecting you.

3. **Financial:** Satisfaction with current and future financial situations

   The American Psychological Association states money is the top cause of stress for Americans and has been since it began its survey in 2007, regardless of economic climate.

   Some tips to help you take the highest care of your financial well-being as a Day One Executive include:

- *Be financially conscious.* Look at and acknowledge your money and honor even the penny.
- *Eliminate negative debt.* Get support to get on top of negative debt so that it does not become debilitating.
- *Have a healthy credit score.* Check it regularly and care for it.
- *Save.* Be proactive in setting aside funds to cover taxes and savings.

- *Build financial acumen.* Read books or take a class to build your financial intelligence to care for your golden eggs.

4. **Intellectual:** Recognizing creative abilities and finding ways to expand knowledge and skills

A survey by the Institute for Corporate Productivity (i4cp) reports 70 percent of employers say their workforce lacks the skills and knowledge needed for the future. This spells opportunity for the Day One Executive. Here are some tips to help you capitalize on and use this to your advantage:

- *Up-skill and re-skill.* It's never been easier to keep your skills sharp and grow your expert and referent power. Even top universities, such as Harvard and MIT, offer free online courses.
- *Tap into your artistic side.* Intellectual skills also include the care you provide to your creative self. Julia Cameron, author of the book *The Artist's Way*, recommends several techniques in her book. One of them, discussed in our interview, includes taking yourself on a weekly "artist's date," a whimsical excursion or activity with no explanation or permission that is fun for you. It could be going on a photo safari, hitting your neighborhood flea market, or trying your hand at watercolors.
- *Learn.* Whether reading, listening to a podcast, or taking a class, committing to a growth mindset can help make your career recession-proof and keep your creativity flowing. Psychologist Carol Dweck's ground-breaking research on growth mindset (versus fixed mindset) shows

how empowering it is to realize we can all learn and grow throughout our lives. All it takes is your commitment to adopt this mindset (Dweck, 2014).

5. **Occupational:** Personal satisfaction and enrichment from one's work

   Most Americans will spend an average of ninety thousand hours at work (Thompson, 2016). Are you gaining satisfaction from all those hours? You have more choice than you may realize in how you invest those hours.

   - *Choose purpose.* There's a famous story of when President John F. Kennedy visited NASA in 1962 and asked a janitor in the hallway what his job was. The janitor replied, "I'm helping to put a man on the moon." This man was cleaning the building but connected his work (rightly so) with the ultimate mission of the organization (Nemo, 2014).
   - *Play to your strengths.* Gallup is the industry leader in strengths-based research, and research over more than two decades is clear: People who use their strengths daily at work are happier and outperform those that don't (Flade and Elliot, 2015).

     You can take the CliftonStrengths assessment and discover your top five strengths for about the price of a movie (Gallup, 2022).

   - *Do what you love.* In my coaching practice, I advise clients seeking greater vocational satisfaction and alignment in their work to do an exercise I call "Do-Great-Love," introduced to me by Angelique Rewers, CEO of BoldHaus.

Here's how it works:

a. Take a sheet of paper or a journal and create three columns. In the left column, write a list of every activity you "do" as part of your job. Include volunteer roles you may have in an organization or your community.

b. In the center column, transfer over only things from the left column at which you are great. Don't be modest here.

c. In the right column, transfer over only those things from the center column that you genuinely love doing. You love doing these so much you would do them for free. Steer your career as much as you can toward this column of work.

6. **Physical:** Recognizing the need for physical activity, healthy foods, and sleep

Everybody has heard the drumbeat about the importance of eating well and getting a good night's sleep. But do you know the power of play? The nurturance of nature? The power of touch? Below are some of my go-to techniques I hope spur you to create your own list.

- *The Power of Touch*
One of the most significant impacts of the COVID-19 pandemic has been the loss of physical touch. Touch is clinically proven to reduce the stress hormone cortisol and increase the body's production of serotonin, oxytocin, and dopamine, leading to better sleep, reduced anxiety, and lower feelings of depression. More frequent hugs

were associated with highly protective immune system responses to viral infection (Yeager, 2020).

Studies have shown somatic techniques activate our parasympathetic nervous system, which correlates with a more relaxed state of being. Access Bars® technique, where a practitioner gently touches thirty-two points on the head, reduces stress, anxiety, and depression (Hope, 2017).

- *Renew with Rest*
  We all have experienced the delta between days with little rest and days where we feel well rested. Certainly, we feel better, feel like we accomplish more, and seem to enjoy the rested days better. It should not be surprising that research overwhelmingly supports the benefits of sleep, summarized comprehensively in "The Extraordinary Importance of Sleep" (Worley, 2018). But would it surprise you to know other than sleep, there are other forms of rest that are also effective at renewing your body and putting a pep in your step?

  Other forms of rest Day One Executives will gift themselves to preserve the golden goose include:

  - *Naps.* Ever wish you could redeem all the naps you tried to get out of in kindergarten? I know I do. Researchers have now made the undisputed case for naps, essentially short bursts of sleep, as beneficial to the body's biochemistry and even productivity and cognitive function (Lamp et al., 2019).

Honor your body when it signals the need for a nap. You're not lazy. Close your office door, go to your car, or find a quiet place away from others and give yourself permission to take a catnap.

– *Waking rest.* Researchers define waking rest as "a period of quiet, reflective thought that allows the brain time to consider and process whatever arises spontaneously." As little as five to twenty minutes once or multiple times per day can provide measurable benefits. Researchers have found the same neurophysiological rhythms present in deep sleep arise during wakeful rest (Brokaw et al., 2016).
You can take a waking rest wherever you are, even seated. Just close your eyes as if you are meditating, or if you can, put your head on your desk.

– *Other forms of rest.* Physician, researcher, and author Saundra Dalton-Smith, MD, outlines seven other types of rest:
  - Active rest (which includes a break for yoga or a walk)
  - Mental rest (short breaks where you might jot down things you want to be sure not to forget)
  - Sensory rest (shutting off screens and devices, taking an Epsom salt bath)
  - Creative rest (includes taking in the wonder of nature, a place you love, or works of art)
  - Emotional rest (allowing yourself to feel all the emotions and be truthful about how you are feeling)

- Social rest (spending time in the companionship of people who reinvigorate you and taking a break from people who exhaust you, even family)
- Spiritual rest (prayer, meditation, or books that connect you with your faith)

- *Power of Play*
  Research consistently demonstrates not only that play is fun, but what kids have known all along: It pays to play. (See the *Harvard Business Review* research and *Fast Company*'s story on three scientific benefits of taking breaks.) Companies and even top universities are catching on. From razor scooters to Legos to whimsical work areas, Google consciously creates environments top engineers the world over find fun (Stewart, 2013). The Massachusetts Institute of Technology (MIT), known for its grueling academic rigor, even encourages students to take regular "brain breaks."

  I learned the power of play in a humbling yet fun way while leading research for the nation's largest counter-terrorism disaster preparedness training program. Our job on the evaluation team was to piece together what was called a "reconstruction"—a minute-by-minute account of what happened in a simulated set of attacks and the ensuing aftermath of disaster, and to make recommendations for national strategy. It was intense, but in the aftermath of the 9/11 terror attacks, its importance spurred us on.

  We routinely worked twelve- to fourteen-hour days, sometimes seven days a week. It wasn't long before our makeshift command center looked like a landfill from fast food. Exhausted and with deadlines looming, the head cognitive psychologist on our team informed me she had purchased tickets for the team to go to a baseball game in Baltimore, Maryland.

"What?" I exclaimed—shocked at the idea as much as by the entire team being on board with what felt to me like a preposterous plan. It felt feckless and irresponsible to even consider approving this. The psychologist clearly had me pegged and wisely cited some research about how taking a break to do something fun lets the brain change gears, and you return even more productive. How could I argue with that?

I reluctantly relented. Next thing I knew, we were in the ballpark laughing as we passed hotdogs and crackerjacks. The work faded from center stage as even those of us who weren't ardent baseball fans were screaming our heads off with any home run by any team.

We returned renewed, refreshed, and bonded on a new level, ready to take on the final sprint to the finish line. The Secretary of the Department of Homeland Security signed out our analysis and delivered it to the White House, and it laid a foundation for what guides our nation's preparedness and response to catastrophic disaster response. My colleague was right, and I never forgot the lesson I learned that day. So take that break to shoot hoops with your kid, water your garden, or as I said to my colleague, "take me out to the ballgame."

7. **Social:** Developing a sense of connection and belonging; having a (good) support system
Belonging is a core human need, especially in distress or transition. Some research places it third in importance after food and shelter. A sense of belonging even exerts a protective effect on health and well-being, especially under conditions of extreme stress (Seppälä and King, 2017). Below are some ways to help yourself gain and feel a healthy sense of belonging:

- *Find a work best friend.* Gallup's research spanning more than a decade is clear: Having a friend at work translates to seven times more engagement with, enthusiasm about, and commitment to work (Gallup, 2022).
- *Join a committee or volunteer.* Connecting with others who have the same goals can go a long way toward creating a community of belonging.
- *Help another person.* Helping others feel welcome and connected will also increase your sense of belonging. With only 36 percent of people engaged at work even after decades of study, this presents an accessible and visible opportunity for you to stand out—and it's far more likely when you feel a sense of belonging at work (Harter, 2021)

If you're not feeling it, consider making a change. You deserve better.

8. **Spiritual:** Expanding one's sense of purpose and meaning in life

Some ways Day One Executives can enhance this include:

- *Choosing purpose.* Humans thrive with purpose, physically as well as emotionally. Research from Cornell University showed students who felt a sense of purpose in their work not only felt greater satisfaction in their lives but were also out sick less than those that didn't feel a sense of purpose in their work. Lead researcher Dr. Antony Burrell hypothesizes a sense of purpose mitigates stress and exerts a physically protective influence. "The findings are mind-blowing," he said, referring to the study (Swift, 2021).
- *Finding, or reconnecting with, a faith community.* One's faith and spiritual home, such as a church, synagogue, temple, or other religious community, can be essential to life. Researchers at the Mayo Clinic found religious involvement and spirituality are associated with better health outcomes, including greater longevity, coping skills, and health-related quality of life (even during terminal illness) and less anxiety, depression, and suicide (Mueller et al., 2001).
- *Seeking out experiences that give you goosebumps.* Speaking of geese, this is the advice of Dacher Keltner, one of the foremost scholars of the emerging science of awe, a long-overlooked emotion: "Opportunities for awe surround us, and their benefits are profound," Keltner said in an article for *Psychology Today* (Stone, 2017).

Watching a waterfall or Olympic athlete can stimulate awe, but so can seeing a butterfly or bumblebee or gazing at a beautiful flower. The experience of awe contributes to enhanced critical and creative thinking faculties, and it's one of the few experiences that pulls us entirely into the present moment.

DO AN ANNUAL ASSESSMENT OF YOUR OWN WELL-BEING WHEEL

You hopefully do an annual physical and dental appointment. If you have a car, you probably take it in for an annual inspection to ensure it's safe to drive. What if you did at least an annual assessment of your well-being?

Many colleges, including Princeton University, have adopted the eight pillars into a "wellness wheel" with student well-being programs. As they write on their website, "Wellness is not merely the absence of illness or distress—it is a lifelong process of making decisions to live a more balanced and meaningful life."

The University of New Hampshire describes well-being as "an optimal and dynamic state that allows people to achieve their full potential" and has a gorgeous "well-being" wheel you can print.

Here's a summary of the well-being wheel technique:

- Draw a circle and divide it into eight pie pieces, the eight pillars, about equidistant apart.
- Draw five smaller concentric circles inside the wheel until you have a small circle at the center (it should look like a dartboard or a spider web).
- Label each pie piece with one of the eight pillars.
- Plot the health of each pillar, with the center of the circle signaling "empty" and the outer ring to represent "full." Nobody gets far for long on a flat tire. This might offer a place to start in terms of making the conscious choice to devote more attention.

- Add some of the ideas of this chapter into each of the wheels. Note the ones you have tried or would like to try. What would you add?

At times, it is natural to find an aspect of your well-being wheel temporarily deprived or even flattened, such as due to a life disruption or stress. Resilience is what helps you absorb those times. The key is to be alert to any area suffering from chronic neglect. Periodically monitoring your wellness wheel can help you see these gaps and take steps to address them.

* * *

Too often, we put ourselves last on our list, powering through. As a Day One Executive, you owe it to yourself and your mission to take the highest care of you. If one thing is true about Aesop's fables, it's that they have stood the test of time. Keep your goose golden, and you will too.

Chapter Checklist:
- Perform an annual assessment of your own well-being wheel.
- Experiment with layering some of the well-being ideas from this chapter or from your life and notice what changes.
- Be open even to ideas previously "way out there" as options for nurturing your best and highest self.

CHAPTER 19

Learn to Walk Through Fire

———

We were supposed to meet by the lake. My friend Maria (from chapter 3, "Know Your Value") needed both nature and nurture after the week she had. Days earlier, someone drove their car through a red light at the entrance to their neighborhood, striking and killing her friend and neighbor, who left behind a shocked and grieving husband who had been driving their car that day and walked away from the accident.

Maria was in shock. She shared that the loss and brutal reminder of the fragility of life hit her on a surprisingly deep emotional and existential level, triggering its own crisis. Maria was walking through fire.

We universally acknowledge grief as one of the most stressful events a person will endure in their lives (Holmes and Rahe, 1967). But there are all kinds of figurative fires that can rage in life. Loss of a job, sudden news of a scary health diagnosis for you or a loved one, sudden extreme stress from any cause, or the loss of a loved one—parent, child, friend, or spouse—are but a few.

Most of us have to keep moving forward even as an inferno rages in our midst. We have to learn to walk through fire.

KEEP YOUR FIRE PROTECTION AT THE READY

Last year, in an admitted personal protective gear binge, I purchased a fire ladder, smoke hood, and fireproof escape cape. My friends laughed, as I'm known for going a bit overboard when it comes to safety matters, fondly known as "safety patrol." But despite the friendly jeers, they all also agree that, literally and metaphorically, fire protection is key when you need to walk through flames.

Reaching out for protective support when you are walking through fire is not a sign you're weak or even strong—it's a sign you're smart. A licensed therapist can be your best ally when you need to walk through fire. "Different types of stressors may require specialized support," said Dr. Pearl Zurich, a licensed clinical psychologist based in McLean, Virginia, who works with many executives, in an interview.

A retired Air Force Lieutenant Colonel and disabled veteran, Dr. Zurich has walked through fire multiple times. She survived a near-death experience in a traumatic automobile crash that left her with permanent disabilities, and she served as a primary caretaker for both of her parents through terminal illnesses—all while holding down a full-time job. The experience of having walked through fire makes her appealing to clients who may otherwise have been reluctant to seek help.

"The particular type of stress may dictate the kind of help you get," she advised. "Everybody knows to call 911 if they are facing a life-threatening medical emergency, but beyond this, people do not always know where to turn for help." Someone experiencing financial stress may benefit from finding a financial counselor. Someone in a domestic violence situation may need to seek a crisis center (she points out crisis centers are usually staffed and able to provide mental health support within twenty-four hours). On July 16, 2022, the United States launched a new three-digit suicide hotline, "988," making it even easier to get help (Substance Abuse and Mental Health Services Administration, 2021).

In Dr. Zurich's case, even though she is a therapist herself, she sought a licensed psychotherapist to support her emotionally through caring for and ultimately saying goodbye to her parents.

"You may receive emotional support through family and friends, but it can be beneficial to have the support of an objective third person who understands how grief works," she said. "Complicated grief can take several forms (i.e., chronic, delayed, or absent) and can happen when you don't fully process the initial grief. It can be a frighteningly spiraling and undulating experience, and a trained counselor can help you process those strong and unpredictable currents of grief." It can help enormously to have support through it and to know you're not alone.

WE WILL ALL HAVE TO WALK THROUGH FIRE

A few years ago, I had my own experience of walking through fire. Someone I had met a few years earlier began stalking me. When he showed up at my home after threatening to do so if I did not respond to him and accede to his demands, my life was turned upside down.

Beyond sheer terror, I was grieving the sudden and stark loss of a sense of safety I had known only days earlier and took for granted. While meeting with detectives, trembling uncontrollably, I never felt more alone in my life. As the rest of the world talked football, I was moving out of my home, with police escort, to a secure location. Months later, I would be the lead witness in a successful criminal prosecution that was as stressful as any of the precipitating events.

Like most people, I didn't have the luxury of taking a year off to process my trauma around this. I had to walk through fire while keeping my small business afloat and continuing to create my future. I sought protective support immediately from legal counsel as well as a licensed psychotherapist to help me process the emotional trauma so that I could move forward and function and hopefully, one day, flourish once again.

BECOME A FIRE WALKER

There are more possibilities than ever for walking through fire. All of that, and the ideas below, helped me bloom again, and they can help you too. You just have to become a fire walker.

PRACTICE MINDFULNESS MEDITATION

So, it just so happens I've literally walked "on" fire. Like Oprah Winfrey and millions of others, I once walked across hot coals at a Tony Robbins seminar. That was the moment I became a believer in mindfulness.

The technique Robbins taught us was to place our focus on three simple words: "Cool, wet moss." We gathered outside, and I can assure you this wasn't any fake fire. Before I knew it, I was gliding over twenty-five feet of searing coals outside of the Palm Beach Convention Center, feeling nothing underneath me except—you guessed it—cool, wet moss. A well-meaning crew of emergency medical technicians tackled me out of this soothing trance, shattering my meditative cocoon in their zeal to hose off any residual coals. Only then did I feel the first sting of a burning ember between my toes.

You don't have to walk on hot coals to experience that kind of meditative peace though. Many meditation techniques are available now, from simple balanced breathing to movement-based meditation, such as Tai chi or nature walks (Harvard Health Publishing, 2014).

Research published in the *Journal of the American Medical Association* (JAMA) found meditation helpful for relieving anxiety, pain, and depression. For depression, meditation was about as effective as an antidepressant (Rutledge and Schneider, 2014).

TAKE A PAUSE

Sometimes, while you may not be able to bring life to a complete halt, you can create the space for what Abby Norman calls a "pause" in her forthcoming book, *The Power of the Pause*. In this space, you can take stock of what support may be required and begin to put those support pillars in place. Free yourself up to do whatever it takes to give yourself the necessary support to get through the situation.

If you've been acting as the CEO of your life, as the first chapter in this section encourages, you are hopefully gifting yourself with options. Take a sabbatical if you can. In my situation described above, I didn't want my circumstance widely known, but I knew I would need more space than usual. I reached out to key clients to let them know I would need to make some schedule adjustments in the coming months, and they were beautifully supportive. I turned up the amplitude of the wellness pillars described in chapter 18, "Take the Highest Care of You."

NURTURE YOUR BODY

While you shouldn't take life too seriously, stress can be deadly serious. It creates deleterious physiological changes in the body (Yaribeygi et al., 2017). What if you could lie down and feel stress melt away? Our bodies require a safe, nurturing touch, and there are many somatic techniques these days that can bring you this. From craniosacral therapy to Access Bars®, from different forms of massage to Reiki, many techniques can offer you the healing power of touch that cannot be overstated in an increasingly detached world.

CLAIM AGENCY

Pioneering psychological researchers in the field of personal agency, Larry Cochran and Joan Laub describe agency as a "combination of human intentions and actions to make things happen."

In their book *Becoming an Agent: Patterns and Dynamics for Shaping Your Life*, Cochran and Laub describe dramatic transformations in people who once saw themselves as victims of circumstance, who felt trapped and helpless. Rather than sit back and passively wait, they chose to live the life of an agent, actively setting goals, striving and overcoming obstacles, and actualizing ideals. They came to feel liberated to "mold the course of their own lives."

Researchers Nancy E. Betz and Gail Hackett (1987) characterize the notion of agency as "proaction, initiative, assertiveness, and persistence." It may look different for you. However it looks for you, claiming agency is when you decide to get in the driver's seat of your life, even after a traumatic event.

I stepped into the power of agency when I agreed to serve as the key witness in the criminal trial of the stalker. The last thing I wanted to do was continue this nightmare, especially when victory was anything but guaranteed. I ultimately agreed to go forward when I learned that if we were successful in securing a conviction and he ever did this to anybody else, it would be an automatic felony. I felt a duty to do everything in my power to stop him from harming someone else. Also, should he ever again engage in criminal behavior, he then would have a criminal record rather than be a first-time offender.

Part of claiming agency is getting help for yourself, just as you would for your best friend, in the face of any threat to your life or well-being. Whatever it is, you are not alone. Writing this book while running a demanding business, I had a series of family health crises strike in succession. I was part way through the Creator Institute program that Georgetown University Professor Eric Koester founded and reached a moment of despair, overwhelmed by the enormity of the project. Ten years into the author's journey, I considered abandoning the book when Professor Koester said, "You don't need more content; you need community." Allow others to support you.

SEEK HELP EARLY

One of the tricky things when you are a resilient person, which you are, is that it can be hard to know when we've crossed the line of what we can weather alone and when we could use some assistance. I've often wondered if only there was a "check engine light" that could come on when it may be time to seek help before it becomes a crisis.

There is!

While friends and family might be the first to sound an alarm, The American Institute of Stress has a simple and easy-to-use online self-checker. Based on the Holmes-Rahe inventory, it has forty-three known stressors. Click any stressors you are experiencing, such as significant changes in work responsibilities, a move, or a major change in the health of a loved one, and it generates a risk score. Interestingly, even "positive" stressors make the list, such as an outstanding achievement. The stress checker lets you see it coming.

By seeing it coming, the stress inventory is the closest thing to a crystal ball in empowering you to stave off the worst health consequences of extreme stress. According to the Holmes-Rahe statistical prediction model, if you score 150 to 299 on the inventory, you run a 50 percent chance of health breakdown in the next two years. If you score three hundred or more, you are running an 80 percent chance. That is the "check engine light" that can alert you to take action now to protect yourself and your future.

The willingness to do this for ourselves is crucial to our grittiest resilience. You are worth it. I'm so glad I took Professor Koester's advice and let my community, which includes many of you, support me. In my case, as I write these words, I'm seeing the light at the end of the tunnel for the very first time in my ten-year author journey.

LET YOURSELF OFF THE HOOK

Faced with a crisis or prolonged stress, it is not reasonable to expect yourself to work or perform at the same level to which you are accustomed. Moreover, it's not kind to yourself. It may be necessary to renegotiate some expectations, downshift a role even temporarily, or set new boundaries for what you will take on and when and where you may work.

The video game industry is notorious for overworking its game developers. Indie game developer Supergiant Games made headlines upending this model by instituting mandatory vacation time that everyone must take.

In an industry that routinely works one-hundred-hour weeks, Supergiant Cofounder and Studio Director Amir Rao says, "Setting reasonable limits with yourself... and the people around you, are essentially the only way you're going to be able to do it over a long period of time" (Jungreis, 2020).

Remember Maria, who was grieving the unexpected loss of her friend and neighbor? She was fortunate to have an executive coach furnished by her company. She was stunned when the coach suggested to her, "You could cut your productivity by 50 percent, and it would still be fine."

This was unthinkable to my friend. It felt terribly irresponsible.

"I only know one speed—full throttle," she said.

What Maria later realized was by throttling back, what felt like shirking contributed as much to her company as it did to her. It kept her from crossing over into burnout.

"Burnout" is a condition in which professionals develop depression-like symptoms from aspects of their occupation, which can manifest as physical, mental, and emotional exhaustion and apathy (Freudenberger, 1974).

In 2019 the World Health Organization acknowledged burnout in its International Classification of Diseases as an occupational phenomenon and pledged to embark on developing evidence-based guidelines on mental well-being in the workplace.

If unaddressed, burnout may affect your job, self-esteem, or your health. The Mayo Clinic identifies four contributing factors to burnout, which can be exacerbated by any other acute stress in your life (Mayo Clinic, 2021):

- You have a heavy workload and work long hours.
- You struggle with work-life balance.
- You work in a helping profession, such as health care.
- You feel you have little or no control over your work.

Empowered by her coach, Maria did two things: She scaled back her expectations of herself, and to her surprise, she discovered her coach was right—nobody noticed. She also renegotiated her workload. She is still happily with the company.

SUPPORTING OTHERS WALKING THROUGH FIRE

As a Day One Executive, when you are not directly walking through fire yourself, you can don your fire cape and support someone who is. Even if you are not personally aware of any such circumstance, the likelihood one or more people in your immediate circle are walking through fire is high. As a result of COVID-19, the Centers for Disease Control and Prevention (CDC) reported an alarming quadrupling in diagnoses of anxiety and depressive disorders in 2020 compared to 2019 (Czeisler et al., 2020).

One of the most potent ways you can support someone walking through fire is being a space of allowance for them. By this I mean not reacting and allowing generous space for them to even be "in the grip," as Naomi L. Quenk, writing for the Myers-Briggs Type Indicator, calls it when we are under extreme stress (Quenk, 2000). This doesn't mean be a doormat or tolerate abuse or disrespect cloaked as stress. It does mean being the potency of you and gifting them a wide berth from a space of caring.

When others see you do this, they will more easily become this space for colleagues in their midst who may be suffering from invisible distress.

* * *

One of the most beloved movies of all time is the 1987 award-winning and Oscar-nominated *The Princess Bride*, directed by Rob Reiner. In the movie, the title star and her true love must traverse a fire swamp filled with all kinds of dangerous hazards. Yes, even in a swamp, Buttercup, the Princess Bride, and her beloved swashbuckling pirate love Westley had to walk through fire.

"We'll never survive," she says.

"Nonsense," Westley says. "You're only saying that because nobody ever has."

If you've seen the movie, you know they make it through the fire swamp and go on to thrive. But they didn't attempt it alone—they helped each other walk through the fire.

Chapter Checklist

- Everybody walks through fire at least once in their life.
- Don't be ashamed or afraid to get help.
- Learn to be a fire walker.
- Use all tools available, even unconventional ones such as Access Bars®.
- Support others as they walk through fire.

CHAPTER 20

Banish the Imposter

——

Nearly one hundred students from one of the world's top consultancies waited impatiently as she awkwardly fumbled with the video conferencing platform audio that just worked perfectly well in the pretest. Her inner voice sneered, *Who do you think you are to teach this class? You can't even figure out this video platform.* She felt like a total imposter—in her own imposter syndrome workshop.

Dr. Pearl Zurich, the clinical psychologist whom we met in the last chapter, was teaching the popular class on this very subject, and the stakes were high. "I created the class because I have felt like an imposter much of my life," she confided. She was the daughter of Chinese American immigrants who fled Communist China, became American citizens, and served the cause of freedom throughout their professional lives as they worked to create a better future for their children. Dr. Zurich's career began at the University of Virginia, where she was in the Reserve Officer Training Corps. She retired from the United States Air Force as a lieutenant colonel after serving as chief mission director for Air Force One. She then made a radical turn into a second career, earning a doctorate in psychology and actualizing her dream of becoming a clinical psychologist. This was after she earned a master's degree from Johns Hopkins University in creative nonfiction, and before she completed her coaching credentials at Georgetown University.

Despite all of this, Dr. Zurich still felt like an imposter. Maybe you have been there too.

Psychologists Pauline Rose Clance and Suzanne Imes first used the term "imposter phenomenon" in a 1978 research paper. Like bellbottom jeans, imposter syndrome was apparently here to stay. They noted three key characteristics of the phenomenon, which they originally observed with women in the workforce but which multiple controlled studies have since come to see include all genders (Eruteya, 2022):

1. Thinking other people have an exaggerated view of your abilities.
2. The fear of being exposed as a fraud.
3. The continuous tendency to downplay your achievements.

Ironically, the feeling of being a fraud is most frequently experienced by high achievers. MIT Sloan Assistant Professor Basima Tewfik, who has conducted field research on impostor syndrome, says even the most successful people like Albert Einstein, former Starbucks CEO Howard Schultz, and the writer Maya Angelou acknowledged feeling that they were imposters (Harrell, 2022). Perhaps it brings some comfort to know we have this in common with such luminaries.

I've struggled with feeling like an imposter as someone who carved a career in a STEM field as a liberal arts major. While I've worked with executives my entire career, been an executive, and extensively researched executives, I wondered, Who am I to think I could empower people to become the executives they were born to be? Just when I thought I finally had put it behind me, this feeling roared back when I became serious about publishing and New Degree Press signed the book. I was terrified to put my work into the broader world.

If you have ever felt like an imposter in a job, you're clearly not alone, as 82 percent of professionals suffer from imposter syndrome according to research published in the *Journal of General Internal Medicine* (Bravata et al., 2020). Dr. Zurich says the biggest surprise for her in leading workshops on this subject that take place across Europe, Asia, and the Americas has been witnessing first-hand what the research shows about imposter syndrome is true: It is a universal experience across genders, roles, and cultures.

The vulnerability that even hard-charging people are willing to show among their peers in these workshops had taken Dr. Zurich off guard. "I'm surprised how much they are willing to share about their personal experience, whether the class size has ten people or 150," she said. It speaks to the yearning to shed this feeling. The workshops have proven to connect people who can otherwise feel painfully alone and embolden them to take risks they might be otherwise reluctant to take. "Hearing the experiences of others normalizes their experiences as they commune and share vulnerably," she said.

Imposter syndrome is resistant to evidence to the contrary. Even receiving the well-deserved promotion does not necessarily vanquish it. Dr. Zurich points out feeling like a fraud can be episodic or chronic. Feeling nervous and like you don't belong when you begin a new role is typical. That is episodic and should subside as you meet new people and fully embrace the position and its unique challenges. Suffering from debilitating and chronic feelings of inadequacy despite achievements is a more concerning sign of imposter syndrome.

Self-doubt is normal, and a healthy dose can inspire you to raise your game. If it stalls your career growth or causes to you forgo taking positive risks (believing it's just a matter of time before people find out you are a fraud), those are signs it's time to banish your inner imposter. Anything is possible when you move that distraction out of your way. Just ask Naomi (not her real name).

ACKNOWLEDGE YOU

Early in her life, even Naomi may not have looked into a crystal ball and seen "future CEO." She was diagnosed with attention deficit hyperactivity disorder (ADHD) in adolescence, and academics were not her jam. Yet by age thirty, Naomi became CEO of an innovative start-up company demonstrating the potential of 5G technology, backed by one of the world's leading providers of technology and communications services with revenues well over $100 billion.

Naomi was ambitious, but top colleges were out of her reach right out of high school. Her first job, a retail gig, didn't necessarily portend the success waiting in the wings for her. Rather than discount her ambition at the urging of any sneering imposter, Naomi simply knew she would not take a traditional path. Being different didn't mean she had to settle for less.

"Many people assume they are a failure if they can't play that game," she said, referring to the cutthroat path many take to get where they want to go. The "top of the crop get the coveted jobs and then fight it out for a decade or two to see who makes it. They work grueling hours, grind it out. Some of them will come out on top with prestigious jobs at large institutions," she explained. "It's a long, difficult path—and it wasn't for me," she said. "You have to know what kind of person you are."

Naomi was aware she loved excelling, and she thrived in an unstructured environment. Her gaze never veered from what she *could* do. Even in her first retail job, she enjoyed shining as the person "who did the best job folding button-down shirts."

Naomi also saw in that retail job that she thrived in ambiguity where many others required certainty. Even though she did not know where it would lead, she claimed, owned, and acknowledged what she had come to appreciate as her capacities: the thrill of excelling, the ability in almost any circumstance to intuitively know what action was required, and the joy of uncertainty—not knowing what each day would bring. In so doing, she banished any would-be inner imposter.

HAVE YOUR BACK

Through will, grit, and persistence, Naomi transferred to New York University (NYU). Through a connection, she received a coveted internship offer at a major investment banking concern on Wall Street. She gave it a whirl but turned it down within weeks because she realized she was miserable. It had none of the energy she knew she required to thrive.

As fortune had it, one day the cofounder of Zipmark, a start-up venture, visited her favorite class on entrepreneurship as a guest speaker. Enthralled by his swashbuckling stories of the early bootstrap days of the company, Naomi was hooked. She did something few other students did: She emailed him after the presentation to explore possibilities.

She had her back.

And then she did something nobody else did after receiving no response. She emailed him again. And again. And one day, she received a response.

The founder invited her to meet the team at their headquarters office in Manhattan. Unable to afford cab fare, Naomi walked twenty New York City blocks—in heels. Out of breath, sweaty, but looking sharp in the only business suit she owned, Naomi walked into a meeting already in progress. The cofounder motioned for her to take a seat.

She felt immediately at home in the unstructured, uncertain, and informal environment of the start-up where everybody pitched in to do whatever was required. A start-up company doesn't need academics. It needs smart people who can perceive what is required and get things done—people like Naomi. It wasn't long before the company named her director of operations. Within a decade and a few job hops later, she was chief executive officer of the 5G incubator environment mentioned above that is shaping technologists' understanding of how people might live, learn, work, and play in the near future.

Learning to trust yourself can seem daunting at first. Like Naomi, you may take a nontraditional path. You may at times have to be willing to walk alone (hopefully not twenty city blocks in high heels). You may have to be willing to pass up a prize opportunity when others can't believe you wouldn't say yes. Most of all, you have to be willing to banish any inner imposter.

Banishing your imposter means having your own back. Honor the affirming whispers only you may hear. Follow the breadcrumb trail only you see.

Banishing your inner imposter can be as simple as not putting yourself down, ruling yourself out, or negotiating against yourself. It may mean claiming, owning, and acknowledging your unique strengths, like Naomi did. It means not becoming discouraged just because you don't look or feel the part, fit other people's mold, or even when you don't get the job or promotion you wanted. It doesn't mean you aren't good enough. You are.

SEVEN TECHNIQUES TO BANISH THE IMPOSTER

Keeping an inner imposter at bay may be a challenge you accept every day. Below are some techniques that can help you keep that bugger at bay. What would you add to this list?

1. Trust what lights you up.
   If it lights you up, you have a capacity there. Trust that. Naomi noticed she enjoyed working retail. That didn't mean she was destined to have a career in folding shirts, but there was an energy there she didn't find in a classroom. It was dynamic, generative, and different every day. She would come to discover entrepreneurial start-ups matched that energy, proving to be a place where she could thrive.

   Take a moment to reflect on your life. Look back on experiences that genuinely light you up and notice where you chose more in that direction. Before I started my consulting company AHA Insight, I started a successful photography business. Telling stories through photographs had always been a passion. The idea of entrepreneurship also intrigued me, but I wasn't ready to quit my job and take what felt like a reckless leap at the time.

   I chose to start a small lemonade stand business called PhotograVIE. It was a play on words with photography and the French word for life. The venture helped me bridge into the future by giving me awareness about running a business while also living more fully by being paid to create a life I loved. Five years later, I closed the business with a smile in my soul, having been honored to tell the stories of dozens of families in pictures, allowing them to both be in the moments of their lives and also be in their photos (rather than taking the photos). The experience gave me the confidence three years later to take the leap into full-time entrepreneurship.

2. Keep choosing you.
Naomi could easily have decided she wasn't destined to fulfill her dreams. She could have concluded her ambitions were outsized and unrealistic. She could have counted herself out before anyone could invite her in.

Rather than focus on things others said she couldn't do, she aggressively watched where she excelled and chose more of that. She gave herself every advantage she could, including the risk she took in writing to the guest speaker from her entrepreneurship class. Like Naomi, choose you every time.

As I write in chapter 17, "Be Unstoppable," recognize a no doesn't always mean no. Sometimes it just means not now—unless you count yourself out. Keep choosing you, even quietly, and be assured others will too.

3. Acknowledge you.
You've been doing amazing things your whole life. You've just been dismissing them. "Imposter syndrome is just temporary memory loss, where you have forgotten all the amazing things about you," confidence coach Tiwalola Ogunlesi said in an interview with the *Harvard Business Review* (Eruteya, 2022).

So often we focus disproportionately on our disappointments. What if we flipped it? Start exercising your "acknowledging muscle" every time you see yourself do anything outside your comfort zone, however seemingly insignificant. Ogunlesi suggests we acknowledge our achievements by completing a "monthly wins tracker" to chronicle our progress. She suggests creating a table with two columns and entering:

- Type of win (big or small)
- Descriptions (what actions you completed)

You may also find it helpful to do a daily reflection at first. I recommend adding a third column. Note how you felt before and after the experience. It can teach you a lot about how to move through debilitating fear and doubt.

Pay attention to your successes, your growth, and the risks you took that paid off. Acknowledge it when you see yourself show up bravely. You possess all the courage, fortitude, and inner wisdom you need to take those risks.

Acknowledgment doesn't work like one thick coat of paint you can suddenly apply in one setting. The acknowledgment we're talking about builds up slowly, step by step, experience by experience. As you increasingly acknowledge yourself, you begin to believe in yourself, and even better, you become believable to you. That will extinguish any inner imposter faster than a ghostbuster proton blaster.

4. Stop comparing yourself.

One of the cruelest things we do is compare ourselves to others or to imagined fantasies about where we "should" be. Even the strongest person in the world fell prey to this and, thus, found himself feeling like a fraud. A former World Record holding power lifter, AJ Roberts is now a motivational speaker along with his wife, Jennie Roberts, since inducted into the Fitness Hall of Fame.

I heard him speak at a conference about eight years ago, where he candidly shared, "My focus drifts to where I think I should be versus where I am today. My thoughts shift to what I am not versus who I am now." Sound familiar?

He shared that his secret for snapping out of this "self-loathing pattern of destruction" can be as simple as stopping this insidious voice in its tracks. "That voice telling you this isn't you," he said, "it's simply a voice, and like anything, it can be tamed."

AJ believes it can be helpful to accept that whatever your goal may be, you don't have control over the goal itself. You have control over the daily choices and actions you set up to hit that goal. Accomplishing your goals will be a natural byproduct of those daily, controllable actions. As you do this, he says, "the thoughts of being an imposter seem to slip away."

What are some of your dreams and targets? What action can you take today to put you within striking distance of it?

5. Have your own back.

The imposter runs rampant when we rely on others for approval and validation. Commit now to having your own back, even when others let you down or fail you altogether. Having your own back means:

- Trusting, rather than dismissing, your awareness.
- Dusting yourself off after what feels like a cataclysmic failure and noticing the awareness you gained or writing it off as a great story.
- Being as kind to yourself as you would be to your best friend.
- Making the seemingly small choices today that can create a different, better tomorrow.
- Asking whether an experience is empowering or disempowering and choosing accordingly.
- Tuning in when you are feeling down or discouraged and asking, "What must I be saying to myself to feel this way? Is this true?"
- Do not give up on yourself or on something that really matters to you, even when the chips are down.

6. See it for what it is.

"Imposter syndrome is a form of psychological defense," Dr. Zurich said, bluntly unmasking the *real* imposter. Her practice focuses on teens and adults from all walks of life, including below average students to high achieving leaders and professionals, all of whom were afflicted with feelings of being a fraud. "Sometimes feeling like a fraud is nothing more than a distraction from deeper feelings that have never been dealt with," she said to me in our interview.

In essence, she explained that our brain tries to protect us from processing emotions that may feel scary. Dr. Zurich says many of us have learned it isn't safe to feel the primary feeling based on reactions from caregivers in our lives. *TIME* magazine named Paul Ekman one of the 100 most influential people in the world, and he tops the list of some of the most influential psychologists of the twenty-first century. A leading researcher in the field of micro expressions, Ekman proposed there are seven emotional expressions universal to people all over the world: happiness, sadness, surprise, fear, anger, disgust, and contempt (Paul Ekman Group, 2022).

As Dr. Zurich explained to me, our bodies are hard-wired to survive, so the mind adapts to provide safety. Self-doubt and projection are two defenses many of us employ regularly to avoid feeling what may be scary or even more forbidden such as anger, disgust, or contempt. She invites clients to be willing to excavate the deeper feeling lurking underneath, from which the fear you are a fraud may be trying to distract you.

Dr. Zurich gives an example of someone whose new boss just gave them some hard-to-hear feedback that their work is not satisfactory:

"The imposter thought would say, 'Yeah, he's right, I'm not good enough,'" she said. "The deeper primary feeling that arises first, however, may be anger," if, for example, the boss failed to give you adequate guidance, subjected you to an unrealistic timeframe, or has unreasonable expectations.

When it doesn't feel safe to feel anger, Dr. Zurich explained, we are brilliantly adaptive. We manufacture secondary feelings such as shame or fear to cover the anger. They may also be unpleasant but feel like safer emotions to feel than anger. Boom, we feel like an imposter.

Thoughts of being unworthy or a fraud can arise essentially to distract us from the feeling of anger. It's all super psychoanalytical, but it can be helpful to understand what may be neurologically going on here by examining what may be triggering the feelings of being an imposter. Rather than believing the feelings of "I'm a fraud," to be true, we empower ourselves to see, know, and believe those feelings don't have to rule our choices.

Feelings of anger, disgust, or contempt often contain important messages for us, if only we are willing to receive them. They may be a signal you are not receiving something you require, that someone is taking advantage of you, or that someone has misled you. What choices could be available if you were willing to be curious about the information those feelings contain?

Rather than make yourself wrong, what action could you take for the highest care of yourself? Techniques such as the multiple brain integration technique (MBIT), described in chapter 5, "Build Decision Intelligence," can help you create the space to receive the information those feelings contain. By treating them as messengers, not threats, you can gain a sense of clarity, even about pragmatic steps you can take on your behalf with astonishing ease.

7. Consider seeking a licensed therapist.

If you find yourself feeling trapped in an unhappy job, staying chronically stuck out of fear of not being good enough, consider reaching out for the services of a licensed psychotherapist. This person has the training and skills to help you work through what may be deeper underlying experiences that may be perpetuating a cycle of imposter syndrome, and you don't have to do this alone. If something stopped your car, would you just stay stuck on the side of the road, or would you get a mechanic to help you get moving again? Sometimes we all need a little help to get out of a rut or fix a flat tire so that we can get moving again.

Dr. Zurich notes there are many therapeutic approaches, including cognitive behavioral therapy (CBT), experiential, and psychodynamic therapies. A CBT therapist may help you change the thoughts and behaviors that trigger the feelings. "Fix the thought, change the feeling" is a way to describe this approach. The psychodynamic orientation helps you better excavate and target primary and secondary feelings that sometimes can do a number on us. Some therapists, like Dr. Zurich, offer an integrated approach that blends psychodynamic, cognitive behavioral, experiential, and mindfulness approaches to help people find self-compassion and clarity. There is so much more available for you now than ever. We don't have to stay stuck.

* * *

Dr. Zurich cautions people to realize that banishing your imposter forever may not be realistic. It may have to be a daily self-care practice. She advises, "It's like brushing your teeth."

Even the strongest man in the world agrees.

AJ Roberts said, "It's important to know that it's like a bear in hibernation. At some point, it will awaken again. And when it does, I'll be ready to do this dance all over again."

As Dr. Zurich said at the start of this chapter, even the most qualified among us can feel like an imposter, so it's not that the Day One Executive doesn't have an inner imposter. They just don't permit it to take up residence. They banish it, and so can you.

Chapter Checklist:

- Feeling like an imposter doesn't make you one. Even Einstein felt like an imposter.
- High achievers tend to feel this the most because they never feel like they are good enough. Feeling like an imposter can push you to acquire more expertise, which can be good up to a point. But when it starts standing in the way of your dreams or desires and making you live in chronic self-doubt, it's time to banish it.
- Claim, own, and acknowledge your uniqueness. Just because you don't approach things the way others do doesn't make you an imposter.
- Have your back.
- If your inner imposter is blocking the door to your dreams, seek the help of a licensed psychotherapist. You deserve better - don't stay stuck!

CHAPTER 21

Commit to You

____

"You're only 10 percent committed to your life," he said so casually I almost missed it.

Gary Douglas is the founder of the personal development modality, Access Consciousness®. It was 2013, and I had just met him. I had no idea what he meant and felt my head spinning.

"What?" I said in disbelief.

"I wonder what would happen if you totally committed to your life," he mused.

As I reflected, I saw that, incredibly, he was correct. I had been living my life half-heartedly. That moment was when I began truly to commit to my life.

Three months later, I took the leap into entrepreneurship I had dreamed about for more than a decade to work full-time with executives leading transformational change. Resigning from the company I had been with for twenty years no longer felt terrifying. It felt liberating.

Five years later, I ran into Gary again in Costa Rica. By chance, we both had chosen to walk alone to the dining hall. We had each opted for roads less traveled, and our paths intersected.

A thunderous monsoon had just passed over, and everything glistened. The streets became mirrors as the sky opened back up, and the sun brought a near blinding brightness as we walked quietly together. "I can see you are now about 80 percent committed to your life!" he said with a happy smile. As is usually the case with any conversation with Gary Douglas, it put me into total question.

I wondered what it would take to commit that last 20 percent…

HOW COMMITTED ARE YOU TO YOU?

The willingness to commit to you doesn't have to be an all or nothing proposition. Every little bit adds up and builds on itself, creating positive momentum in your life. Where have you committed to you? What has that created for you?

Committing to me has gifted me:

- The courage to start my company, something I had dreamed my entire life of doing but never yet been willing to do.

- The bravery to pursue justice to its fullest extent to protect the world from a dangerous stalker (see chapter 19, "Walk Through Fire").
- The voice to speak up when I was passed over for a promotion that two male colleagues received, for which we were equally qualified.
- The stamina to write this book to empower more people to have greater choice, autonomy and agency in their lives.
- The permission to pursue dreams that otherwise felt out of reach to me.

BUILD YOUR SELF-ESTEEM

Committing to you is about living into your fullest potential and space of possibility. Self-esteem nurtures, and is nurtured by, a commitment to you. As one of the world's foremost self-esteem researchers, Nathaniel Branden, PhD, wrote in his classic book, *The Six Pillars of Self-Esteem:*

When we have unconflicted self-esteem, joy is our motor, not fear. It is happiness that we wish to experience, not suffering that we wish to avoid. Our purpose is self-expression, not self-avoidance, or self-justification. Our motive is not to "prove" our worth but to live our possibilities.

He calls self-esteem the immune system of consciousness. Like our physical immune systems, we can build our immune system of consciousness. How exciting is that?

You don't have to wait for self-esteem to start committing to you. Start choosing toward you today, and your self-esteem will naturally grow. The following sections offer some approaches to help you commit to you.

BE BOLD

Dictionary.com defines "bold" as:

- Not hesitating or fearful in the face of actual or possible danger or rebuff.
- Not hesitating to break the rules or propriety; forward; impudent.
- Necessitating courage and daring; challenging.
- Beyond the usual limits of conventional thought or action; imaginative.
- Striking or conspicuous to the eye; flashy; showy.

Whether making a fashion statement or trying something new, seeing yourself in bold action can be exhilarating. Appropriate boldness is sometimes about choosing to go beyond the definitions we have ever had of who we are. It's choosing to be more of us.

Boldness isn't universally considered a singularly positive trait. Awesome is a fine line. In the twelfth century, the root word was associated with "audacious, presumptuous, over-stepping usual bounds." By the thirteenth century, it took on a meaning of requiring or exhibiting courage, and it also referred to people or things that stood out, both in an admiring and disparaging sense (Online Etymology Dictionary, 2022).

The Hogan personality assessment cites boldness as a potential derailer when it takes the form of overconfidence, entitlement, or fantasized talent (Hogan, 2014). This is why I refer to *appropriate* boldness. Like any great power, boldness must be balanced and tempered.

- Boldness not tempered by a willingness to listen to others and humility will veer into arrogance.
- Boldness not informed by accurate awareness will careen into recklessness.
- Boldness must be used with extreme care. We should reserve it for the moments that call for it.

But when a circumstance calls for boldness, nothing less will do. As a leader, you may find yourself thrust into a role for which you do not feel prepared, requiring you tap inner boldness. Doing so can reveal capacities you may not even realize you possess.

This happened for me. I told the story earlier in the book about leading top official counterterrorism preparation and response research that would shape national policy. What I didn't share was how I got the job.

One of my mentors was a nationally-known research scientist selected to lead the evaluation. He opened the door to me to be an analyst on incredibly meaningful research. The week prior to the kickoff meeting, he announced he would not be able to lead the project after all.

He told the client that I would be taking his place. I was utterly petrified, as I had never led anything like this. I felt totally inadequate leading a team of PhD research scientists.

The deal had been done, he said. The client was expecting me to show up at the kickoff meeting and lead, and he was confident I had what it took to succeed. He was known for throwing people into the deep end of the pool as a way of developing talent, but I felt I had just been dropped into the middle of the ocean.

Walking into the kickoff meeting with fifty leaders and contractors from the newly-formed Department of Homeland Security required every molecule of boldness I could summon. Talk about feeling like an imposter! In the aftermath of those terrible attacks, there was no time for self-doubt. The people gathered in the room expected a leader to show up. The mission required me to step up and step into more of me.

The work became some of the most fulfilling and meaningful of my career with an incredible team. It revealed capacities I never realized I possessed and may never have accessed had I been able to stay in my comfort zone. It was then I learned once and for all I didn't need to know it all, because I most certainly didn't. I saw firsthand the magic comes from tapping the brilliance of an incredible team, which we had. To my surprise, I brought skills and abilities they valued. My gratitude continues to flow to this mentor and to that team.

Boldness does not always require a stage, nor an audience. We may summon it in a private conversation with one person, negotiating a salary, or in our own private decision-making.

It may be required to save your life or someone else's life. Most of all, it is a part of your internal resilience. It can be an energy that can allow you to persevere after rejection, failure, or extreme adversity. Boldness is required to take any risks where we might otherwise feel afraid, certain we will do it wrong or do it badly.

Decades later, I would hear the most liberating words of my career: Do it anyway.

BE WILLING TO "DO IT WRONG, DO IT BADLY, DO IT ANYWAY"

Christel Crawford is an international empowerment coach. She encourages people worldwide to "do it wrong, do it badly, and do it anyway." As she told me in an interview, "You can't move forward in your career or life if you are constantly stuck needing to do it right. If you give yourself total permission to do it badly, suddenly, you are free." I continue to discover something she said to me to be true: "It usually turns out what you create is so much more brilliant than what you thought."

Christel told me a story of when she built her current worldwide business. "I was in quite a pickle," she said, describing how she moved across the country with $500 of credit to her name—and no job. A high school dropout from an abusive home, she knew her life needed to be different, but she had no idea what that would look like or how to get where she so desired to go.

"Somewhere in us, we do know," Christel said in our interview. "If you are having a pull toward something, you *do* know. Those pulls, pings, and those pressure moments are your personal breadcrumb trail to something you would never have been able to cognitively design from a logical point of view."

It may be different for you, but Christel experiences connecting with her knowing as a centered sensation in her body "that permeates down to the ground. It expands your world," she said.

Christel followed her own breadcrumb trail and "whipped together a worldwide challenge with a terrible landing page with way too many choices." But she generated her first $900 in revenue online. She kept going. Three years later, Christel has a thriving worldwide business growing daily with tens of thousands of followers on social media. The most rewarding aspect for her, though, is that she is living fully into her purpose.

"I had no idea what I was doing," she says, reflecting back on those early hard times. "But I just said to myself, are you willing to do this wrong?" Committing to you, she said, is about "guiding yourself forward into a future for which you have no reference points. All these things come in to hack that to pieces, such as doubt and fear that distract you from what you can truly choose that you don't even know you can choose, but somewhere in there you know you can choose it."

Christel added that in its purest form, "knowing doesn't have any doubt in it." In her words, "It's true. Unless you are willing to do it wrong, do it badly, and just do it anyway, nothing ever changes." Knowing is an inner confidence, and choosing for you is confidence building.

BEHAVE YOUR WAY INTO CONFIDENCE

Confidence isn't a feeling. It's a product of a consistent choice of behaviors. Developing confidence requires choosing beyond a feeling that might otherwise limit us. Research suggests this can be disproportionately true for women, but it can afflict any of us.

Confidence is directly correlated with our choice-making and, thus, can be a direct influence on our ability to progress in our career. A 2016 survey of 8,400 adults by Bain & Company and LinkedIn revealed 75 percent of men—but only 63 percent of women—enter the workforce with the confidence they can rise into senior management. Lower confidence levels "undermine important career-building behaviors, including the willingness to seize opportunities." Their research shows "women are less likely than men to seek out an opportunity if they know their supervisor might not be fully supportive, to make decisions that could be perceived as risky, or to voice an opinion with which others may not agree" (Artabane et al., 2017).

This is where boldness is required. Christel's and my choice to say yes to something we had never done before was an example of a bold choice that was a gateway to confidence. Rather than waiting until we felt confident, we took bold action. In both of our cases, it was a predicate choice for our present careers and callings.

DON'T FAKE IT UNTIL YOU MAKE IT

Feeling like you are faking it is natural as you build your confidence. In fact, 70 percent of people report feeling they are a fraud, because they have not internalized their successes along their developmental paths. (See chapter 20, "Banish the Imposter," for more on this.)

Many books and well-meaning individuals advise you can "will" your way into confidence. You likely heard the advice to "fake it 'til you make it." Do not heed this advice. "Faking" can lead to hollow confidence not rooted in substantial self-witnessing of bold moves and your ability to recover and keep moving forward.

In my experience, there is only one pathway: You must choose and behave your way into authentic confidence.

THREE DOORWAYS TO CONFIDENCE

True, authentic confidence in one's abilities comes through three doorways:

1. Choose through fear. Feel the fear and do it anyway. Confidence is a direct and automatic byproduct of choosing through fear in the direction of your dreams and witnessing yourself doing this.
2. Act with integrity. Through integrity of your thoughts, words, and deeds, confidence blooms.
3. Have your own back. Having your own back and season with a healthy dash of vulnerability, and you are both bold and beautiful.

Let's see what's behind these doors.

1. **Choose through fear.**
You make a deposit in your own self-trust account every time you choose through fear in the direction of your dreams. You don't have to risk it all to build this muscle. You can start small.

The story I told in chapter 17, "Be Unstoppable," of choosing to climb those terrifying stairs to enter that cave in Cibola National Forest was an example of me choosing through fear. Choosing for you does not have to mean clinging to a rickety metal staircase precariously dangling from a cliff. It can be having a difficult conversation, saying yes to that new assignment for which you may feel unprepared, or, like Christel, pursuing a dream with nothing but your moxie available as your initial resources. Each time you choose this, you commit to more of you.

2. **Act with integrity.**
Authentic confidence is rooted in integrity *with you.* The first definition of integrity in almost any English dictionary pertains to honesty and morals. My preferred definition, however, can usually be found a little deeper. In the *Collins* dictionary, "the state of being a united whole" is the second definition. In *Merriam-Webster,* the third entry is "the quality of state of being complete or undivided."

Our integrity with ourselves and others begins with not divorcing ourselves. There is a witness to everything you think, say, and do. That witness is you.

Research shows the brain adapts to even small self-serving lies, so they get easier and more automatic if you are not consciously guarding, choosing, and protecting your integrity (Garrett et al., 2016). Integrity issues don't have to get big to corrode your confidence. They can be as subtle as incongruences in your own thoughts, words, and deeds—or actions. New Year's resolutions are often perfect examples of this. When we don't keep our promises to ourselves, we see it. It erodes our confidence.

Set aside for a moment the moralistic aspects of integrity. You deserve nothing less than the highest integrity with yourself. Since it powers authentic confidence, it is the wind in your sails. Why would you carelessly give this away?

Research shows we have three distinct neurological centers of activity: our head, heart, and gut. If you have ever had the experience of feeling torn, then you have experienced at least two of these "brains" at work, possibly in opposition. If you have ever said or done something and then felt a pit in your stomach, you likely had a desire to take it back or make it right—to regain that sense of inner congruence. Incongruence seeps confidence.

Disharmony exacts a subtle but pervasive psychological toll, and it steals in the night from your confidence. The antidote to this is to be your own vigilant and present witness. Check in with yourself regularly, and immediately set it right when you notice you are out of integrity (yes, you may have to take bold action to set that right).

Don't be afraid to go back on something you previously said. "I know I told you yesterday this was acceptable. It isn't. Here's why." You may pay a price in the short-term, but in the long-term, as you guard your integrity, your power will grow.

3. Have your own back.

I'm a fan of the television series 24, produced by and starring Kiefer Sutherland. The show won over fifty Emmy awards during its run from 2001 to 2010 (Cochran and Surnow, 2001-2010). The lead character, Jack Bauer, exemplifies committing to your life.

Jack acted from a place of integrity with himself—even at grave risk. He always had his own back, even when others failed him. Viewers were gripped because they knew, no matter what, Jack Bauer would never give up on himself.

More than a decade into my career, I needed to have my back when I chose to step off the fast-track. Deeply unhappy, I had come to see I didn't want the very thing I had worked so hard to attain: I wanted to support top executives leading big changes in the world, but I didn't want to be one myself. I was at a career crossroads and feeling a lot of pressure because the company I was with had invested substantially in me as a high potential future leader.

Desperate for some direction in the midst of this career crisis, I met with a career coach who recommended I take the Myers-Briggs Type Indicator. I had taken it earlier in my management rise, but this time the results were different. "There must be some mistake," I said to the career coach. I gazed in disbelief at results that suggested I was an "introvert" and, even worse (in my mind at the time), a "feeler."

"This will be career-ending," I said to her. She laughed and helped me gain a more accurate perspective of the information staring me in the face. It was, but not for the reasons I feared.

The results affirmed something I had been unwilling to acknowledge about me. It took enormous energy for me to pursue and sustain an identity not true for me. That was the moment I chose to step off the career ladder—or rather, make a lateral move on the career lattice.

I felt an immediate sense of relief. It was the moment I began reinventing myself—or, more accurately, reconnecting with my authentic self that had been there all along, waiting for me to commit to my life. This choice came at a cost for which I hadn't fully factored. I became invisible in the corporate rubric.

I told myself I didn't care because the reward of new-found joy in my work more than offset the purely financial rewards of my previous path, as I moved into executive coaching and facilitation work where I felt fully me.

That was true until management overlooked me for a promotion that two equally-qualified male counterparts received. For a half-decade, the three of us were a bankable team who together helped the company rake in revenues with winning proposals, elevate brand awareness, and protect profits by intervening on projects running off the rails.

At that moment, I saw the price I was paying to "be me." I would be violating integrity with myself if I did not demand parity in this. I approached an executive in my chain of command who affirmed we were indeed equal contributors, but was unwilling to go to bat for me. That was a moment of choice for me, and I chose to have my own back.

I researched the criteria for being named a corporate officer and drafted a promotion justification letter. I approached the executive again, this time with the letter, and asked if he would sign it. To his everlasting credit, he did. The company named me a corporate officer the following quarter.

AN ONGOING QUEST

Committing to your life is a choice to dare greatly, to quote the title of the bestselling book by shame researcher and beloved author Brené Brown. Committing to your life takes guts and isn't always pretty. I wish I could say it's a "one and done" choice, but it's not. Committing to you is an ongoing quest, and it is not always easy. Things won't always go the way you want.

The good news, though, is that it doesn't require having all, or even any, of the answers. As Christel shared, "If you think anybody else can tell me where I'm going, I can't even tell me where I'm going," she said, laughing.

Christel has committed to her life and is still choosing this today. She's all in.

I'm happy to say, at this point in my life, I am too.

Are you?

* * *

As a Day One Executive, whatever your deepest dreams, desires, or ambitions might be for your life, know they are in reach. You don't have to wait for someone else to make you an executive. You already are, and you can bring this forward on day one.

You only have to choose it.

Chapter Checklist:

- Ask yourself, how committed are you truly to your life and living? What would it look like to commit to yourself at 100 percent?
- Consciously choose to build your self-esteem, the immune system of consciousness.
- Be willing to do it wrong, do it badly, and do it anyway.
- Guard your integrity.
- Be willing to have your own back.

Acknowledgments

——

Writing a decent book is a lot of work. It is a wildly creative, lonely, gritty, grueling endeavor—and so worth it. But the writing part is truly only a small part of what it takes to bring a book into the world. *The Day One Executive* would not have made it into your hands (or ears) or those of future Day One Executives without the generosity, love, and support of *you*. If you are even reading this, I thank you, because you have supported the book.

Additionally, I wish to extend my profound gratitude to the individuals listed below, without whose support this book would not have come into being:

MY FAMILY
This book would not have been possible without the devotion and support of my parents, Judge H. Jere Armstrong and Jeanne, who were my first writing coaches and role models for what it means to be an executive. They shared their unparalleled razor-sharp editorial acumen generously and often on

short notice. I feel so blessed to have had them by my side as my most present, unyielding cheerleaders.

I would like to acknowledge my sister Ashley, my first and forever friend and my lifelong creative partner and business advisor; my brother-in-law Dave and my beloved "nephies" Henry, Arthur, Leo; Turtle, Birdie, and Cookie—you are joy to the world.

MY FRIENDS

This book would not have been written without the encouragement, inspiration, generosity, caring, and grace of my friends—you were witnesses to the work, and I am forever grateful:

- To Pam, fifteen years ago, in a particular conversation, you planted a seed in me about my own legacy that became the driving force for this book. You've been by my side ever since, tirelessly cheering me on and checking in on me, sometimes daily. Thank you for the countless ways you've been there for me always and in all ways my cherished friend, and in this, the most meaningful and challenging endeavor of my life.
- To Bilge, you served as my unofficial chief editor and witness to the work of this mammoth inaugural undertaking. Thank you for jumping into the trenches with me, and so generously sharing your editorial brilliance to liberate the book's most impactful ideas. Peter kept my technology going even after I fried a computer. From saving my campaign video, to sacrificing nights and weekends helping me restructure chapter after chapter, to opening

your home to me as a writing retreat and cocoon and keeping me fed and watered, you mid-wived my legacy. Thank you for your cherished friendship.

- To Pearl, Suzie, Beth, Amy, JKD, Shana, Jocelyn, Jen, Kristen, and Levent, thank you for being there for me with your support, faith, and persistent encouragement in this seemingly never-ending journey every step of the way.

MY HIVE OF MENTORS

I would not have been able to write this book without your guidance and mentorship throughout my career.

- Thank you to every person who allowed me to tell parts of their stories, offering us candid, unguarded access to what the path of the executive really looks like.
- I am forever grateful to my earliest hive of mentors who took me under their wings and then let me fly with them and whose examples more than words showed me the path of the Day One Executive: David and Mike, you showed me how to not lose me and custom-create a fulfilling career. Fred, Cindy and Steve, Bruce, Terry, Dianne and Bonnie, you taught me excellence and let me learn from you, some of the best teachers and mentors anywhere. Chuck, Jo, and Nick, you taught me about customer service, which is at the heart of any Day One Executive.
- I am grateful every day for clients, colleagues, and fellow coaches who inspire me, have graced me with the great privilege and opportunity to observe them in action, teach me daily, and invited me through their examples into greater vulnerability.

THE BETA READERS

Thank you to all of the book's beta readers who generously gifted me their priceless time and helped separate the wheat from the chaff with content. If the book is at all good, it is due in equal measure to you.

I wish to specifically and especially acknowledge a handful of people who went deep with me on the book and were willing to tell me the unvarnished truth about what to keep and what to cut: Bilge Emrich, Dr. Pearl Zurich, Tara Ramsey, Jana Lynott, Nicholas Viers, and my sister. You helped me turn lead into gold.

THE BOOK'S EARLIEST SUPPORTERS

Thank you to every person who supported this book in the publisher's pre-order campaign in 2021. This book would not exist without you. Your financial support to the publisher sent a powerful message early that the book concept was viable.

Even more than that, your kind and generous support became the wind in my sails I didn't know I needed. On the longest, loneliest nights and the hardest days, I felt you cheering me on, pulling me through. My eyes welled with tears as each of your names sailed over my computer screen. While I knew the book needed the support of my community, I had no idea how much I did too. From the bottom of my heart (and book), I thank you (in alphabetical order by last name):

Jerry Abrams
Mary Mosope Adeyemi

Judge and Mrs. H. Jere Armstrong
Lorenza Arnal
Mine Astarlioglu
Levent Atay
Jocelyn Bauer
Peter Michael Beck
Andrea Berkley
Michelle Birkenstock
Jenna Blade
Kristen Boehme
Jan and Steve Bouch
Trent Bowers
Rebecca Brewster
Dom Brightmon
Michele Brown
Dee Burke
Carmine Carpanzano
Ramona Cedeño
Sara and Benjamin Davis
Debbie Deaton, MSN, RN, NPD-BC
Anthony DeLeon
Sara DeWitt
Michelle Dimaio
Jennifer Dixon
Elizabeth Dornblaser
CD
Bilge and Peter Emrich
Jennifer Graham
Douglas Green, Jr.
Judge and Mrs. William P. Greene
Carolyn O'Neill Griffin
Mark Groene

John Groene
Jody Groene
Mary Harper
Terrell Hebert
Donnie Hill
BH
Kim Howard
Rachel Hudson
Rebecca Hulse
Pamela Johnson Viers
Beatriz Jones
Jennifer Jordan
Si Kailian
Bryan Katz
Lorraine Kennett
Amy Williams Kiser
Eric Koester
Ann Koh
Jill Kreiger
Claudia Mounsey Lau
Christopher Leibig
Kyle Longton
Jana Lynott
Cynthia Maronet
Jordan Matthews
Jen Maurillo
SM
Betsy McLoughlin
Merri Micale Mueller
Seth Miller
Shana Montesol Johnson
Tracey Naples

Luci Nardone
Abby Norman
Allison Ohori
Elizabeth Rose Overacre
Lori Palmer
Stephanie Patton
Laura Pehota
Karen Perry
Paula Harahan Polglase
Amanda Presgraves
Tara Ramsey
Jeanne Raymond
Nina H. Regan
Joe and Kelly Sequenzia
John Skarvelis
Ashley and David Skatoff
Jerry C. Skelly
Adam Slayton
Julie Soutuyo
Erika Stellato
Jennifer Swanson
James Szuch
Ann Tassey
Suzanne Poling Turner
Pamela Johnson Viers
Golda Villa
Melissa Waters
Karen Weiss
Rebecca White
Krista Wilkerson
Mohammed Yousuf
Traci Zimmerman

John and Lucy Zozzaro
Deeann Zukowski
Pearl Zurich, PsyD
Chris Zurich

THE CREATOR INSTITUTE AND NEW DEGREE PRESS
This book would not have been possible without the irrepressible vision, blazing brilliance, and staggering generosity of Georgetown University professor Eric Koester and the Creator Institute. Professor Koester lives what he teachers. He gave me the blueprint I needed to bring this book to fruition.

Early in the process he told me, "You don't need more content, you need community," and he was exactly right. Even when I was willing to let myself down and give up, I saw how much energy he was pouring into all of us in the cohort, and I was not willing to let him down. I extend gratitude to the entire team at the Creator Institute and New Degree Press, whose high-quality artists, editors, and advisors created an alchemy that brought my book into vibrant being.

MY EDITORS AND ASSISTANT
I'm paraphrasing, but a wise person once said to me that writing a book is the easy part. The real work is in the editing. I should have known then to run, and because of the editors below, I'm so glad I didn't:

- I am profoundly grateful to Sandy Huffman of New Degree Press. You understood the vision of the book from day one and stuck by me through day one thousand. A brilliant, generous, honest, thorough, and compassionate editor, your eagle eye and profound caring for the book's message and for me have helped the book shine. From your own wealth of experience, you know what it takes to bring a project such as this to fruition. I had no idea, but I know this: I could not have done it without *you*!

- Stacey Covell of One Word Editing created the nearly two hundred citations in record time and also lent her editorial chops to the first half of the book, strengthening its voice and helping me find mine.
- Betsy McLoughlin—you sprinkled fairy dust across all twenty-one chapters and the introduction. You delivered exactly what was required and then some, blowing me away with your mad editorial skills.

I wish to also express my gratitude to Jennifer Houser, who has been a gift of an executive assistant and program coordinator, flawlessly interacting gracefully on my behalf and keeping wheels of my business and the book turning when I was neck deep in thousands of words while supporting executives in their highest stakes engagements. A double-certified National Academy of Sports Medicine (NASM) personal trainer, entrepreneur, and fellow JMU Duke, Jennifer is an incredibly versatile Day One Executive. I had no idea writing a book is an Ironman Triathlon event—it's no wonder Jennifer showed up on the scene and proved to be the perfect fit for both the book and the business!

Last but not least, I am grateful to God, the first and ultimate Day One Executive, who created by spoken and written word, has made all things possible in my life and career, and carries all creations to completion, including this book.

Appendix

――――

INTRODUCTION

Neal, Stephanie, and Rosey Rhyne. *Leadership Transitions Report.* Global Leadership Forecast Series. Development Dimensions International, Inc., 2021.

Training Industry. "Leadership: The Leadership Training Market." Updated November 20, 2020. https://trainingindustry.com/wiki/leadership/the-leadership-training-market/.

CHAPTER 1

Accenture. "Poor Customer Service Is Top Reason Consumers Switch Service Providers, Accenture Survey Finds." Accenture. July 2005. https://newsroom.accenture.com/subjects/customer-relationship-management/poor-customer-service-is-top-reason-consumers-switch-service-providers-accenture-survey-finds.htm.

Anthony, Scott D. "Kodak's Downfall Wasn't About Technology." *Harvard Business Review*, July 15, 2016. https://hbr.org/2016/07/kodaks-downfall-wasnt-about-technology.

Bonini, Sheila, and Steven Swartz. "Profits with purpose: How organizing for sustainability can benefit the bottom line." McKinsey & Company, July 2014. https://www.mckinsey.com/business-functions/sustainability/our-insights/profits-with-purpose-how-organizing-for-sustainability-can-benefit-the-bottom-line.

Deloitte. "Deloitte: Seven Trends Impacting Retail and Consumer Products Industries Amid a Global Pandemic and Beyond." Cision, June 17, 2020. https://www.prnewswire.com/news-releases/deloitte-seven-trends-impacting-the-retail-and-consumer-products-industries-amid-a-global-pandemic-and-beyond-301078384.html.

Handy, Charles. "What's a Business For?" *Harvard Business Review*, December 2002. https://hbr.org/2002/12/whats-a-business-for.

Lund, Susan, Anu Madgavkar, Jan Mischke, and Jaana Remes. "What's Next for Consumers, Workers and Companies in the Post-COVID-19 Recovery." *McKinsey Global Institute*. May 18, 2021. https://www.mckinsey.com/featured-insights/future-of-work/whats-next-for-consumers-workers-and-companies-in-the-post-covid-19-recovery.

Lunn, Peter D., and Sean Lyons. "Consumer Switching Intentions for Telecoms Services: Evidence from Ireland." *Heliyon* 4, no. 5 (2018). https://doi.org/10.1016/j.heliyon.2018.e00618.

Mcaleer, Brendan. "Watch Jean-Claude Van Damme Do Epic Splits Riding Two Volvo Trucks." *Road and Track*, November 14, 2013. https://www.roadandtrack.com/car-culture/videos/a6024/volvo-and-jean-claude-van-damme/.

Memmott, Mark. "How'd They Do That? Jean-Claude Van Damme's 'Epic Split.'" *NPR*, November 16, 2013. https://www.npr.org/sections/thetwo-way/2013/11/16/245607276/howd-they-do-that-jean-claude-van-dammes-epic-split.

Pisani, Joseph. "Better.com CEO to Take Time Off After Zoom Firings." *Wall Street Journal*, December 10, 2021. https://www.wsj.com/articles/better-com-ceo-to-take-time-off-after-zoom-firings-11639165125.

Ruderman, Marian N., and Patricia J. Ohllott. *The Realities of Management Promotion*. Greensboro: Center for Creative Leadership, 1994.

Tarek, Shams. "Kodak EasyShare One review: Kodak EasyShare One." CNET, November 8, 2005. https://www.cnet.com/reviews/kodak-easyshare-one-review/.

Verizon. "Bell Atlantic is now Verizon Communications Inc." Bell Atlantic, June 30, 2000. https://www.verizon.com/about/sites/default/files/bellatlantic/index.html.

Verizon. "Hinshaw Named Chief Information Officer of Verizon Wireless." VerizonNews Archives, October 19, 2005. https://www.verizon.com/about/news/vzw/2005/10/pr2005-10-19.

Vermeulen, Freek. "Companies Don't Always Need a Purpose Beyond Profit." *Harvard Business Review,* May 8, 2019.

CHAPTER 2

Davis, Kate. "Reconciling the Views of Project Success: A Multiple Stakeholder Model." *Project Management Journal* 49, no. 5 (October 2018): 38–47. https://doi.org/10.1177/8756972818786663.

Fleming, Victor, dir. *The Wizard of Oz.* 1939; Culver City, CA: Metro-Goldwyn-Mayer Studios Inc.

Hardy-Vallee, Benoit. "The Cost of Bad Project Management." Gallup, February 7, 2012. https://news.gallup.com/businessjournal/152429/cost-bad-project-management.aspx.

Hopmere, Michael, Lynn Crawford, and Michael S. Harré. "Proactively Monitoring Large Project Portfolios." *Project Management Journal* 51, no. 6 (December 2020): 656–69. https://doi.org/10.1177/8756972820933446.

Lloyd, James. "How Have the Egyptian Pyramids Lasted So Long?" *BBC Science Focus Magazine*, March 11, 2014. https://www.sciencefocus.com/science/how-have-the-egyptian-pyramids-lasted-so-long/.

PM Zone. "The Golden Triangle." Accessed September 1, 2022. https://beingaprojectmanager.com/nuggets/project-management-golden-triangle/.

Project Management Institute, Inc. "PMI® Certifications." *Certifications*. Accessed March 5, 2022. https://www.pmi.org/certifications.

Scheiner, Michael. "The Project Management Triangle (Iron Triangle) & Its Elements Explained". CRM.org, July 29, 2022. https://crm.org/news/project-management-triangle.)

Shah, Ishita Viren. "Comparison of Stakeholder Management and Change Management Factors in Managing Successful Versus Unsuccessful IT Projects." (master's thesis, Purdue University, 2016). 813. https://docs.lib.purdue.edu/open_access_theses/813.

CHAPTER 3

Brzezinski, Mika. *Knowing Your Value: Women, Money, and Getting What You're Worth.* New York: Hachette Books, 2011.

Encyclopedia Britannica Online. s.v. "Steve Wozniak." Accessed September 18, 2022, https://www.britannica.com/biography/Stephen-Gary-Wozniak.

Glassdoor Team. "How to Ask for a Raise." *Glassdoor,* July 26, 2022. https://www.glassdoor.com/blog/guide/how-to-ask-for-a-raise/.

Kaplan, Robert S., and P. D. Norton, "The Passive-Aggressive Organization." *Harvard Business Review* 83, no. 10 (2005): 82–157.

Kershner, Irvin, dir. 1980. *The Empire Strikes Back.* Los Angeles, CA: Twentieth Century-Fox Film Corporation.

Merriam-Webster.com. s.v. "effective". Accessed July 6, 2022. https://www.merriam-webster.com/dictionary/effective.

Merriam-Webster.com. s.v. "efficient." Accessed July 6, 2022. https://www.merriam-webster.com/dictionary/efficient.

Milasas, Simone. "Create, Connect, Move." 2019. SoundCloud, 5:45. https://soundcloud.com/simonemilasas/create-connect-move.

Milasas, Simone. *Joy of Business: What if Business is the Adventure of Living?* Santa Barbara, CA: Access Consciousness Publishing Company, 2013.

Rewers, Angelique. Presentation at the Velocity Training Conference, Boca Raton, FL, 2013.

Slater, Daniel. "Elements of Amazon's Day 1 Culture." Amazon Web Services (AWS), Accessed September 18, 2022. https://aws.amazon.com/executive-insights/content/how-amazon-defines-and-operationalizes-a-day-1-culture/.

CHAPTER 4

Associated Press, "Pepsi Termed No. 1 Seller," The New York Times. January 28, 1986. https://www.nytimes.com/1986/01/28/business/pepsi-termed-no-1-seller.html.

"Become a More Strategic Leader." *Wharton @ Work*, January 2017. https://executiveeducation.wharton.upenn.edu/thought-leadership/wharton-at-work/2017/01/become-a-more-strategic-leader/.

Clark, Dorie. "If Strategy Is So Important, Why Don't We Make Time for It?" *Harvard Business Review*, June 21, 2018. https://hbr.org/2018/06/if-strategy-is-so-important-why-dont-we-make-time-for-it.

Giles, Lionel. *Sun Tzu On the Art of War*. Abingdon: Routledge, 2013.

Harvard Business School, "Strategy." *Institute for Strategy and Competitiveness*. Accessed on August 18, 2022. https://www.isc.hbs.edu/strategy/Pages/default.aspx.

Horwath, Rich. *The Strategic Thinking Manifesto*. Strategic Thinking Institute, n.d. https://www.strategyskills.com/pdf/The-Strategic-Thinking-Manifesto.pdf.

Javetski, Bill. "Leading in the 21st century: An interview with Michael Useem." McKinsey & Company, September 1, 2012. https://www.mckinsey.com/featured-insights/leadership/an-interview-with-michael-useem.

Kahney, Leander. "John Sculley on Steve Jobs: The Full Interview Transcript." Cult of Mac, October 14, 2010. https://www.cultofmac.com/63295/john-sculley-on-steve-jobs-the-full-interview-transcript/.

Knowledge at Wharton Staff. "What Makes a Successful CEO." *Knowledge at Wharton*, April 4, 2018. https://knowledge.wharton.upenn.edu/article/crack-c-suite-code/.

Little, Becky. "How the 'Blood Feud' Between Coke and Pepsi Escalated During the 1980s Cola Wars." History.com. June 11,

2019, updated March 12, 2020. https://www.history.com/news/
cola-wars-pepsi-new-coke-failure.

Mintzberg, Henry, Bruce Ahlstrand, and Joseph Lampel. *Strategy
Safari: A Guided Tour Through the Wilds of Strategic Management.* New York: Free Press, 2005. https://henrymintzberg-
books.com/product/strategy-safari.

Porter, Michael. "What is Strategy?" *Harvard Business Review*,
November-December 1996. https://hbr.org/1996/11/what-is-
strategy.

Robbins, Stever. "The Executive Mindset." Harvard Business
School, June 19, 2006. https://hbswk.hbs.edu/archive/the-ex-
ecutive-mindset.

Sculley, John. "Legendary CEO, Apple, Pepsi-Cola Co." Wharton
Leadership Lecture Series." Philadelphia, PA. Streamed live
on April 5, 2018. YouTube video, 16:40.

Sorensen, Jesper B. and Glenn R. Carroll. *Making Great Strategy.*
New York, NY: Columbia Business School Publishing, 2021.

Terdiman, Daniel. "John Sculley Spills the Beans on Firing Steve
Jobs." CNET, September 9, 2013. https://www.cnet.com/tech/
tech-industry/john-sculley-spills-the-beans-on-firing-steve-
jobs/.

The Wharton School, University of Pennsylvania. "Professor
Harbir Singh on Creating a Strategic Mindset." *Strategy and
Innovation.* Accessed on August 16, 2022. https://executiveed-

ucation.wharton.upenn.edu/for-individuals/program-topics/
strategy-and-innovation/.

U.S. Department of Defense, Joint Force Development, *Joint Doc-trine Note 2-19: Strategy.* December 10, 2019. https://www.jcs.mil/Portals/36/Documents/Doctrine/jdn_jg/jdn2_19.pdf.

Useem, Michael. "You're your Leadership Moment." Knowledge at Wharton, March 30, 2020. https://knowledge.wharton.upenn.edu/article/its-your-leadership-moment/.

CHAPTER 5

Armstrong, April. "How A Better Decision Process Equals Better Decisions—And Higher Trust." Forbes, August 2, 2022. https://www.forbes.com/sites/forbescoachescouncil/2022/08/02/how-a-better-decision-process-equals-better-decisions-and-higher-trust/?sh=5f171e45360d.

Bilalic, Merim, Peter McLeod, and Fernand Gobet. "Expert and novice problem solving strategies in chess: Sixty years of citing de Groot (1946)." *Thinking and Reasoning* 14. (November 2008). https://doi.org:10.1080/13546780802265547.

Botelho, Elena Lytkina, Kim Rosenhoetter Powell, Stephen Kincaid, and Dina Wang. "What Sets Successful CEOs Apart." *Harvard Business Review*, May-June 2017. https://hbr.org/2017/05/what-sets-successful-ceos-apart.

Brodbeck, Felix C., Rudolf Kerschreiter, Andreas Mojzisch, and Stefan Schulz-Hardt. "Group Decision Making under Condi-tions of Distributed Knowledge: The Information Asymmetries

Model." *The Academy of Management Review* 32, no. 2 (2007): 459–79. http://www.jstor.org/stable/20159311.

Brousseau, Kenneth R., Michael J. Driver, Gary Hourihan, and Rikard Larsson. "The Seasoned Executive's Decision-Making Style." *Harvard Business Review*, February 2006. https://hbr.org/2006/02/the-seasoned-executives-decision-making-style.

Butler, Declan. "Tomorrow's world: technological change is accelerating today at an unprecedented speed and could create a world we can barely begin to imagine." *Nature* 530, no. 7591 (2016): 398–401. https://doi.org/10.1038/530398a.

Concordia University-St. Paul. "Seven Steps of the Decision Making Process." February 10, 2017. https://online.csp.edu/resources/article/decision-making-process/.

Cypher, Maria. "Meet Our Team of Naming Experts." *Catchword*. Accessed March 5, 2022. https://catchwordbranding.com/team/.

Das Behl, Arpita. "Groupthink: The Role of Leadership in Enhancing and Mitigating the Pitfall in Team Decision-Making." *Northwestern University School of Education and Social Policy*, 2012. https://www.sesp.northwestern.edu/masters-learning-and-organizational-change/knowledge-lens/stories/2012/groupthink-the-role-of-leadership-in-enhancing-and-mitigating-the-pitfall-in-team-decision-making.html.).

Davenport, Thomas H. "Was Steve Jobs a Good Decision Maker?" *Harvard Business Review*, October 13, 2011. https://hbr.org/2011.

Forman, Ernest. "Make Important Decisions Better with Structured Decision Making." *Expert Choice*. Accessed on April 1, 2022. https://www.expertchoice.com/blog/make-important-decisions-better-with-structured-decision-making.

Haden, Jeff. "Neuroscience Reveals How Steve Jobs Made Better Decisions, Faster." *Inc.* Magazine, June 25, 2020. https://www.inc.com/jeff-haden/neuroscience-reveals-how-steve-jobs-made-better-decisions-faster.html.

Ive, Jony. "Jony Ive on What He Misses Most About Steve Jobs." *Wall Street Journal*, October 4, 2019. https://www.wsj.com/articles/jony-ive-steve-jobs-memories-10th-anniversary-11633354769.

Janis, Irving L. *Victims of Groupthink: A Psychological Study of Foreign Policy Decisions and Fiascoes.* Boston: Houghton Mifflin, 1972.

Kinni, Theodore. "How to Pressure Test Your Strategic Vision." Stanford Business, January 15, 2021. https://www.gsb.stanford.edu/insights/how-pressure-test-your-strategic-vision.

Kolbe Corp. "Kolbe A™ Index: Instinctive Strengths Assessment." 2021. https://kolbe.com/kolbe-a-index.

Lerner, Jennifer S., Ye Li, Piercarlo Valdesolo, and Karim S. Kassam. "Emotion and Decision Making." *Annual Review of Psychology* 66, no.1 (2015): 799–823 First published online as a Review in Advance on September 22, 2014. doi: 10.1146/annurev-psych-010213-11504.

mBraining.com. "mBraining Info." 2022. https://www.mbraining.com/mbraining/mbraining-info.

McKinsey & Company. "Decision making in the age of urgency." 2019. https://www.mckinsey.com/business-functions/people-and-organizational-performance/our-insights/decision-making-in-the-age-of-urgency.

Medina, Carmen. "The Potential of Integrating Intelligence and Intuition." *The Cipher Brief*, June 10, 2022. https://www.thecipherbrief.com/the-potential-of-integrating-intelligence-and-intuition.

National Security Institute. "Carmen Medina." Advisory Board. Accessed September 26, 2022. https://nationalsecurity.gmu.edu/carmen-medina/.

Scopelliti, Irene, Carey K. Morewedge, Erin McCormick, H. Lauren Min, Sophie Lebrecht, and Karim S. Kassam. "Bias Blind Spot: Structure, Measurement, and Consequences." *Management Science* 61, no. 10 (2015): 2468–86. http://www.jstor.org/stable/24551537.

Soosalu, Grant, Suzanne Henwood, and Arun Deo. "Head, Heart, and Gut in Decision Making: Development of a Multiple Brain Preference Questionnaire." *SAGE Open* 9, No. 1 (January 2019). https://doi.org/10.1177/2158244019837439.

Surowiecki, James. *The Wisdom of Crowds: Why the Many Are Smarter Than the Few and How Collective Wisdom Shapes Business, Economies, Societies and Nations.* New York City: Doubleday, 2004.

The Myers and Briggs Foundation. "My MBTI Personality Type: MBTI Basics." 2022. https://www.myersbriggs.org/my-mbti-personality-type/mbti-basics/

CHAPTER 6

Agrawal, Anupam, and Caroline Rook, "Global Leaders in East and West—Do All Global Leaders Lead in the Same Way?" (Faculty & Research Working Paper, INSEAD, 2013.). https://sites.insead.edu/facultyresearch/research/doc.cfm?did=52985.

Anterasian, Cathy, Gerhard Resch-Fingerlos, and Robert Stark. "Understanding executive potential: The underappreciated leadership traits of the most successful executives—and why they're important." SpencerStuart, December 2020. https://www.spencerstuart.com/research-and-insight/understanding-executive-potential-the-underappreciated-leadership-traits.

Association for Talent Development. "ATD Research: The Role of Learning in Change Management." Association for Talent Development Press Release, November 6, 2014. http://www.prweb.com/releases/2014/11/prweb12308646.htm.

Bandiera, Oriana, Andrea Prat, Stephen Hansen, and Raffaella Sadun. "CEO Behavior and Firm Performance," Journal of Political Economy 128, no. 4 (April 2020): 1325–1369. doi:10.3386/w23248.

Bandiera, Oriana, Stephen Hansen, Andrea Prat, and Raffaella Sadun. "A Survey of How 1,000 CEOs Spend Their Day Reveals What Makes Leaders Successful." *Harvard Business Review*,

October 12, 2017. https://hbr.org/2017/10/a-survey-of-how-1000-ceos-spend-their-day-reveals-what-makes-leaders-successful.

Crowe, Cameron, dir. *Jerry Maguire.* 1996; TriStar Pictures/Gracie Films, 1996.

Drucker, Peter F. *The Effective Executive: The Definitive Guide to Getting the Right Things Done.* NYC: Harper Business. 2006.

Fæste, Lars, Martin Reeves, and Kevin Whitaker. "The Science of Organizational Change." BCG, May 2, 2019. https://www.bcg.com/featured-insights/winning-the-20s/science-of-change.

Gartner. "Organizational Change Management." *Insights.* Accessed December 7, 2021. https://www.gartner.com/en/human-resources/insights/organizational-change-management.

Harrison, Theo. "The Kubler Ross Change Curve: Understanding The 5 Stages of Change." *Mind Journal,* accessed September 22, 2022. https://themindsjournal.com/kubler-ross-change-curve.

Kotter, John P. "Leading Change: Why Transformation Efforts Fail." *Harvard Business Review,* May-June 1995. https://hbr.org/1995/05/leading-change-why-transformation-efforts-fail-2.

Porter, Michael. "Operational Effectiveness vs. Strategy—Institute for Strategy and Competitiveness." *Harvard Business School,* Accessed June 3, 2022. https://www.isc.hbs.edu/strategy/business-strategy/Pages/operational-effectiveness-vs-strategy.aspx.

Prosci. "Thought Leadership Articles: Best Practices in Change Management." Accessed July 17, 2022. https://www.prosci.com/resources/articles/change-management-best-practices.

Shoemaker, Paul, J. H., Steve Krupp, and Samantha Howland. "Strategic Leadership: The Essential Skills." *Harvard Business Review*, January-February 2013. https://hbr.org/2013/01/strategic-leadership-the-esssential-skills.

Stanford Law School. "Maggie Wilderotter." 27th Annual Stanford Directors' College 2022. Accessed September 22, 2022. https://conferences.law.stanford.edu/directorscollege2022/speakers/maggie-wilderotter/.

U.S. Office of Personnel Management. Senior Executive Service. *Policy, Data, Oversight.* Accessed April 2, 2022. https://www.opm.gov/policy-data-oversight/senior-executive-service/executive-core-qualifications/.

von Kapff, Marcus. *How to Successfully Integrate New Technologies.* JP Morgan Chase and Co., 2020. https://www.jpmorgan.com/content/dam/jpm/commercial-banking/documents/digital-solutions/Digital%20Solutions_Phased%20Approach%20Guide_FINAL_ADA.pdf.

Watkins, Michael D. "10 Reasons why organizational change fails." IMD, January 2020. https://www.imd.org/research-knowledge/articles/10-reasons-why-organizational-change-fails/.

Weber, Emma, Patricia Pullman Phillips, and Jack Phillips. *Making Change Work.* London: Kogan Page, 2016.

William Bridges Associates—Transition Management Leaders. "Bridges Transition Model." *About.* Accessed December 7, 2022. https://wmbridges.com/about/what-is-transition/.

Zhexembayeva, Nadya. "Three Things You're Getting Wrong About Organizational Change." *Harvard Business Review,* June 9, 2020. https://hbr.org/2020/06/3-things-youre-getting-wrong-about-organizational-change.

CHAPTER 7

Aminov, Iskandar, Aaron De Smet, and Gregor Jost. "Decision Making in the age of urgency." McKinsey & Company, April 30, 2019. https://www.mckinsey.com/business-functions/people-and-organizational-performance/our-insights/decision-making-in-the-age-of-urgency.

Drucker, Peter F. The *Effective Executive: The Definitive Guide to Getting the Right Things Done.* New York: HarperCollins e-books, 2009.

Federal Judiciary. "About the Supreme Court." Accessed September 28, 2022. https://www.uscourts.gov/about-federal-courts/educational-resources/about-educational-outreach/activity-resources/about.

Hubbard, Thomas N. "Research: Delegating Can Increase Your Earnings." *Harvard Business Review,* August 12, 2016. https://hbr.org/2016/08/research-delegating-more-can-increase-your-earnings.

International Olympic Committee. "Olympic champion Mattek-Sands celebrates the dramatic evolution of tennis through the ages." News. August 24, 2020. https://olympics.com/ioc/news/olympic-champion-mattek-sands-celebrates-the-dramatic-evolution-of-tennis-through-the-ages.

Kotter, John P. "Leading Change: Why Transformation Efforts Fail." *Harvard Business Review*, May-June 1995. https://hbr.org/1995/05/leading-change-why-transformation-efforts-fail-2.

Neilson, Gary L., Karla L. Martin, and Elizabeth Powers. "The Secrets to Successful Strategy Execution." *Harvard Business Review*, June 2008. https://hbr.org/2008/06/the-secrets-to-successful-strategy-execution.

Port, Michael. *Book Yourself Solid: The Fastest, Easiest, and Most Reliable System for Getting More Clients Than You Can Handle Even if You Hate Marketing and Selling.* New York: John Wiley & Sons, Ltd. Edition, 2006.

Porter, Michael E., and Nitin Nohria. "How CEOs Manage Time." Harvard Business Review, July-August 2018. https://hbr.org/2018/07/how-ceos-manage-time#how-ceos-manage-time.

Women Corporate Directors. "Maggie Wilderotter." Accessed September 1, 2022. https://www.womencorporatedirectors.org/WCD/Events/WCD_Global_2019/bios/Maggie_Wilderotter.aspx.

CHAPTER 8

Brown, Brené. *Dare to Lead: Brave Work. Tough Conversations. Whole Hearts.* New York: Random House, 2018.

Buckingham, Marcus, and Ashley Goodall. "The Feedback Fallacy," *Harvard Business Review*, March-April 2019. https://hbr.org/2019/03/the-feedback-fallacy.

Cameron, Julia. *The Artist's Way: A Spiritual Path to Higher Creativity.* New York: J.P. Tarcher/Putman, 2002.

Covey, Stephen R. *The 7 Habits of Highly Effective People: Powerful Lessons in Personal Change.* Cambridge, UK: Free Press, 2004.

Covey, Stephen M. *The Speed of Trust: The One Thing that Changes Everything.* New York: Simon and Schuster Audio, 2008.

Cumming, Emily A. "An investigation into the relationship between emotional intelligence and workplace performance: an exploratory study." (Master's thesis, Lincoln University, 2005). http://researcharchive.lincoln.ac.nz/handle/10182/2417.

Dishman, Lydia. "The complicated and troubled history of the annual performance review." Fast Company, November 7, 2018. https://www.fastcompany.com/90260641/the-complicated-and-troubled-history-of-the-annual-performance-review.

Eurich, Tasha. "What Self-Awareness Really Is (and How to Cultivate It)." *Harvard Business Review*, January 4, 2018. https://hbr.org/2018/01/what-self-awareness-really-is-and-how-to-cultivate-it.

FourWeekMBA. "The Competing Value Framework in a Nutshell." *FourWeekMBA*. Accessed April 2, 2022. https://fourweekmba.com/competing-values-framework/.

Gilbert, Elizabeth "Editorial Review on Amazon." Review of *The Artist's Way*, by Julia Cameron. Amazon.com. https://www.amazon.com/Artists-Way-Spiritual-Higher-Creativity/dp/1585421472.

Goleman, Daniel, and Richard E. Boyatzis. "Emotional Intelligence Has 12 Elements. Which Do you Need to Work On?" *Harvard Business Review*, February 6, 2017. https://hbr.org/2017/02/emotional-intelligence-has-12-elements-which-do-you-need-to-work-on.

Gregersen, H. B., Allen J. Morrison, and J. Stewart Black. "Developing leaders for the global frontier." *Sloan Management Review* 40, no. 1 (Fall 1998): 21–32.

Grenny, Joseph and Brittney Maxfield. "How Leaders Can Ask for the Feedback No One Wants to Give Them." *Harvard Business Review*, July 29, 2019. https://hbr.org/2019/07/how-leaders-can-ask-for-the-feedback-no-one-wants-to-give-them.

Kawasaki, Guy. "Angela Duckworth: MacArthur 'Genius' Grant Winner, Researcher, and Author of *Grit: The Power of Passion and Perseverance*." February 10, 2021. In *Guy Kawasaki's Remarkable People* Podcast. Produced by Guy Kawasaki. Podcast, 49:16. https://podcasts.apple.com/us/podcast/angela-duckworth-macarthur-genius-grant-winner-researcher/id1483081827?i=1000508469993.

Neitlich, Andrew. *Elegant Leadership: Simple Strategies, Remarkable Results*. Newbury, UK: Chatham Business Press, 2001.

Quinn, Robert E., and John Rohrbaugh. "A Spatial Model of Effectiveness Criteria: Towards a Competing Values Approach to Organizational Analysis." *Management Science* 29, no. 3 (1983): 363-377. https://doi.org/10.1287/mnsc.29.3.363.

Reiner, Rob, dir. *A Few Good Men*. 1992; Boulevard, Culver City, CA: Columbia Pictures, 1992.

Rock, David, Josh Davis, and Beth Jones. "Kill Your Performance Ratings," *Strategy+Business*. Autumn 2014. https://www.strategy-business.com/article/00275?gko=c442b.

Smith, Pete. *Dare to Matter: Choosing an Unstuck and Unapologetic Life of Significance*. Kindle eBooks, 2017. Kindle.

Tjan, Anthony K., Richard J. Harrington, and Tsun-Yan Hsieh. *Heart, Smarts, Guts, and Luck: What It Takes to Be an Entrepreneur and Build a Great Business*. Boston: Harvard Business Review Press, 2012.

Truninger, Margarida, Xavier Fernández-I-Marín, Joan M. Batista-Foguet, Richard E. Boyatzis, and Ricard Serlavós. "The Power of EI Competencies Over Intelligence and Individual Performance: A Task-Dependent Model." *Frontiers in Psychology* 9 (2018): 1532. https://doi.org/10.3389/fpsyg.2018.01532.

Van Velsor, Ellen, and Jean Brittain Leslie. "Why Executives Derail: Perspectives across Time and Cultures." *The Academy of Man-*

agement Executive (1993-2005) 9, no. 4 (1995): 62–72. http://www.
jstor.org/stable/4165289.

Zhou, Yi, and Hongbo Shao. "The Responding Relationship
between Plants and Environment is the Essential Principle
for Agricultural Sustainable Development on the Globe."
Comptes Rendus Biologies 331, no. 4 (2008: 321–328. https://doi.
org/10.1016/j.crvi.2008.01.008.

CHAPTER 9

Angelou, Maya (@DrMayaAngelou). "When someone shows you
who they are, believe them the first time." Twitter, June 12, 2015.
5:01 p.m. http://t.co/7rks11m11C.

Berra, Yogi, and David H. Kaplan. *You Can Observe a Lot by
Watching: What I've Learned About Teamwork from the Yan-
kees and Life.* Hoboken: Wiley, 2009.

Chia, Jasmine, and Samuel Hagen. "The Org Chart as Political
Map-Making." EPIC, April 23, 2020. https://www.epicpeople.
org/org-chart-as-political-map-making/.

Fisher, Roger, and Daniel Shapiro. *Beyond Reason: Using Emotions
as You Negotiate.* New York: Penguin, 2006.

Grossman, Robert J. "What Is Culture?" *HR Magazine,* February
2, 2009. https://www.shrm.org/hr-today/news/hr-magazine/
Pages/0209grossman1.aspx.

Mintzbert, Henry. *Power In and Around Organizations.* Engle-
wood Cliffs: Prentice Hall, 1983.

Princeton University. "What is Ethnography?" *Undergraduate.* Accessed June 17, 2022.

Rokeach, Milton. *The Nature of Human Values.* New York: Free Press, 1973.

Voss, Chris. *Never Split the Difference: Negotiating as if Your Life Depended on It.* New York: Harper Business, 2016.

CHAPTER 10

Caltrans. "California Makes $1.18 Billion Transportation Investment." Caltrans press release, June 24, 2021. https://dot.ca.gov/news-releases/news-release-2021-018.

French, John R. P. and Bertram Raven. "The Bases of Social Power." In *Studies in Social Power*, edited by D. Cartwright, 150–167. University of Michigan, 1959. http://www.communication-cache.com/uploads/1/0/8/8/10887248/the_bases_of_social_power_-_chapter_20_-_1959.pdf.

Grant, Adam. Give and Take: Why Helping Others Drives Our Success. London: Penguin Books, 2014.

McCormick, Tyler H., Matthew J. Salganik, and Tian Zheng. "How Many People Do You Know? Efficiently Estimating Personal Network Size." *Journal of the American Statistical Association* 105 (2010): 59–70. 10.1198/jasa.2009.ap08518.

Ruderman, Marian N. and Patricia J. Ohlott. *The Realities of Management Promotion.* Greensboro: Center for Creative Leadership. 1994. https://www.ccl.org/wp-content/uploads/2015/04/RealitiesMgtPromotion.pdf.

CHAPTER 11

Bates, Suzanne. "The Science of Influence: The Three Dimensions of Executive Presence." Bates Communications, December 5, 2013. https://www.bates-communications.com/articles-and-newsletters/articles-and-newsletters/topic/strategy-to-execution.

Beeson, John. "Deconstructing Executive Presence." *Harvard Business Review*, August 22, 2012. https://hbr.org/2012/08/de-constructing-executive-pres.

Dagley, Gavin R. and J. Cadeyrn. "Understanding Executive Presence Perspectives of Business Professionals." *Consulting Psychology Journal: Practice and Research* 66, no. 3 (2014): 197-211.

Das, Devika. "Executive Presence & Biases: 8 Biases and how you can use them to be more influential." *Core Executive Presence* website, July 27, 2020. https://www.coreexecutivepresence.com/post/executive-presence-biases-8-biases-and-how-you-can-use-them-to-be-more-influential

Duan, Mary. "Improve Your Executive Presence." *Stanford Business*, September 27, 2017. https://www.gsb.stanford.edu/insights/improve-your-executive-presence.

Fillipkowski, Jenna. *Executive Presence: Desired but Ill-Defined.* Cincinnati: Human Capital Institute, 2020. https://tracom.com/wp-content/uploads/2020/02/HCIReportTalentPulse-TRACOM.pdf.

Florentine, Sharon. "Executive presence: The key to unlocking your leadership potential." *CIO*, January 17, 2020. https://www.cio.com/article/201528/executive-presence-the-key-to-unlocking-your-leadership-potential.html.

Hewlett, Sylvia Ann, Lauren Leader-Chivée, Laura Sherbin, and Joanne Gordon with Fabiola Dieudonné. *Executive Presence: Key Findings*. New York: Center for Talent Innovation, 2013. https://www.talentinnovation.org/_private/assets/Executive-Presence-KeyFindings-CTI.pdf.

Hietanen, Jari K. (2018). "Affective Eye Contact: An Integrative Review." *Frontiers in psychology* 9 (2018): 1587. https://doi.org/10.3389/fpsyg.2018.01587.

Swaminathan, Nikhil. "How to Win an Election: Make a Good First impression (in Less than 250 Milliseconds)." *Scientific American*, October 23, 2007. https://www.scientificamerican.com/article/how-to-win-an-election-ma/.

CHAPTER 12

Covered Speakers Bureau. "Jocko Willink—Highly Decorated Navy Seal Officer." Topical Keynote Speakers & Experts—Entrepreneurs, Business & Leadership. Accessed September 22, 2022. https://coveredspeakers.com/topical-keynote-speakers-and-experts/jocko-willink-decorated-navy-seal-officer/.

Covey, Stephen M. *The Speed of Trust: The One Thing that Changes Everything*. New York: Simon and Schuster Audio, 2008.

Mendoza, Martha, and Juliet Linderman. "U.S. Medical Supply Chains Failed, and COVID Deaths Followed." Frontline-PBS. org, October 6, 2020. https://www.pbs.org/wgbh/frontline/article/us-medical-supply-chains-failed-covid-deaths-followed/.

Willink, Jocko, and Leif Babin. *Extreme Ownership: How U.S. Navy SEALs Lead and Win*. New York: St. Martin's Press, 2015.

CHAPTER 13

Amazon Staff. "What is an Amazon bar raiser?" Amazon, October 30, 2019. https://www.aboutamazon.com/news/workplace/amazon-bar-raiser.

Dastin, Jeffrey. "Amazon hikes average U.S. starting pay to $18, hires for 125,000 jobs." *Reuters*, September 14, 2021. https://www.reuters.com/business/exclusive-amazon-hikes-starting-pay-18-an-hour-it-hires-125000-more-logistics-2021-09-14/.

Goldsmith, Marshall. *What Got You Here Won't Get You There: How successful people become even more successful*." New York: Hyperion, 2007.

Hancock, John Lee, dir. *The Founder*. 2016; New York: Film Nation Entertainment.

Kawasaki, Guy. "Mark Manson." April 28, 2021. In *Guy Kawasaki's Remarkable People Podcast*. Produced by Guy Kawasaki. Podcast, 46:10. https://guykawasaki.com/mark-manson/.

Lombardi, Vince. "Famous Quotes by Vince Lombardi." *Vince-Lombardi.com*. Accessed March 5, 2021. http://www.vincelombardi.com/quotes.html.

Maze, Jonathan. "McDonald's, once a Tech Laggard, Becomes a Digital Sales Leader." *Restaurant Business*, April 28, 2022. https://www.restaurantbusinessonline.com/financing/mcdonalds-once-tech-laggard-becomes-digital-sales-leader.

MoMA. "Paul Cézanne." *Arts and artists*. Accessed October 1, 2021. https://www.moma.org/artists/1053#fn:2.

Palmer, Annie. "Amazon will overtake Walmart as the largest U.S. retailer in 2022, JPMorgan predicts." CNBC, June 11, 2021. https://www.cnbc.com/2021/06/11/amazon-to-overtake-walmart-as-largest-us-retailer-in-2022-jpmorgan.html.

Presgraves, Amanda. "Playing Big: How I Measure My Proudest Moments in 2021." Brainwaves (blog). January 11, 2022. http://www.amandapresgraves.com/new-wave/2022/1/11/playing-big-how-i-measure-my-proudest-moments-in-2021.

Zheng, Lily. "We're Entering the Age of Corporate Social Justice." *Harvard Business Review*, June 15, 2020. https://hbr.org/2020/06/were-entering-the-age-of-corporate-social-justice.

CHAPTER 14

Center for Creative Leadership. "Keep a Promising Career on Track & Prevent Derailment." *Leading Effectively Articles*. February 16, 2020. Accessed July 14, 2022. https://www.ccl.org/articles/leading-effectively-articles/5-ways-avoid-derailing-career/.

Chamorro-Premuzic, Tomas. "Could Your Personality Derail Your Career?" *Harvard Business Review*, September-October 2017. https://hbr.org/2017/09/could-your-personality-derail-your-career.

Eurich, Tasha. "What Self-Awareness Really Is (and How to Cultivate It)." *Harvard Business Review*, January 4, 2018. https://hbr.org/2018/01/what-self-awareness-really-is-and-how-to-cultivate-it.

Hogan-The Dark Side. "Dive into the Darkside." *Home*. Accessed March 3, 2022. https://www.hogandarkside.com/#.

Korn Ferry. "Detecting Derailers: Korn Ferry Institute Study Shows How to Find Warning Signs Before High Potentials Go Off Track." Korn Ferry press release, September 5, 2015. https://www.kornferry.com/about-us/press/detecting-derailers-korn-ferry-institute-study-shows-how-to-find-warning-signs-before-high-potentials-go-off-track#.

Lybarger, John, S. *Coaching Public Service Leaders: Seven Practices Good Leaders Master*. Bloomington: Author Solutions Inc., 2019.

Van Velsor, Ellen, and Jean Brittain Leslie. "Why Executives Derail: Perspectives across Time and Cultures." *The Academy of Management Executive (1993-2005)* 9, no. 4 (1995): 62–72. http://www.jstor.org/stable/4165289.

CHAPTER 15

Armstrong, April. "Don't Just Ask Somebody. Ask YOUR Body.", *AHA Insights|the Blog* (blog), January 31, 2018. https://www.aprilarmstrong.live/post/manage-your-blog-from-your-livesite.

Businessolver. "The State of Workplace Empathy." Resources. Accessed November 24, 2021. https://www.businessolver.com/resources/state-of-workplace-empathy.

Douglas, Gary M. "Whose Lies Are You Living?" *Gary M Douglas* (blog). September 27, 2014. https://garymdouglas.com/whose-lies-are-you-living/.

Framingham Heart Study. *Three Generations of Health Research*, n.d. https://www.framinghamheartstudy.org/.

Garrett, Geoffrey. "What I Learned at Wharton's CEO Academy." *Wharton Magazine*, December 7, 2017. https://magazine.wharton.upenn.edu/digital/what-i-learned-at-whartons-ceo-academy/.

Geiger, A. W., and Gretchen Livingston. "8 facts about love and marriage in America." Pew Research Center, February 13, 2019. https://www.pewresearch.org/fact-tank/2019/02/13/8-facts-about-love-and-marriage/.

Hasbro. "Kids Have Spoken! Hasbro Introduces First Kid-Sources THE GAME OF LIFE Game with New Career Choices." Hasbro press release, April 23, 2015. https://investor.hasbro.com/news-releases/news-release-details/kids-have-spoken-hasbro-introduces-first-kid-sourced-game-life.

Kukolic, Siobhan Kelleher. "How Little Time You Spend Doing What You Hate." Medium, July 24, 2018. https://medium.com/thrive-global/how-little-time-you-spend-doing-what-you-hate-bb669d0874a7)

Lee, Allen. "The 20 Highest Selling Board Games of All Time." Money Inc, August 30, 2019. https://moneyinc.com/highest-selling-board-games-of-all-time/.

Miller, Hannah L. "Why is Empathy Important as a Business Leader?" LEADERS, July 6, 2022. https://leaders.com/articles/personal-growth/why-is-empathy-important/.

Rohn, Jim. "Creating the Right Attitude for Success." *Creating the Right Attitude for Success* (blog), October 16, 2017. https://www.jimrohn.com/attitude-for-success/.

Russell, Emily Evans. "Energy Shopping to Create Your Life." Emilyevanrussell.com. Accessed May 12, 2022. https://www.emilyevansrussell.com/energy.

Seligman, M. P. *Authentic Happiness: Using the New Positive Psychology to Realize Your Potential for Lasting Fulfillment.* New York, NY: Free Press, 2002.

Stockton, Carla. "The World of the Widow: Grappling with Loneliness and Misunderstanding." *The Guardian*, October 5, 2015. https://www.theguardian.com/lifeandstyle/2015/oct/05/widows-women-bereavement-spouses.

U.S. Census Bureau. "Marriage and Divorce." *Families and Living Arrangements.* Accessed August 1, 2022. https://www.census.gov/topics/families/marriage-and-divorce.html.

Willink, Jocko, and Leif Babin. *Extreme Ownership: How U.S. Navy SEALs Lead and Win.* New York: St. Martin's Press, 2015.

CHAPTER 16

Buehler, Roger, Dale Griffin, Kent C. H. Lam, and Jennifer Deslauriers. "Perspectives on prediction: Does third-person imagery improve task completion estimates?" *Organizational Behavior and Human Decision Processes* 117, no. 1 (2012): 138–149. doi:10.1016/j.obhdp.2011.09.001.

Forsyth, Darryl K., and Christopher D. B. Burt. "Allocating time to future tasks: The effect of task segmentation on planning fallacy bias." *Memory & Cognition* 36, no. 4 (2008): 791–798. doi:10.3758/MC.36.4.791.

Kawasaki, Guy. "Cassie Holmes: Applying the Science of Happiness to Life." September 7, 2022. In *Guy Kawasaki's Remarkable People Podcast.* Produced by Guy Kawasaki. Podcast, 60:02. https://guykawasaki.com/cassie-holmes-applying-the-science-of-happiness-to-life/.

Kruse, Kevin. "Why A Personal Assistant Should Be Every Entrepreneur's First Hire." *Forbes*, June 20, 2016. https://www.forbes.com/sites/kevinkruse/2016/06/20/why-a-personal-assistant-should-be-every-entrepreneurs-first-hire/?sh=224647c7e9a7.

Perry, Tony. "J. Robert Beyster dies at 90; founder of defense giant SAIC." Los Angeles Times, December 23, 2014. https://www.latimes.com/local/obituaries/la-me-robert-beyster-20141224-story.html.

Porter, Michael E., and Nitin Nohria. "How CEOs Manage Time." *Harvard Business Review*, July-August 2018. https://hbr.org/2018/07/how-ceos-manage-time.

CHAPTER 17

Armstrong, April. "The Cave You Fear to Enter." *April Armstrong* (blog), April 25, 2019. https://www.aprilarmstrong.live/post/the-cave-you-fear-to-enter.

Carleton, R. Nicholas. "Fear of the unknown: One fear to rule them all?" *Journal of Anxiety Disorders* 41, (2016): 5–21.) https://www.sciencedirect.com/science/article/pii/S0887618516300469.

Cramer, Ginny. "JMU lands in the top 75 ranking for public national universities." James Madison University, September 12, 2022. https://www.jmu.edu/news/2022/09/12-usnews_rankings.shtml.

Drevitch, Gary. "The Thing We Fear More Than Death: Why Predators are responsible for our fear of public speaking." *Psychology Today*, November 29, 2012. https://www.psychologytoday.com/us/blog/the-real-story-risk/201211/the-thing-we-fear-more-death.

Equally Able Foundation. "Meet Our Team: Our Founder Mohammed Yousuf." 2022. https://equallyable.org/our-team/.

James Madison University. "James Madison University Selects Jonathan R. Alger as Sixth President." *New President.* Accessed September 15, 2022.

Kross, Ethan, Marc G. Berman, Walter Mischel, Edward E. Smith, and Tor D. Wagner. "Social rejection shares somatosensory representations with physical pain." *PNAS* 108, no. 15 (2011): 6270–6275. https://www.pnas.org/doi/full/10.1073/pnas.1102693108.

Mohr, Tara Sophia. "Why Women Don't Apply for Jobs Unless They're 100% Qualified." *Harvard Business Review*, August 25, 2014. https://hbr.org/2014/08/why-women-dont-apply-for-jobs-unless-theyre-100-qualified.

National Social Anxiety Center. "Public Speaking Anxiety." *Social Anxiety.* Accessed Jul 17, 2022. https://nationalsocialanxietycenter.com/social-anxiety/public-speaking-anxiety/.

Nicholl, Don, Michael Ross, and Bernard West, creators. *Three's Company.* Aired 1976–1984, on CBS.

Osbon, Diane K., ed. *Reflections on the Art of Living: A Joseph Campbell Companion.* New York: HarperCollins, 1991.

Rodriguez, Tori. "Descendants of Holocaust Survivors Have Altered Stress Hormones." *Scientific American*, March 1, 2015.https://www.scientificamerican.com/article/descendants-of-holocaust-survivors-have-altered-stress-hormones/.

Times Higher Education. "Most-Recommended Universities in the United States." *The Student.* October 15, 2019. https://www.

timeshighereducation.com/student/best-universities/most-rec-ommended-universities-united-states.

Walsh, Neale Donald. *Conversations with God: An Uncommon Dialogue*. London: Hodder & Stoughton, 1997.

CHAPTER 18

Aesop and Milo Winter. "The Goose & the Golden Egg." *The Aesop for Children*. Chicago: Rand, McNally & Co., 1919. Accessed September 25, 2022. http://read.gov/aesop/091.html.

American Psychological Association. "American Psychological Association Survey Shows Money Stress Weighing on Americans' Health Nationwide." American Psychological Association press release. Accessed September 28, 2022. https://www.apa.org/news/press/releases/2015/02/money-stress.

Brokaw, Kate, Ward Tishler, Stephanie Manceor, Kelly Hamilton, Andrew Gaulden, Elaine Parr, and Erin J. Wamsley. "Resting state EEG correlates of memory consolidation." *Neurobioogy of Learning and* Memory 130 (2016): 17–25). doi: 10.1016/j.nlm.2016.01.008.

Cameron, Julia. *The Artist's Way: A Spiritual Path to Higher Creativity*. New York: J.P. Tarcher/Putman, 2002.

Chappell, Bill. "4-Day Workweek Boosted Workers' Productivity By 40%, Microsoft Japan Says." NPR, November 4, 2019. https://www.npr.org/2019/11/04/776163853/microsoft-japan-says-4-day-workweek-boosted-workers-productivity-by-40.

Confino, Jo. "Google's Head of Mindfulness: 'Goodness is Good for Business." *The Guardian*, May 14, 2014. https://www.theguardian.com/sustainable-business/google-meditation-mindfulness-technology.

Dalton-Smith, Saundra. "The 7 types of rest that every person needs." IDEAS.TED.COM. https://ideas.ted.com/the-7-types-of-rest-that-every-person-needs/.

Dweck, Carol. "The power of believing that you can improve." December 17, 2014. Ted video, 10:11. https://www.ted.com/talks/carol_dweck_the_power_of_believing_that_you_can_improve.

Flade, Peter, Jim Asplund, and Gwen Elliot. "Employees Who Use Their Strengths Outperform Those Who Don't." Gallup, October 8, 2015. https://www.gallup.com/workplace/236561/employees-strengths-outperform-don.aspx.

Gallup. "Find the CliftonStrengths Assessment That's Right for You." *CliftonStrengths*. Accessed April 10, 2022. https://www.gallup.com/cliftonstrengths/en/253868/popular-clifton-strengths-assessment-products.aspx.

Gallup. "Gallup Daily: U.S. Employee Engagement." *Poll*. Accessed May 4, 2022. https://news.gallup.com/poll/180404/gallup-daily-employee-engagement.aspx.).

Harter, Jim. "U.S. Employee Engagement Rises Following Wild 2020." Gallup, February 26, 2021. https://www.gallup.com/workplace/330017/employee-engagement-rises-following-wild-2020.aspx.)

Hope, Terrie. "The Effects of Access Bars on Anxiety and Depression." *Energy Psychology: Theory, Research, and Theory* 9, no. 2 (2017). doi 10.9769/EPJ.2017.9.2.TH.

Institute for Corporate Productivity (i4cp). "Study: Only 30% of Companies Say Their Employees Have Needed Skills, But Few Understand Workforce Capabilities Today." i4cp press release, September 30, 2021. https://www.i4cp.com/press-releases/study-only-30-of-companies-say-their-employees-have-needed-skills-but-few-understand-current-capabilities.

Kobrin, Mel. "Promoting Wellness for Better Behavioral and Physical Health." SAMHSA, 2017. https://mfpcc.samhsa.gov/ENewsArticles/Article12b_2017.aspx.

Lahiri, Gaurav, and Jeff Schwartz. "Well-being: A strategy and a responsibility—2018 Global Human Capital Trends." Deloitte, March 28, 2018. https://www2.deloitte.com/global/en/insights/focus/human-capital-trends/2018/employee-well-being-programs.html.

Lamp, Amanda, Maxwell Cook, Rhiannon N. Soriano Smith, and Gregory Belenky. "Exercise, nutrition, sleep, and waking rest?" *Sleep* 42, no. 10 (2019): zsz138. https://doi.org/10.1093/sleep/zsz138.

Massachusetts Institute of Technology. "Brain Breaks." *Doing Well.* Accessed November 28, 2021. https://doingwell.mit.edu/best_practices/brain-breaks.

Mueller, P. S., D. J. Plevak, and T. A. Rummans. "Religious Involvement, Spirituality, and Medicine: Implications for Clinical

Practice." *Mayo Clinic proceedings* 76, no. 12 (2001): 1225–1235. DOI: 10.4065/76.12.1225.

Children and Nature Network. *Connecting with Nature to Care for Ourselves and the Earth: Recommendations for Decision Makers* brochure. New York, 2018. https://natureforall.global/wp-content/uploads/2020/12/ConnectingwithNature.pdf.

Nemo, John. "What a NASA Janitor Can Teach Us About Living a Bigger Life." The Business Journals, December 23, 2014. https://www.bizjournals.com/bizjournals/how-to/growth-strategies/2014/12/what-a-nasa-janitor-can-teach-us.html.

PandoDaily. "PandoMonthly: The best advice Warren Buffett ever gave Jeff Bezos." January 11, 2013. Video, 1:21. https://www.youtube.com/watch?v=wI5ILNp2WLA.

Princeton University: U Matter. "Wellness Wheel & Assessment." *Action matters.* Accessed May 12, 2022. https://umatter.princeton.edu/action/caring-yourself/wellness-wheel-assessment.

Salesforce. "The Leader's Guide to Employee Well-being." *Resource Center.* Accessed December 7, 2021. https://www.salesforce.com/resources/guides/wellness-playbook-employee-wellbeing-guide/.

Santa Clara University School of Law. "8 Pillars of Wellness." *Student Services,* Accessed December 7, 2021. https://law.scu.edu/studentservices/8-pillars-of-wellness/.

Seppälä, Emma, and Marissa King. "Having Work Friends Can Be Tricky, but It's Worth It." *Harvard Business Review,* August

8, 2017. https://hbr.org/2017/08/having-work-friends-can-be-tricky-but-its-worth-it.

Stanford Medicine. "The Belonging Project." *Special Initiatives.* Accessed March 5, 2021. https://med.stanford.edu/psychiatry/special-initiatives/belonging.html.).

Stewart, Henry. "Five Big Companies Who Swear by Mindfulness." *LinkedIn*, August 17, 2015. https://www.linkedin.com/pulse/five-big-companies-who-swear-mindfulness-henry-stewart/.

Stewart, James B. "Looking for a Lesson in Google's Perks." *New York Times*, March 15, 2013. https://www.nytimes.com/2013/03/16/business/at-google-a-place-to-work-and-play.html.

Stone, Emma. "The Emerging Science of Awe and Its Benefits." Psychology Today, April 27, 2017. https://www.psychologytoday.com/us/blog/understanding-awe/201704/the-emerging-science-awe-and-its-benefits.

Swarbrick, Margaret. "A Wellness Approach to Mental Health Recovery." In *Recovery of People with Mental Illness: Philosophical and Related Perspectives*, edited by Abraham Rudnick, Chapter 3. United Kingdom: Oxford University Press, 2012. https://doi.org/10.1093/med/9780199691319.001.0001.

Swift, Jackie. "The Benefits of Having a Sense of Purpose." Cornell Research, Accessed December 7, 2021. https://research.cornell.edu/news-features/benefits-having-sense-purpose.)

Taylor, Chloe. "Aesthetics and Well-Being: How Interior Design Affects Your Happiness." *Psychology Tomorrow*, July 2, 2016. https://psychologytomorrowmagazine.com/aesthetics-and-well-being-how-interior-design-affects-your-happiness/.

Thompson, Karl. "What Percentage of Your Life Will You Spend at Work?" ReviseSociology, August 16, 2016. https://revisesociology.com/2016/08/16/percentage-life-work/.

University of New Hampshire. "The Well-Being Wheel: Wellness vs. Well-Being: What's the Difference?" *Wellness/Self-Care*. Accessed October 4, 2021. https://www.unh.edu/health/well-being-wheel.

Worley, Susan L. "The Extraordinary Importance of Sleep: The Detrimental Effects of Inadequate Sleep on Health and Public Safety Drive an Explosion of Sleep Research." *P&T* 43, no. 12 (2018): 758–763. https://www.ncbi.nlm.nih.gov/pmc/articles/PMC6281147/.

Yeager, Ashley. "Losing Touch: Another Drawback of the COVID-19 Pandemic." *The Scientist*, May 19, 2020. https://www.the-scientist.com/news-opinion/losing-touch-another-drawback-of-the-COVID19-pandemic-67542.

CHAPTER 19

Betz, Nancy E., and Gail Hackett. "Concept of agency in educational and career development." *Journal of Counseling Psychology* 34, no. 3 (1987): 299–308. https://doi.org/10.1037/0022-0167.34.3.299.

Cochran, Larry, and Joan Laub. *Becoming an Agent: Patterns and Dynamics for Shaping Your Life*. Albany: State University of New York Press, 1994.

Czeisler, M. É., R. I Lane, E. Petrosky, et al. "Mental Health, Substance Use, and Suicidal Ideation During the COVID-19 Pandemic—United States, June 24–30, 2020." Morbidity and Mortality Weekly Report 63, no. 32 (2020):1049–1057. DOI: http://dx.doi.org/10.15585/mmwr.mm6932a1.

Freudenberger, Herbert J. "Staff Burn-Out." *Journal of Social Issues* 30, (1974): 159–165. https://doi.org/10.1111/j.1540-4560.1974.tb00706.x.

Harvard Health Publishing. "What meditation can do for your mind, mood, and health." *Staying Healthy*. July 16, 2014. https://www.health.harvard.edu/staying-healthy/what-meditation-can-do-for-your-mind-mood-and-health-.

Holmes, T. H., and R. H. Rahe. "The Social Readjustment Rating Scale." *Journal of Psychosomatic Research* 11, no. 2 (1967): 213–218.

Jungreis, Max. "The cofounder of Supergiant." Insider, November 24, 2020. https://www.businessinsider.com/supergiant-video-game-studio-hades-conquered-nintendo-switch-workload-burnout-2020-11.

Mayo Clinic. "Job burnout: How to spot it and take action." *Healthy Lifestyle—Adult Health*. June 5, 2021. https://www.mayoclinic.org/healthy-lifestyle/adult-health/in-depth/burnout/art-20046642.

Norman, Abby. "The Power of the Pause." (Potomac, MD: New Degree Press, forthcoming 2023).

Quenk, Naomi L. *In the Grip: Understanding Type, Stress, and the Inferior Function.* Oxford: Oxford Psychologists Press, 2000.

Reiner, Rob, dir. *The Princess Bride.* 1987; Beverly Hills, CA: Act III Communications.

Rutledge, Thomas, Paul Mills, and Robert Schneider. "Meditation Intervention Reviews." *JAMA Intern Med.* 174, no. 7 (2014): 1193. doi:10.1001/jamainternmed.2014.1419.

Substance Abuse and Mental Health Services Administration (SAMHSA). "988 Suicide & Crisis Lifeline." *Find Treatment.* Accessed December 7, 2021. https://www.samhsa.gov/find-help/988.

The American Institute of Stress. "The Holmes-Rahe Stress Inventory." *The Holmes-Rahe Stress Inventory.* Accessed December 7, 2021. https://www.stress.org/holmes-rahe-stress-inventory.

World Health Organization. "Burn-out an 'occupational phenomenon': International Classification of Diseases." *Departmental News.* May 28, 2019.https://www.who.int/news/item/28-05-2019-burn-out-an-occupational-phenomenon-international-classification-of-diseases.

Yaribeygi, Habib, Yunes Panahi, Hedayat Sahraei, Thomas P. Johnston, and Amerihossein Sahebkar. "The impact of stress on body function: A review." *EXCLI Journal* 16, (2017): 1057–1072. https://doi.org/10.17179/excli2017-480.

CHAPTER 20

Alley. "Let's Do Launch." 2022. https://alley.co/.

Bravata, Dena. M., Sharon. A. Watts, Autumn. L. Keefer, et al. "Prevalence, Predictors, and Treatment of Impostor Syndrome: A Systematic Review." *Journal of General Internal Medicine* 35, no. 4 (2020): 1252–1275. doi:10.1007/s11606-019-05364-1.

Clance, Pauline Rose and Suzanne Ament Imes. "The Imposter Phenomenon in High Achieving Women: Dynamics and Therapeutic Intervention." *Psychotherapy: Theory, Research & Practice* 15, no. 3 (1978): 241–247. https://doi.org/10.1037/h0086006.

Eruteya, Kess. "You're Not an Imposter. You're Actually Pretty Amazing." *Harvard Business Review*, January 3, 2022. https://hbr.org/2022/01/youre-not-an-imposter-youre-actually-pretty-amazing.

Harrell, Eben. "Imposter Syndrome Has Its Advantages." *Harvard Business Review*, May-June 2022. https://hbr.org/2022/05/impostor-syndrome-has-its-advantages.

Paul Ekman Group. "What are emotions?" *Universal Emotions*. Accessed September 23, 2022. https://www.paulekman.com/universal-emotions/.

CHAPTER 21

Artabane, Julie Coffman, and Darci Darnell. "Charting the Course: Getting Women to the Top." Bain & Company, January 31, 2017. https://www.bain.com/insights/charting-the-course-women-on-the-top.

Branden, Nathaniel. *The Six Pillars of Self-Esteem*. New York: Bantam Books, 2012. Kindle.

Britannica. "24." *TV & Radio Shows & Networks*. July 17, 2020. https://www.britannica.com/topic/24-TV-series.

Clance, Pauline Rose. "Imposter Phenomenon (IP)." *Paulineroseclance.com*. Accessed May 12, 2022. https://paulineroseclance.com/impostor_phenomenon.html.

Cochran, Robert, and Joel Surnow, creators. *24*. 2001–2010, on Fox. https://www.imdb.com/title/tt0285331/?ref_=ttfc_fc_tt.

Collins Dictionary. s.v. "integrity." Accessed March 5, 2022. https://www.collinsdictionary.com/dictionary/english/integrity.

Dictionary.com. s.v. "bold." Accessed March 5, 2022. https://www.dictionary.com/browse/bold.

Garrett, Neil, Stephanie C. Lazzaro, Dan Ariely, and Tali Sharot. "The brain adapts to dishonesty." *Nature Neuroscience* 19, no. 12 (2016): 1727–1732).

Hogan. *Supplement Form 5: Hogan Development Survey*. Tulsa: Hogan Press, 2014. http://www.hoganassessments.com/sites/default/files/uploads/HDS_Subscale_Technical_Supplement.pdf.

Keller, Helen. *Let Us Have Faith*. New York: Doubleday & Company, 1940.

Merriam-Webster.com. s.v. "integrity." Accessed March 5, 2022. https://www.merriam-webster.com/dictionary/integrity.

Online Etymology Dictionary. s.v. "bold (adj.)" Accessed September 25, 2022. https://www.etymonline.com/word/bold.

Made in United States
Troutdale, OR
12/23/2023

16385916R00232